Ink, Stink Bait, Revenge, and Queen Elizabeth

Ink, Stink Bait, Revenge, and Queen Elizabeth

A Yorkshire Yeoman's Household Book

Steven W. May and Arthur F. Marotti

Cornell University Press
Ithaca and London

First published 2014 by Cornell University Press
First printing, Cornell Paperbacks, 2014
Printed in the United States of America

Library of Congress Cataloging-in-Publication Data

May, Steven W., author.
Ink, stink bait, revenge, and Queen Elizabeth : a Yorkshire yeoman's household book / Steven W. May and Arthur F. Marotti.
pages cm
Includes bibliographical references and index.
ISBN 978-0-8014-5355-7 (cloth : alk. paper)
ISBN 978-0-8014-5656-5 (pbk. : alk. paper)
1. Hanson, John, 1517–1599—Notebooks, sketchbooks, etc.
2. English literature—Early modern, 1500–1700—History and criticism.
3. Manuscripts, English—England—Yorkshire. 4. England—Social conditions—16th century—Sources. I. Marotti, Arthur F., 1940– author.
II. Title.
PR421.M28 2014
820.9'003—dc23 2014029089

Cornell University Press strives to use environmentally responsible suppliers and materials to the fullest extent possible in the publishing of its books. Such materials include vegetable-based, low-VOC inks and acid-free papers that are recycled, totally chlorine-free, or partly composed of nonwood fibers. For further information, visit our website at www.cornellpress.cornell.edu.

Cloth printing 10 9 8 7 6 5 4 3 2 1
Paperback printing 10 9 8 7 6 5 4 3 2 1

Contents

Illustrations

Abbreviations

BL	British Library, London
CP	Cause Papers of the Consistory Court, Borthwick Institute, University of York
EEBO	*Early English Books Online*, http://eebo.chadwyck.com/home
HM	Huntington Library Manuscript
ODNB	*The Oxford Dictionary of National Biography*, ed. H. C. G. Matthew and Brian Harrison, http://www.oxforddnb.com
OED	*Oxford English Dictionary*, http://www.oed.com
PRO	Public Record Office, Kew
STC	A. W. Pollard and G. R. Redgrave, *A Short-Title Catalogue of Books Printed in England, Scotland, and Ireland and of English Books Printed Abroad 1475–1640*, 2nd ed., rev. W. A. Jackson, F. S. Gerguson, and Katharine F. Pantzer, 3 vols. (London: Bibliographical Society,1976–91)
Wing	Donald Wing, comp., *Short-Title Catalogue of Books Printed in England, Scotland, Ireland, Wales, and British America, and of*

English Books Printed in Other Countries, 1641–1700, 3 vols. (New York: Index Committee of the Modern Language Association of America, 1972–94)

WYAS West Yorkshire Archive Service

Acknowledgments

We are grateful, first, to Dr. Arnold Hunt, curator of manuscripts at the British Library, for calling Hanson's manuscript to our attention, for providing valuable background information about it, and for facilitating our access to a digital copy of it. Dr. Alan Bryson gave helpful advice on a number of topics relevant to our study. Completion of this project was greatly facilitated by the generous support of the Arts and Humanities Research Council through its funding of the "Early Modern Poetry" project at the University of Sheffield and by research funds from Wayne State University. For information helpful for our discussion of the Elizabeth Armada thanksgiving ballads (in chapter 2), we are grateful to Dr. Natalie Mears of the University of Durham for useful suggestions growing out of her AHRC-funded project "British State Prayers, Fasts and Thanksgivings, 1540s–1940s." We are also grateful to one of the anonymous Cornell University Press readers for valuable suggestions for revision, including the advice that we interpret the use of the term "citizens" in the Armada thanksgiving ballads in terms of the delicate relations between royal authority and London civic laws and liberties. Finally we thank *English Literary Renaissance* and Brill Publishers for permission to use material from the following works: Steven W. May and Arthur F. Marotti, "Two Lost Ballads of the Armada Thanksgiving Celebration [with texts and illustration]," *English Literary Renaissance* 41, no. 1 (Winter 2011): 36–68, and Steven W. May, "Queen Elizabeth's Performance at Paul's Cross in 1588," in *Paul's Cross and the Culture of Persuasion in England, 1520–1640*, ed. Torrance Kirby and P. G. Stanwood (Leiden, Neth.: Brill, 2014), 300–313.

Ink, Stink Bait, Revenge, and Queen Elizabeth

Introduction

Description and Provenance of the Hanson Manuscript

In 2007 the British Library acquired a fifty-folio manuscript that was among the muniments of the Spencer-Stanhope family of Cannon Hall, Yorkshire (now British Library Additional MS 82370). The name John Stanhope occurs on folio 1 of the manuscript, which initially led us to suppose that the sixteenth-century family patriarch of that name had compiled the anthology. We discovered, however, that the dominant hand throughout belonged to Stanhope's yeoman neighbor, John Hanson of Rastrick, Yorkshire (1517–99).[1] Hanson worked as a scrivener and legal agent, drawing up deeds and wills and handling other forms of legal business despite his apparent lack of legal training. Just when he began to compile his household book or over what period of time is uncertain: completed

1. See Steven W. May, "Matching Hands: The Search for the Scribe of the 'Stanhope' Manuscript," *Huntington Library Quarterly* 76, no. 3 (Autumn 2013): 345–75.

by 1589 at the earliest, it is almost entirely an Elizabethan anthology, containing a wide variety of texts—literary and nonliterary, prose and verse, secular and spiritual. It is a rare example of the provincial anthology that records works of local interest that seldom or never penetrated the main networks of scribal transmission connecting London with the two universities. It includes the following contents:

ff. 1–11v: recipes for different-colored inks and for catching fish and fowl, as well as other utilitarian material
ff. 12–18v: a prose account of the mid-fourteenth-century feud between the Eland and Beaumont families
ff. 19–26v: two lost broadside ballads describing Queen Elizabeth's procession through London to give thanksgiving at St. Paul's for the Armada victory (24 November 1588) (these are separated by an excerpt from King Philip II of Spain's proclamation against William of Nassau [1584] in which the Spanish king's assumed titles are flaunted)
ff. 27–29v: proverbs and maxims in couplets taken from the *Preceptes of Cato* (4 eds., 1550–77)
ff. 30–31v: a copy of Sir John Constable's "byerley bouke," a binding agreement with tenants of the Lordship of Clyfton in Yorkshire, 25 October 1554[2]
f. 32: a verse calendar beginning "Circumstantly thre kynges cam by.nyght"
ff. 33–42: a ballad about the Eland-Beaumont feud beginning "what welthye wyghtes can here attayn"
f. 42: a verse Decalogue beginning "No gods but one, shalt thowe adore"
ff. 42v–43v: an epitaph for Sir Henry Savile (d. 1558) beginning "No wyght can well Dyscryve"
ff. 44–45v: an epitaph for Mr. Henry Savile of Thornhill (d. 1569) beginning "O earth earth take unto [thee] heare"
f. 45v: Queen Elizabeth's poem "The dowt of future foos"
f. 46: poem attributed to Queen Elizabeth, "Now leave and let me Rest"
ff. 46v–47v: a Nativity poem beginning "When Jesus was borne in bethleem"

2. The "byerley" (by our law) book specified what tenants could and (mostly) could not do with regard to the public space, pasture, trees, livestock, and so forth on the manor in question.

ff. 47v–49: Thomas Churchyard's epitaph of the Earl of Pembroke (d. 1570) beginning "synce playnts wante powere"
f. 49: a poem by Churchyard but here attributed to Queen Elizabeth, "I Lost a losse," and a Latin epigram on Emperor Frederic from Foxe's *Acts and Monuments* beginning "Si probitas sensus, virtutum gracia"
f. 49v: Thomas, Lord Vaux's poem "I lothe that I Dyd love"
f. 50: a list of tenants of the Netherwood House and lands in Rastrick, Yorkshire
f. 50v: a list of the counties of England and Wales with the number of parishes in each

As can be seen from this list, the manuscript contains both utilitarian and literary items. Its literary highlights include the long narrative poem about some of the sensational events associated with a mid-fourteenth-century Yorkshire feud between the Eland and Beaumont families, a conflict that spread from southwest Yorkshire into Lancashire and is independently documented in the historical record.[3] It also contains poetry from the metropolitan center and the royal court, including two unique copies of ballads describing Queen Elizabeth's procession through London after the victory over the Spanish Armada, two poems attributed to the Queen herself, and some other verse by courtly writers copied from either manuscript or print sources. It is this intersection between the local and the national and between popular and elite cultures that makes this manuscript particularly interesting, for the collection reflects material embedded in the cultural memory of its provincial compiler and readers while demonstrating the dissemination of material from the cultural center to the periphery.

The physical features of the manuscript are as follows. Its original vellum binding (209 × 155 mm) is torn and stained, and its paper (206 × 152 mm) has many pages that are dog-eared or torn, some with water staining; folios 1–14 form a single gathering followed by folio 15, of different paper stock, pasted in with text missing in the midst of the prose narrative of the

3. The historical documents related to this feud are discussed in J. M. Kaye, "The Eland Murders, 1350–51: A Study of the Legend of the Eland Feud," *Yorkshire Archaeological Journal* 51 (1979): 61–79.

Eland-Beaumont feud. The codex is completed by two additional gatherings, folios 16–31 and 32–50. The original format was apparently three quarto gatherings of four leaves each with a single quarto gathering inserted in the final one, now missing one leaf, and indistinguishable in the binding. Between folios 7 and 8 can be seen stubs of two vellum leaves sewn into the binding; between folios 23 and 24, 32 and 33, and 36 and 37, single vellum stubs have been sewn into the binding, with "Matheum Marshe henri" written in a sixteenth-century secretary hand on the last of these. About a quarter of the leaf has been torn out along the lower outer margin of folio 49.

Chain lines throughout are horizontal, and there are at least two pot watermarks—one with band initials "I B" and the other with "I V," all in the middle gutter.[4] There is some writing on the front vellum cover ("Historia[e] / Historia / de boemed [Beaumont] / cum Eland")[5] and the inside of the back cover ("The Text" and "the man is blest that"). On folio 1 the name "John Stanhope" is written in red ink, then deleted. Seven hands are represented in the manuscript: Hand A, belonging to John Hanson and responsible for more than 95 percent of the anthology's content, is a rounded, mid-sixteenth-century, secretary hand with many archaic forms and gratuitous flourishes.[6] The remaining hands appear sporadically in the document. Hand B (on ff. 7v, 10v, 50v) is an angular secretary hand with double cross-stroked majuscules, an open-loop *h* and *y* descenders, a back-ascending terminal *s*, and angled second foot on the *w*. Hand C is a rounded cursive italic at the bottom of folios 7v and 26v, with a left-hooking *d* ascender, epsilon *e*, and a broad-stroke foot to the *k*. Hand D (on ff. 1, 26, 43v, 49v) is an angular cursive italic. Hand E (on the pasted-in replacement, f. 15) is a rounded cursive italic, using "wn" for "when," terminal *s*

4. The former resembles no. 2885 (date 1575) in J. S. G. Simmon and Bé van Ginnekan-Van de Kasteele, eds., *Likhachev's Watermarks in English-Language Version*, vol. 2, *Plates and Indexes* (Amsterdam: Paper Publication Society, 1994). It also resembles POT 089.1 (date 1552) and POT 352.1 (date 1578) in the University of Delaware's online Thomas L. Gravell Watermark Collection, http://www.gravell.org. The tops of the pot watermarks are visible in the gutters of ff. 1, 2, 4, 11, 25, 27, 29, 31, 33, 35, 41, 43, and 49, the bottoms in the gutters of ff. 7, 8, 13, 16, 18, 20, 22, 38, 40, 46, and 48.

5. This obviously relates to the ballad and prose history of the Eland-Beaumont feud found within the manuscript.

6. For a close-up analysis of the features of this hand and identification of the scribe, see May, "Matching Hands."

with a final looped ascender, and a minuscule secretary *p*. Hand F (bottom of f. 46) is a mixed rounded cursive, with an angled minuscule *p* descender and a back stroke *s* descender. Hand G (inside back cover), is a regular secretary/mixed hand.

In the past several decades, there have been notable editions of sixteenth- and seventeenth-century English manuscript miscellanies, largely poetical collections: for example, Ruth Hughey's edition of the massive Harington family Arundel Harington manuscript (1960); Steven May's edition of Henry Stanford's anthology (1988); Peter Seng's edition of the Tudor songs and ballads found in British Library Cotton Vespasian MS A-25 (1978); Ernest Sullivan, Jr.'s edition of two manuscripts close to John Donne and his circle, the Dalhousie (now Texas Tech) Manuscripts (1988); Edward Doughtie's edition of the musician John Lilliat's poetical collection (Bodleian Rawlinson Poetry MS 148) (1985); Jean Klene's edition of *The Southwell-Sipthorpe Commonplace Book* (1997); Deborah Aldrich-Watson's edition of Constance Aston Fowler's anthology (Huntington MS HM 904) (2000); Thomas Olsen's edition of *The Commonplace Book of Sir John Strangways (1645–1666)* (2004); John Gouws's edition of Nicholas Oldisworth's manuscript collection; and Michael Denbo's edition of Pierpont Morgan Library MS MA 1057 (2012).[7] Some of these contain prose along with poetry. Nearly all these collections were compiled by elite

7. Ruth Hughey, ed., *The Arundel Harington Manuscript of Tudor Poetry*, 2 vols. (Columbus: Ohio State University Press, 1960); Steven W. May, *Henry Stanford's Anthology: An Edition of Cambridge University Library Manuscript Dd.7.75* (New York: Garland, 1988); Peter J. Seng, ed., *Tudor Songs and Ballads from MS Cotton Vespasian A-25* (Cambridge, MA: Harvard University Press, 1978); Ernest W. Sullivan II, ed., *The First and Second Dalhousie Manuscripts: Poems and Prose by John Donne and Others, A Facsimile Edition* (Columbia: University of Missouri Press, 1988); Edward Doughtie, ed., *Liber Lilliati: Elizabethan Verse and Song (Bodleian MS Rawlinson Poetry 148)* (Newark: University of Delaware Press; London: Associated University Presses, 1985); Jean Klene, ed., *The Southwell-Sibthorpe Commonplace Book: Folger MS. V.b.198*, Renaissance English Text Society, 7th ser., vol. 20 (Tempe, AZ: Medieval & Renaissance Texts & Studies, 1997); Deborah Aldrich-Watson, ed., *The Verse Miscellany of Constance Aston Fowler: A Diplomatic Edition*, Renaissance English Text Society, 7th ser., vol. 25 (Tempe, AZ: Arizona Center for Medieval and Renaissance Studies, 2000); Thomas G. Olsen, ed., *The Commonplace Book of Sir John Strangeways (1645–1666)*, Renaissance English Text Society, 7th ser., vol. 29 (Tempe, AZ: Arizona Center for Medieval and Renaissance Studies, 2004); John Gouws, ed., *Nicholas Oldisworth's Manuscript (Bodleian MS. Don.c.24)*, Renaissance English Text Society, 7th ser., vol. 34 (Tempe, AZ: Arizona Center for Medieval and Renaissance Studies, 2009); Michael Denbo, ed., *The Holgate Miscellany: An Edition of Pierpont Morgan Library Manuscript, MA 1057*, Renaissance English Text society, 7th ser., vol. 35 (Tempe, AZ: Arizona Center for Medieval and Renaissance Studies, 2012).

or at least genteel scribes.[8] Surviving manuscript compilations from yeoman households are very few. Families of the gentry and aristocracy had the means of preserving texts they valued in muniment rooms, libraries, and other household spaces, while those further down the social ladder were less likely to pass on such objects to succeeding generations.

The Hanson manuscript is a particular kind of manuscript miscellany sometimes termed a household or family book—the kind of collection kept in the home ready to receive utilitarian information (such as recipes for ink, records of real estate transactions, medical receipts, etc.).[9] Household books contained not only material to be consulted but often also texts to be read at family gatherings: good candidates in the Hanson manuscript would be the prose and verse versions of the Eland-Beaumont narrative, the two Armada thanksgiving ballads, and the Decalogue and Nativity poems. This miscellany belonged to a world in transition from orality to script, one in which literacy rates were increasing rapidly, even among women and the lower classes. Texts, such as ballads, could become part of the oral tradition, and individual works, whether popular, elite, or aimed at "the middling classes," were often read aloud in familial or other social

8. Sir John Harington, for example, compiled the Arundel Harington manuscript; MS Dd.5.75 was written by the household chaplain of the Carey family, lords Hunsdon; the scribe of *Liber Lilliati*, John Lilliat, was vicar choral of Wells Cathedral.

9. On the different types of "household books" see Julia Boffey, "Bodleian Library, MS Arch. Selden. B.24 and Definitions of the 'Household Book,'" in *The English Medieval Book: Studies in Memory of Jeremy Griffiths*, ed. A. S. G. Edwards, Vincent Gillespie, and Ralph Hanna III (London: British Library, 2000), 125–34. Boffey, 127, distinguishes "practically-oriented collections from those that also contain 'literary' material, of however unsophisticated a kind"—a characterization that fits the Hanson manuscript. There is another composite manuscript from the late fifteenth century assembled by another middle-class man who also served as a legal scrivener; it has the mixture of utilitarian and literary material that characterizes some household books. See Cameron Louis, ed., *The Commonplace Book of Robert Reynes of Acle: An Edition of Tanner MS 407* (New York: Garland, 1980). In discussing the spread of literacy into the middle class in thirteenth- through fifteenth-century England, M. B. Parkes, "The Literacy of the Laity," in *Literature and Western Civilization: The Mediaeval World*, ed. David Daiches and Anthony Thorlby (London: Aldus Books, 1973), 562–63, 569, highlights the pragmatic literacy of the legal professionals. He cites several surviving manuscript compilations of legal and other middle-class professionals (Bodleian MSS Douce 132 and 137, Selden Supra 74, Digby 86, and Ashmole 61 and British Library MSS Harley 2253, Egerton 1995) that contain mixtures of professional material with religious/moral texts, practical advice, and recreational items such as romances, saints' lives, and lyric poems. Though not all of these are household books, their heterogeneity resembles that of Hanson's collection.

gatherings; sometimes these were texts of great length, such as Sidney's *Arcadia*.[10]

Hanson's Anthology and Provincial Manuscript Culture

The Hanson compilation provides another window into the nature of scribal culture in the provinces as opposed to those centered in London and the universities that we associate, almost exclusively, with the transmission of literary manuscripts. Yet the royal court, the Inns of Court, Oxford, and Cambridge could boast no more than a few thousand writers at any one time. Whatever its literate population, all of London drew from a citizen base of fewer than 150,000 potential writers and collectors during Elizabeth's reign—that in a nation of more than four million. Even allowing for lower, even much lower, rates of literacy in the countryside, numbers alone dictate that most scribal culture, even literary culture, on a page-by-page basis, must have been produced outside the centers manuscript scholars have tended to credit with virtually all of it.

The near invisibility of the dominant rural origins of the age's manuscript production is due to several factors too complicated to address here in detail. In brief, the key to document preservation is the stability of permanent archives. The papers of the educated elite were far more likely to end up in some family's muniment room than were those of the nation's cottagers, despite the latter's increasing literacy. Their wooden houses burned or had to be replaced, and even solid middle-class families lacked the room over the centuries to store letters and papers other than vital legal documents. What little remains of outlying Renaissance scribal culture was for the most part acquired by (if not generated within) prosperous families on their way up. The key to the survival of their papers was the economic transition from wooden-framed house to a family seat of brick or stone. All the rest of this rural scribal culture, including the no doubt voluminous writings of the lower classes, has perished.

---

10. See William Nelson, "From 'Listen Lordings' to 'Dear Reader,'" *University of Toronto Quarterly* 46 (1976–77): 110–24, and Roger Chartier, "Leisure and Sociability: Reading Aloud in Modern Europe," trans. Carol Mossman, in *Urban Life in the Renaissance*, ed. Susan Zimmerman and Ronald F. E. Weisman (Newark: University of Delaware Press, 1989), 103–20.

The following comparison of four regional manuscripts with Hanson's household book places his collection in its local context; in doing so, it reveals that during Elizabeth's reign provincial scribes created miscellanies displaying as great a diversity of content as their urban counterparts. Such a limited sample cannot, of course, establish that these documents are representative of the rural genre as a whole. They are rare survivals, and while many more miscellanies of the type no doubt remain to be discovered, their sum can hardly amount to more than a small fraction of the total regional output. John Hanson's West Yorkshire neighbor, John Kay of Woodsum, compiled several household books during Elizabeth's reign; those most resembling Hanson's are now Folger Library MSS X.d.446 (c. 1564–92), and X.d.449 (c. 1570–92). Thomas Brampton of Kenton, Suffolk, created a similar document from an older account book, now Bodleian Library MS Gough Norfolk 43 (compiled c. 1585–1603). Bodleian MS Tanner 175 is another book of estate records transformed to a household book between c. 1590 and 1608 by Henry Gurney, yeoman farmer of Great Ellingham, Norfolk. Bodleian MS Ashmole 48 is not a household book but an anthology dominated by poetry that nevertheless shares several important characteristics with the Hanson manuscript.[11] It was connected with if not written in part by the minstrel Richard Sheale of Tamworth, Staffordshire. Its datable entries suggest that it was compiled between about 1557 and 1565.

Similar contents, genres, and even identical works crop up in these four regional miscellanies. Kay, Brampton, and Gurney, for example, record births, deaths, and marriages, very typical "household book" entries, unlike those of Hanson or of the compiler of MS Ashmole 48. These three scribes and Hanson do include practical business records in their miscellanies, however. Kay records repair of a chapel in Huddersfield Church and numerous payments, loans, and rentals (X.d.449, p. 7; X.d.446 passim). Brampton and Gurney include rentals, expenses, and copies of official

11. Gurney's anthology is analyzed by Steven W. May, "Henry Gurney, a Norfolk Farmer, Reads Spenser and Others," *Spenser Studies* 20 (2005): 183–223. Thomas Wright edited the verse in the Ashmole MS under the title *Songs and Ballads with other Short Poems, Chiefly of the Reign of Philip and Mary* (1860; repr., New York: Forgotten Books, 1970). Our references to poems in Ashmole 48 follow Wright's numbering. For a recent discussion of Ashmole 48, see Andrew Taylor, *The Songs and Travels of a Tudor Minstrel: Richard Sheale of Tamworth* (York, UK: University of York, 2012).

letters. Equally practical is Hanson's copy of the "byerley bouke" and his list of tenants on folio 50 of his manuscript. Ashmole 48 lacks these utilitarian entries but does include two horoscopes, while multiple recipes are found in the Brampton and Gurney collections. Gurney includes one recipe for making ordinary ink (f. 28); the others are all medicinal, in contrast with Hanson's emphasis on colored inks and paint, fishing, and fowling. Gurney entered Latin verse and prose into MS Tanner 175 (ff. 48v–49, 135v), as did Brampton (ff. 46, 42v, 49v–50), while Latin passages also appear in Kay's volumes,[12] suggesting that these three scribes were on an educational level roughly equivalent to Hanson's.

All four scribes copied excerpts from printed works into their anthologies, as did Hanson. At least thirteen of the seventy-seven poems preserved in MS Ashmole 48 were copied from printed broadsides.[13] Henry Gurney transcribed most of the dedicatory and commendatory poems from Spenser's *Faerie Queene* into MS Tanner 175, although most of its 620-odd poems are Gurney's own compositions. Thomas Brampton copied aphorisms from William Baldwin's bestseller, *A Treatise of Moral Philosophy*, which saw seventeen editions between 1547 and 1600. And, like Hanson, Brampton was attracted to Thomas Churchyard's unsophisticated verse, copying on folio 1v "A good description of a freende" from *A pleasaunte Laborinth called Churchyardes Chance* (1580, *STC* 5250). On folio 56, Brampton copied poems concerning friendship from Nicholas Breton's *A Floorish upon Fancie*.[14]

Brampton, Gurney, and Kay interacted in similar ways with the agronomist poet Thomas Tusser, whose *Hundreth* (later, *Five Hundreth*) *Points of Good Husbandry* was even more popular than Baldwin's *Treatise*, going through eighteen editions between 1557 and 1599. In anapestic tetrameter couplets, Tusser provided practical advice for managing a farm, its crops and livestock. His passages of moral and religious exhortation notwithstanding, the book's appeal was almost exclusively agrarian, precisely intended for such land managers as Brampton, Gurney, Kay—and Hanson.

12. Folger MS X.d.446, p. 20; X.d.449, p. 12; Bodleian MS Gough Norfolk 43, ff. 42v, 49v–50.

13. Hyder E. Rollins, "Concerning Bodleian MS. Ashmole 48," *Modern Language Notes* 34 (1919): 343–49.

14. *STC* 3654–55, three editions, 1577–c. 1585.

Brampton copied out Tusser's "Posies for thine owne bed Chamber," subscribing them "per me Thomaom Brampton Jr. 1594" (f. 31v). Gurney took nothing directly from this work, but he wrote anapestic tetrameter verses entitled "Tusser Imitated" on several occasions (ff. 82v, 106, 186, 187v). Kay wrote eight lines of fourteener couplets entitled "Myne Opynyon of Tusser and Parfreman Lytle voloms" (f. 3v, the latter reference, apparently, to Thomas Palfreyman's pirated editions of Baldwin's *Treatise*). Kay also wrote a 586-line "necessarye lesson" modeled in part on Tusser exhorting that "Howsbandye to be observyd by hym that dwelleth at woodsom yf he entend to Releve the poor and manteyne Hospitalitie" (pp. 7–20).

Hanson's interest in local magnates emerges in his verse epitaphs for Sir Henry Savile and his heir, Henry Savile, plus the references to the Savile family in both accounts of the Eland-Beaumont feud. Brampton and the scribe of Ashmole 48 were likewise concerned with local gentry and nobility.[15] Poem 51 in the Ashmole collection celebrates men at arms from the north country who served in Scotland in 1558, including the earls of Cumberland, Northumberland, and Shrewsbury. Poem 56 is Sheale's verse "epithe [epitaph] off the dethe off the ryghte honorable lady Margrete countes off Darbe." Brampton copied out the charges leveled against Thomas Howard, Duke of Norfolk in 1572, and against Philip Howard, Earl of Arundel in 1589 (ff. 34–36, 32v). He included as well, on folio 41, a text of the very popular song by Francis Kenwelmarsh, "of the Right noble Earle Walter Erle of Essex" the night before he died (1576), plus a unique elegy for his father, Walter Devereux, Viscount Hereford (d. 1558).[16] The motive for Brampton's interest in the Devereux family is unclear, for, while the Howards were highly influential in East Anglia, the Devereux sphere of influence was on the border of Wales. Gurney, too, copied the song sung by Earl Walter but took his version from *The Passions of the Spirit* (*STC* 3682.5, 1599), another book possibly written by Nicholas Breton; here the song is simply entitled "A Praier." Gurney composed a eulogy in verse for

15. See Taylor's discussion of Sheale's relationships with the Stanley family in *Songs and Travels*, 40–81.

16. Earl Walter's song, beginning "O heavenly God, O Father dear, cast down thy tender eye" (EV 17058), was first printed in the first edition of the *Paradise of Dainty Devices* (1576), where it is attributed to F[rancis] K[inwelmarsh]. Reprinted in all later editions of the *Paradise*, it appears in another seventeen Elizabethan manuscripts and two further printed sources.

Lord Burghley (f. 48v), but neither he nor John Kay included tributes to regional magnates in their household books.

The Hanson, Brampton, and Ashmole 48 collections also preserve "elite" texts that illustrate how widely even court-centered works were disseminated through the national transcription networks. Hanson acquired a text of Queen Elizabeth's poem beginning "The doubt of future foes," plus a second poem attributed to her in court-related miscellanies. Brampton obtained a copy of the Earl of Essex's poetic tirade against Sir Walter Ralegh (beginning "Muses no more, but mazes be your names") and a lament by Sir Henry Goodere with the answer by Thomas Norton (ff. 27v, 53v). These last two poems concern Goodere's assistance to Mary, Queen of Scots, in her intrigues with the Duke of Norfolk, and it is the Norfolk connection that probably explains Brampton's interest in these works. But all three poems are very much centered in London and the court. The Ashmole manuscript includes unique copies of two poems by Henry, Lord Morley and a copy of "I lothe that I Dyd love" by Thomas, Lord Vaux. Unlike Hanson's text of the latter poem, however, the Ashmole version was not copied from Tottel's *Songs and Sonnets*. It might derive from a lost broadside version of the poem entered in the Stationers' Register in 1563–64, or it may, with at least four other manuscripts, represent independent scribal circulation of the text and therefore an ultimately aristocratic point of origin.

The Ashmole anthology most closely resembles Hanson's manuscript in its emphasis on ballads, an interest taken up by none of the other three scribes. Although the Ashmole text of the ballad of "Chevy Chase" is the earliest extant version of the work, it was probably copied from print. From the standpoint of scribal culture it is thus, with most of the other ballads in the collection, the same kind of text as Hanson's copies of the two printed broadsides describing the Armada victory celebration late in 1588. Print texts were often copied into manuscript collections. However, poem 17 in the Ashmole manuscript, the story of the West-Darcy feud, is as much a "folk" ballad as that of the Eland-Beaumont feud. It recounts events that occurred in Yorkshire in 1556. Its remote rural setting lessened its appeal as a broadside for the London or national market; like the ballad of the Eland-Beaumont feud, it is the kind of verse narrative that circulated in a fairly limited region. It could have gained little traction with collectors outside the locality where the West and Darcy families held sway, and it is no wonder that the Ashmole copy is a unique text.

Hanson's household book thus shares with these four regional miscellanies a broad spectrum of contents marked by the inclusion of practical information and memoranda, locally circulated texts (whether recipes, epitaphs, or ballads), verse and prose taken from the national, even court-centered networks of scribal circulation, and texts copied from a variety of printed sources. Sheale, Gurney, Kay, and Brampton add to this variety by including their own verse in their miscellanies, something Hanson cannot be shown to have done (although his authorship of the verse Decalogue and the Nativity poem is not out of the question). Such regional collections therefore preserve a rich heritage of texts whose literary and social importance remains largely unstudied. They testify not only to rural tastes and interests but also to the significant volume and variety of transcribed discourse that circulated far from the urban, university, and aristocratic environments we ordinarily associate with elite scribal culture.

The Main Compiler and His Family

Additional MS 82370, for the most part an Elizabethan miscellany, descended from the early seventeenth century among the papers of the Spencer-Stanhope family of Elland, Yorkshire, a hamlet then some few miles southwest of Leeds. Of the seven hands we have identified in the codex, five probably belonged to members of the Stanhope family. The John Stanhope who signed his name on folio 1 was probably John Stanhope III (1629–93), grandson of the family patriarch John Stanhope of Horsforth (c. 1525–93). He is the only family member of that name whose handwriting we have not seen and who is likely to have written in an italic of this type. Neither he nor the four as-yet-unidentified scribes were significant contributors to the anthology's overall text. Their longest entry is the inserted feud narration on folio 15 that replaces the original leaf 15.

Most or all of the manuscript's remaining forty-nine folios are in a single old-fashioned secretary hand. Given the anthology's strictly Elizabethan contents, the elder John Stanhope at first seemed the most likely compiler. However, we were unable to find any examples of his handwriting among the family papers at Sheffield City Archives or the West Yorkshire Archive Service, Bradford. Instead, after locating several legal documents that

Stanhope signed with his mark, we reluctantly concluded that the family's patriarch was illiterate.[17] Neither does the manuscript's dominant hand resemble that of the next two generations of Stanhope heirs, Walter and John II.[18] The manuscript was instead compiled by the Stanhopes' neighbor and relative by marriage, John Hanson (1517–99) of Woodhouse in the hamlet of Rastrick, also of the parish of Elland.[19] Whereas John Stanhope was a newcomer to Yorkshire in the mid-sixteenth century, the Hansons can be traced back to Roger of Rastrick, resident of Elland in 1251. Heirs male of this family were designated "de Rastrick" until the mid-fourteenth century, when Henry de Rastrick's son, John, took the name Hanson, a contraction of "Henry's son."[20] Our scribe was the sixth consecutive family heir named John.[21] His mother was Agnes, eldest daughter of John Savile of Newhall. Savile represented a cadet branch of the Yorkshire family whose senior members had been seated at Thornhill since the late fourteenth century. Both the Henry Saviles commemorated on folios 42v–45v had served in Parliament and as sheriffs of Yorkshire as well as in other important offices. The Hansons of Tudor Rastrick were a well-connected, prosperous yeoman family.

By 1549 John Hanson had married Margaret, daughter and co-heir of Thomas Woodhead. Their first son, another John (1549–1621), was followed by two more sons and three daughters. Margaret died in June 1571; on 13 October 1572 Hanson married his second wife, also named Margaret, daughter of Robert Wade and widow of Edward Farrer. Their daughter,

17. These are three acknowledgments of debt dated 28 October 1590 and 2 November 1592. WYAS, Bradford, SpSt/5/4/2/2, SpSt/5/1/28.

18. Hugh Owen, *Stanhope, Atkinson, Haddon & Shaw, Four North Country Families* (Chichester, UK: H. Owen, 1985), plate 7, provides a facsimile of a holograph letter written in 1620 by Walter Stanhope (1574–1660). See also Walter's hand in WYAS, Bradford, SpSt/10/7/2. Owen provides a facsimile of the hand of John Stanhope II (1608–75) from the Bradford Archive, SpSt 6/1/8; it also appears passim in SpSt/4/12/2, e.g., f. 2, although this legal memorandum book is a jumble of many other hands as well.

19. The case for Hanson's hand in MS Add. 82370 is made in May, "Matching Hands." The control document is WYAS, Calderdale, KM 255, a grant of 1562 in which Hanson identifies himself as the scribe.

20. J. Horsfall Turner, *Biographia Halifaxiensis: or, Halifax Families and Worthies*, 2 vols. (Bingley, UK: T. Harrison, 1883), 1:230.

21. George John Armytage, "Ancient Pedigree of Hanson of Restrick," *Yorkshire Archaeological Journal* 1 (1870): 80–81.

Judith, was baptized in the parish church 13 June 1574.[22] Upon his father's death in 1554, John senior had inherited Woodhouse, the family home, and the principal Hanson properties in and around Rastrick and Elland. He was recognized throughout his adult lifetime as a responsible, productive local citizen. In 1559 he was appointed constable of Rastrick, a post he also held in 1580.[23] His citizenship, however, was exercised in a decidedly rural environment. The hamlets of Rastrick and Elland were bounded on the north by Leeds and on the east by Wakefield. Halifax to the west and Huddersfield to the south were larger towns but scarcely more than hamlets themselves.

Cloth making and the wool trade were, increasingly, the economic mainstays of the entire area, although it is not clear that senior members of the Hanson family were in any sense of the word "clothiers." A majority of the bequests in the will of Hanson's father, however, were sheep parceled out to his children and grandchildren.[24] Hanson's will also reflects the centrality of farming in his life and the lives of his extended family. He bequeathed to his heir, John, two wagons, two plows, a coulter, and three yokes. His son-in-law, William Deyne (Judith's husband), received a wagon, plow, coulter, and other farming equipment plus "my Spelded oxe at Swillington."[25] Hanson's household book likewise bears witness to his rural lifestyle with more than forty recipes for catching fish, frogs, rabbits, and fowl.

Other recipes, however, point to Hanson's literate, quasi-legal occupations. The anthology opens with five recipes for making ink, then turns to making colored inks and paint, such as the instructions "To make whyte color to portrey on paper or parchement" (f. 4). There are recipes "To make glewe for bookes" (ff. 5r–v, 7v)—specifically, to glue parchment

22. John William Clay, ed., *The Registers of Elland, Co. Yorkshire*, 2 vols. (Leeds, UK: J. Whitehead and Son, n.d.), 1:31, 41; Joseph Hunter, *Familiae Minorum Gentium*, ed. John W. Clay, vol. 2, Harleian Society Visitation Series 38 (London: Harleian Society, 1895), 1214–15; www.familysearch.org.

23. Joseph Horsfall Turner, *History of Brighouse, Rastrick, and Hipperholme* (Bingley, UK: T. Harrison and Sons, 1893), 43; Hunter, *Familiae*, 2:1215.

24. Borthwick Institute, University of York, Probate Register 14, f. 222r–v.

25. Will of John Hanson, Borthwick Institute, University of York, Probate Register 27, ff. 669–72.

membranes together—to cleanse a soiled book (f. 5v), and to make "a sasse [sauce] for pryntyng of bookes wythe gold" (f. 6v). These entries suggest that Hanson was involved with writing and illuminating manuscripts. The colors of the various inks and paints suggest a particular interest in heraldry and the depiction of coats of arms. No manuscripts of this kind compiled by Hanson have come to light, but his son's heraldic manuscript with beautifully colored coats of arms and genealogical notes on royal and noble English families is preserved at the Calderdale record office.[26]

How the elder Hanson learned to read and write remains mere guesswork, for there is no record of his education. He was proficient enough in Latin to appreciate and copy into his anthology a Latin epigram (f. 49), as well as to adapt and transcribe numerous Latin legal documents. He probably had at least the equivalent of a grammar school education, although it was not until 1621 that his son and heir founded the first grammar school in Rastrick by a provision in his will.[27] John senior's name does not appear on the rolls of either university or the Inns of Court. Given the very fragmentary nature of the latter records for the first half of the sixteenth century, it is entirely possible that Hanson spent time at one of the Inns or received rudimentary legal training at one of the subordinate Inns of Chancery, for which no membership records survive.

Whatever the source of his legal education, there is ample evidence that Hanson performed the duties of scrivener and law clerk. He identified himself as the scribe of two legally binding vellum documents, an indenture dated 26 May 1561 and a bond dated 11 May 1562. In addition, his hand can also be found in a number of other contemporary legal documents.[28] He witnessed numerous deeds, grants, and indentures the substance of which did not otherwise concern him, and he was frequently

26. WYAS, Calderdale, SPC: 118, a folio volume with Latin epitaph for Sir John Savile, the elder John Hanson's first cousin (d. 1607, ff. 130–30v), and Gabriel Savile's epitaph in English verse for Henry Savile (d. 1569).

27. William Page, *Victoria County History, York*, 3 vols. (London: Constable, 1907–13), 1:482. John Hanson the younger endowed the school with lands worth twenty shillings per annum (will dated 14 August 1621).

28. WYAS, Calderdale, KM: 255, witnessed "Iohis Hanson scriptoris," and KM: 271/1, subscribed "Ioh*ne* hanson scriptore." Hanson also transcribed, inter alia, KM: 256, KM: 275a, 275b, KM: 287, KM: 292/1, KM: 324, KM: 334, KM: 346, KM: 296*, KM: 370, and KM: 392.

granted power of attorney in property transactions during the 1560s.[29] This responsibility was apparently related to his office as grave (or administrative officer) of Rastrick. Hanson's seat at Woodhouse was part of the Manor of Wakefield, itself belonging to the Duchy of Lancaster. The manor was divided into twelve now-obsolete administrative units known as graveships, one of which was Rastrick. Graves were elected annually from among the landowners in each graveship.[30] At the manor courts and leet courts, graves represented their fellow tenants in whatever transfers of land came before the courts. The published court rolls show that John Hanson senior served as grave in 1551 and his son, John junior, in 1583–85, although the elder Hanson must also have held the office during the 1560s when he was frequently called upon to represent his neighbors in the royal court.[31]

John Hanson was thus a trusted participant in some of the weightiest legal matters of rural southwest Yorkshire. In 1585, for example, Hanson, his son Thomas of Rastrick, another Thomas Hanson (of Toythill), and Thomas Thornhill "prised & estemed" the inventory of goods and livestock owned by a recently deceased widow, Elizabeth Thornhill.[32] Depositions in a court case of 1574 reveal how the Hansons, father and son, were entrusted to draw up original legal documents. When the heirs of Richard Sunderland of High Sunderland near Halifax contested certain provisions of his will, the Hansons found themselves in the thick of the controversy. The elder Hanson was deposed 14 May 1574; he testified that Sunderland had sent for him about a year before, requesting that he "bring with him pen inck and paper to take a note for making certeyn writinges." The next

29. Hanson witnessed the following documents among others (now located in the Armytage archive at Calderdale) to which he was not otherwise a party: KM/S: 254* (grant, 1560); KM: 275 (covenant, 1562); KM/S: 279* (sale, 1562); KM: 289 (sale, 1565); KM: 313 (bond, 1567); KM: 369 (grant, 1574); KM: 390 (sale, 1577); KM: 408 (grant, 1579); KM: 422 (sale, 1581). Hanson exercised power of attorney in the following transactions: KM: 287 (grant, 1565); KM/S: 319* (grant, 1568); KM: 324, 337 (grants, 1568); KM: 320, 321, 339; and KM/S: 345* (grants, 1569).

30. These were always tenants in chief, who held their lands directly from the Crown rather than from a subordinate tenant.

31. Ann Weikel, ed., *The Court Rolls of the Manor of Wakefield from October 1550 to September 1552* (Leeds: Yorkshire Archaeological Society, 1989), 83; Ann Weikel, ed., *The Court Rolls of the Manor of Wakefield from October 1583 to September 1585* (Leeds: Yorkshire Archaeological Society, 1984), 6, 12, 120–21 passim.

32. Peter C. D. Brears, ed., *Yorkshire Probate Inventories 1542–1689*, Yorkshire Archaeological Society Record Series, vol. 134 (Kendal: Yorkshire Archaeological Society, 1972), 54–55.

day Hanson went with John the younger to Sunderland's house, where "the testator shewed this examinant that he had sent for him . . . to make a Draught of his will and to have his counsell in the devising and disposing of his landes and goodes." Hanson promised to have the will "fayre writen into ~~parchment~~ paper" within a week's time, then urged Sunderland to invite "Mr Thomson of Eshold to desire him to come over about the same tyme that his better counsaill might be had concerninge the same matter" (*CP* G.1695, p. 44). On June 1 the Hansons returned to High Sunderland, where, with Thomson's advice, they added a codicil to the will (*CP* G.1695, pp. 44–45). Whether such work was a sideline or the main source of income for the elder Hanson and his son, clearly their joint occupation as scriveners and informal legal counsel was an important part of their livelihood. Moreover, Hanson's youngest son, Nicholas (c. 1562–1613), was formally trained in the law, for his monumental inscription describes him as "one of the Attornies of the Common Pleas, Servant to Sir John Savile, Baron of the Chr. [Exchequer]."[33] This probably explains why Hanson appointed Nicholas, rather than his heir, John junior, the coexecutor of his will, along with his widow, Margaret.

To the extent that Hanson practiced law, he belonged to what C. W. Brooks terms the "lower branch" of the Elizabethan legal profession.[34] While the "upper branch" consisted of serjeants-at-law, barristers, and others qualified to plead in the central law courts at Westminster, clients in local provincial courts were often represented by persons with little or no legal training. Scriveners in particular were often consulted in such matters because they drew up legal documents and thus knew (or ought to know) something about what they copied. When Hanson advised Richard Sunderland to obtain Thomson of Eshold's counsel regarding his will, he was apparently defining his own role in such legal proceedings by referring his client to a trained lawyer. As a trusted law clerk, Hanson could originate legally binding documents, but, since he was not trained in the law, he very responsibly urged his client to consult someone who was as he

33. Turner, *Biographia*, 1:182. Savile was appointed Baron of the Exchequer in 1598 and reappointed by James I in April 1603. See David Ibbetson, "Savile, Sir John (1546–1607)," *ODNB*, http://www.oxforddnb.com/view/article/24741?docPos=2.

34. Brooks, *Pettyfoggers and Vipers of the Commonwealth, the 'Lower Branch' of the Legal Profession in Early Modern England* (Cambridge: Cambridge University Press, 1986), 2–4.

and his son drafted Sunderland's will in final form. The degree to which scriveners such as Hanson practiced law caused Brooks to doubt whether they "and the other professional, semi-professional, and amateur provincial practitioners should be classified as lawyers in the same sense as those who were trained at the inns of court."[35]

Hanson encouraged his eldest son in these same scribal, quasi-legal occupations by bequeathing to him "my booke of statutes Rastall translation . . . and which of all my president [precedent] bookes he will chuse over and above all such prefermentes as I have bestowed upon him."[36] William Rastell's *Collection of all the Statutes*, first published in 1557, was a substantial compendium in alphabetical order of virtually every subject treated by English law since Magna Carta. This abridgement had seen seventeen editions by the time of Hanson's death in 1599. The fact that Hanson owned multiple precedent books also testifies to his creation of legal documents. The most popular printed collection of model documents appeared first in 1543, entitled *A newe boke of Presidentes in maner of a Register*, with a preface by Thomas Phayer (Phaer), the translator of Virgil's *Aeneid*. It provided sample texts for a broad spectrum of legal documents in Latin and English and had been reprinted at least twenty-nine times by 1599. But John the younger also received at least one of his father's "home-made" precedent books. This is a substantial folio of approximately two hundred leaves bound in parchment and entitled on the front cover "Liber Joh[ann]is Hanson ex dono Joh[ann]is Hanson patris sui." Its contents include copies of bills, replications, answers, and rejoinders as used to pursue a case through the courts, along with sample documents showing the form of depositions, tax, tithing, and other records. Some entries, however, have no direct bearing on the Hansons' scribal undertakings, such as the notes on which species of fish inhabit certain rivers (information relevant to the section of the household book dealing with fish baits) and lists of the natural resources of certain Welsh counties. Nearly all the manuscript's contents are in the hand of John Hanson senior and provide an exact match with the dominant hand of Additional MS 82370.[37]

35. Ibid., 44–46.

36. Will, Probate Register 27, f. 671v.

37. WYAS, Bradford, SpSt 1/2.

Hanson's maternal relatives, the Saviles of Bradley, were involved with a number of his legal transactions. Members of the senior branch of this family, among the most affluent and powerful gentry in Yorkshire, were the subjects of several key entries in Hanson's miscellany. In addition to the two Savile epitaphs, the Eland-Beaumont feud narratives in prose and verse are patronage pieces addressed to the Saviles. Through marriage in the fourteenth century to the only surviving Eland heir, the Saviles reaped long-term benefits from the destruction of the house of Eland. Both Henry Savile of Over Bradley, Hanson's uncle, and John Savile, Henry's son and heir (the future Baron of the Exchequer), witnessed the grant that Hanson transcribed and signed as witness in 1562 (WYAS KM: 255). Hanson and his uncle had also witnessed a quitclaim on 25 September 1561 (WYAS KM: 261/2). Hanson witnessed a bill of sale occasioned by the death of Henry Savile of Thornhill in 1569 that included payment of ninety pounds to Henry's first cousin, Dorothy Savile, daughter of his uncle, Henry of Bradley (WYAS KM: 349). On 14 September 1590 both Hanson senior and his son John witnessed the sale of property in the manor of Clifton to the elder Hanson's first cousin, John Savile of Bradley (WYAS KM: 502). Before attaining his post in the Court of Exchequer, the younger Savile had been educated at Oxford and the Middle Temple and was called to the bar in 1573. He became a founding member of the Society of Antiquaries and was created serjeant-at-law in 1594.[38] He was certainly well qualified to advise Hanson about his quasi-legal activities in and around Elland. Other learned relatives among the Saviles included John's brothers Thomas (d. 1593), fellow of Merton College, Oxford, and Sir Henry (also Hanson's first cousin), the classical scholar and friend of Ben Jonson who became provost of Eton College in 1595.[39]

Along with most of his Savile relatives, Hanson seems to have been a loyal Church of England Protestant. His convictions could be called into question by the mnemonic verses for remembering the saints' days in each month that he copied into his household book (f. 32r–v) from one or another edition of the Catholic *Primer* of Salisbury Use. But no Catholic

38. Ibbetson, "Savile, Sir John (1546–1607)."

39. Hunter, *Familiae*, 2:1213–14; William Dugdale, *The Visitation of the County of Yorke . . . MDCLXV*, Surtees Society, vol. 36 (1859) (London: J. B. Nicholas and Sons, 1859), 346.

sympathies are necessarily implied by this, for the Elizabethan liturgy, the *Book of Common Prayer*, also recognized saints' days. Moreover, their citation in legal documents, especially for dates upon which payments fell due annually, probably explains Hanson's transcription of these poetically pedestrian lines. Hanson's copy of the King of Spain's style (f. 22v) may also look suspicious at first glance, but its placement in between the two ballads celebrating the Armada's defeat (ff. 19–22, 23–26v) renders it a taunting reminder that, for all his imperial grandeur, Philip had suffered a military defeat by the island where he had once nominally reigned as king. Moreover, Hanson edited out the original decree's insulting allegations against the Protestant William of Orange. In his will, Hanson left to John the younger his copy of "my bible in latyne of Jeromes translation" (Will, f. 671v), an imperfect version of scripture by Protestant standards but hardly heterodox. Hanson's will also records his gift of the first part of the "actes and monumentes of the Church" (Will, f. 671), to his grandson Robert; this was, of course, John Foxe's massive compendium of Protestant propaganda, usually referred to as the "Book of Martyrs." Hanson's will further specified with regard to his last rites, "that holie Church have her dutie according to the lawes and statutes of this realme" (Will, ff. 669–70v). Neither his serious regard for religion nor his allegiance to the national Protestant church is doubtful.

Hanson's intellectual interests, religious and otherwise, can be reconstructed from his household book and from additional bequests in his will. His religious concerns are further witnessed by two unique poems in the anthology, the Ten Commandments in English verse (f. 42), and a narrative in quatrains of the Three Kings' journey to present gifts to the baby Jesus (f. 32). The inclusion of two poems attributed to the Queen (ff. 45v–46) testifies to Hanson's loyalty to the Crown. Indeed, he also credited Elizabeth with at least the final quatrain, if not the entire epitaph for William, first Earl of Pembroke, a broadside poem clearly attributed to Thomas Churchyard in the printed source. Hanson's concern with practical advice and moral instruction, so typical of the age, is witnessed by the eighty-six couplets he copied from the *Preceptes of Cato* (ff. 27–29v). In addition, he willed to his son Thomas "the Breviarie of health Compiled by Doctor board" (Will, f. 671v): six editions of Andrew Borde's compendious listing of ailments with their causes and remedies appeared between 1547 and 1598. Two bequests in Hanson's will testify to his interest in history. He left to his eldest son "my boke called supplimentum Cronicarum" (Will, f. 671v), perhaps John Stow's *Summary of English Chronicles*, which was reprinted six times between 1565 and 1590. His son Thomas also received his copy of "Langueth Cronicle" (Will, f. 671v), an "epitome" summarizing world history from the Creation. The narrative, often referred to as Cooper's *Chronicle*, was continued by several authors from the reign of Henry VIII into that of Elizabeth. Thomas Lanquet's name, however, was retained on the title page of the work, which saw five editions between 1549 and 1565.

Where Hanson was not copying from printed sources, the language of his household book reflects his own dialect and that of the northern region in which the manuscripts he copied circulated. The *OED* classifies several usages as Scottish: "louped" for "leaped" in the Eland-Beaumont prose narrative (f. 18), and "Dyscryve" for "write down" in the epitaph for Sir Henry Savile (f. 42v, now obsolete except in Scots). Among the recipes on folios 1–11v we find "kelyinges" (keelings, f. 5), Scottish and northern dialect for codfish, and "suddle," Scottish and northern English dialect for "stain" or "sully" (f. 7v). Some of Hanson's spellings are characteristically Scottish. The *OED* recognizes "waik" (f. 3v) as a Middle English and Scots form of "weak." By a ratio of about three to one, Hanson spells "wood" with two *d*'s, a fifteenth- or sixteenth-century Scottish spelling, while his consistent spelling "heigh" for "high" disappears except in Scotland after the fifteenth century.[40] Among the four similar regional anthologies we have compared with this one, our impression is that Ashmole MS 48 most resembles it in the occurrence of northern dialect words. John Kay's anthologies, also products of Yorkshire (Folger Library MSS X.d.446 and X.d.449), present many unusual spellings, but the vocabulary is less distinctively northern than Hanson's.[41] Other unusual dialect words that crop up in Hanson's manuscript are cited in the glosses and textual notes.

The extent of Hanson's property and wealth at his death is difficult to estimate, especially since he had previously conferred on his heir, John, "landes tenamentes and hereditamentes" that are accordingly unspecified

40. Under "Heichland," the online *Dictionary of the Scots Language*, http://www.dsl.ac.uk, records "Heigh land men" for "highland men" as late as 1615.

41. Linguistically, the miscellanies compiled in East Anglia by Thomas Brampton and Henry Gurney seem to us very similar to the London and South Midlands "standard" Elizabethan dialect.

in his will. To his second son, Thomas, he left property in Greetland and the Manor of Clifton, with smaller outlying parcels. Nicholas, his third son, also received property in the Manor of Clifton plus land, houses, and outbuildings in Batley, Woodson, Hipperholme, Brighouse, and Elland. His youngest daughter, Judith, wife of William Deyne, inherited property in Clifton but also a cottage with gardens and other land in Worsbrough, a town more than fifteen miles southeast of Rastrick. Of his monetary bequests, nearly all were expressed in shillings and pence and included several pounds in "matching funds" for repairs to local roadways and a bridge, contingent upon the community's raising like sums for the work. The priest who delivered his funeral sermon was to receive ten shillings and the parish poor, twenty-three shillings, four pence (Will, ff. 669, 670v–71). Hanson bequeathed a few pounds or shillings to each of ten grandchildren, four nephews and one niece, his three daughters-in-law, plus four of his wife's children by Edward Farrar and two of their grandchildren. Even after he distributed more than sixty-seven pounds received from Margaret's brother, Robert Wade, his total bequests in coin came to less than one hundred pounds (Will, ff. 671v–72), an amount that was substantial for a yeoman family and indicative that the Hansons were destined to enter the gentry class and become armigerous under the Stuarts.

Hanson had opened his household book by transcribing some ninety recipes for such active lifetime pursuits as the indoor activities of writing, painting, and repairing manuscripts, on the one hand, and such outdoor activities as fishing and fowling on the other. Toward the end of his anthology he copied a very popular lyric by Thomas, Lord Vaux, that may have consciously served as his farewell to all these things toward the end of his life: "I lothe that I Dyd love / in youthe that I thought swete / as tyme Requyres for my behove / me thynkes they are note mete" (f. 49v). His final entries on folio 50 concern the lands and tenants connected with Netherwood House, the Hanson property occupied by his brother, Edward (d. 1601), among other tenants;[42] they are in a different ink from the poem on folio 49v and were perhaps jotted down at an earlier date.

42. *Index of Wills in the York Registry, A.D. 1594 to 1602*" Yorkshire Archaeological Society Record Series 24 (Leeds, UK: Yorkshire Archaeological Society, 1898), 46.

John Hanson's will of 11 June 1599 (proved 20 August), makes no mention of his manuscript household book.[43] Its transfer to the Spencer-Stanhope archive was made possible by the marriage of his granddaughter, Mary, to Walter Stanhope (1574–1660) on 17 November 1600. The daughter of John Hanson the younger, she had been christened 18 April 1574. She bore Walter at least nine children and died in 1618, probably as a result of complications of childbirth, for her infant daughter, Catherine, died in the same year. The Stanhopes, like the Hansons, were prosperous yeoman stock ascending socially during Elizabeth's reign. In 1630 Walter was fined sixteen pounds for refusing to attend Charles I's coronation and to absorb the expense of being knighted.[44] Possibly Mary herself brought her grandfather's household book into the Stanhope household, but she does not seem to have been a particular favorite with him. The elder Hanson remembered her in his will with a bequest of forty shillings, the same amount given to each of her three sisters (Will, f. 671). More likely the manuscript attracted the notice of her eldest son, John Stanhope, upon her father's death in 1621.[45] As one of John Hanson's four heirs he might easily have claimed the booklet as a family memento owned by his grandfather and largely compiled by his great-grandfather.

Organization of the Book

In the chapters that follow we offer (though not in the order in which they appear in the manuscript) semidiplomatic texts of most of the contents of Hanson's household book. Although many of the texts we have edited are followed by textual collations and, in some cases, genealogical

43. Ibid., 46.

44. Familysearch.org ; Owen, *Stanhope, Atkinson, Haddon & Shaw*, 11 and app. 1; William Easterbrook Preston and Joseph Hambley Rowe, eds., *A Transcript of the Early Registers of the Parish of Guiseley, in the County of York, 1584–1720; Together with a Transcript of the Early Registers of the Chapelry of Horsforth with Notes on Guiseley Families* (Bradford, UK: Percy Lund, Humphries, 1913), 105.

45. In his will (proved 8 November 1621), Hanson designated as his heirs his two living daughters and the eldest sons of his deceased daughters Mary and Margaret. Yorkshire Archaeological Society, Leeds, DD 12/II/16/1.

analyses of their manuscript and/or print transmission (familiar features of critical editions), we have chosen an unconventional format that gives equal weight to the edited texts and to their literary and cultural analyses. Whereas traditional editions disperse interpretive material and contextual information into general introductions, footnotes, and sometimes separate commentary sections, we have chosen instead to consolidate analyses and interpretations in the sections that precede the edited texts, discussing important topics related both to the compiler's interests and choices affecting the makeup of his household book and to the ways the texts he collected might be understood. We discuss particular genres Hanson collected and the sources from which he drew particular items, emphasizing the compiler's interests and tastes. We reflect on what this scribe's presentation of a quite heterogeneous gathering of texts tells us about the scribal culture upon which he drew in forming his household book, and, finally, we interpret the works Hanson collected in the contexts of both local and national cultures. We were particularly conscious of the need to introduce and provide an extensive discussion of the historical and literary contexts of both the Eland-Beaumont prose and poetic narratives and the two Armada thanksgiving ballads, so the introductory material in chapters 1 and 2 is quite elaborate. Ultimately the most valuable parts of these chapters are the edited texts, since they are important ones that either had been lost or had faded into oblivion. They need to be read and interpreted, however, within the contexts of the local and national cultures that produced and used them, and so we provide extensive prefatory comments.

The works included in the remaining three chapters require less historical and cultural analysis, but we attempt to contextualize them adequately. Chapter 3, in five separate sections, considers poems and prose excerpts from five different printed sources, interspersing textual and contextual analyses with the presentation of the texts. Chapter 4, dealing with texts that Hanson derived from manuscript sources, separately discusses and presents five different texts or sets of texts: the two epitaphs for the Savile family members; the two poems attributed to Queen Elizabeth, both of which require textual analyses and stemmata; the verse Decalogue; the Nativity poem; and the seventeenth-century lyric fragment transcribed in a later hand. Chapter 5, dealing with the utilitarian material found both at the start of the manuscript and in later sections, deals first with the recipes for different-colored inks, fish bait, fowl trapping, and other "how to" material found in the first eleven folios of the manuscript, but it presents only a representative selection of this material rather than a complete set of these texts. It concludes with separate discussions of and edited texts of the "byerley bouke," some real estate notes, and the list of English and Welsh counties. The conclusion highlights the importance of John Hanson's household book as a revealing cultural document. It is a rare example of a provincial compilation made by someone below the educational and social status of most collector-scribes from the period. The fact that this manuscript contains both lost and important neglected texts makes it all the more valuable and worth our study.

Editorial Principles

For the prose and poetic items in the manuscript, we present an old-spelling text (as in quotations from primary sources), but we have normalized *i/j* and *u/v* and expanded all contractions, including the terminal loop abbreviation for *es/us/is*, the superscript abbreviation for *er*, and the various contractions for *ro, re*, and *er* formed with minuscule *p*. Abbreviated words have been expanded but the ampersand (&) retained. We have preserved the light punctuation of the original, including Hanson's occasional use of the virgule or slash (/) as a period. Deletions are indicated by strikethroughs, and hypothetical corrections and emendations appear in square brackets. Illegible or missing text is marked by angle brackets (< >). Above-the-line texts are marked by insertion carets (^). Line breaks in the transcription agree with those on the page for entries in both prose and verse. Our glosses depend on the *OED*'s online version unless otherwise acknowledged.

1

The Eland-Beaumont Feud

This news which is called true is so like an old tale that the verity of it is in strong suspicion.

(Shakespeare, *The Winter's Tale*, 5.2.25–26)

Roughly a third of the Hanson manuscript is given over to recording two versions of a mid-fourteenth-century revenge story centered on a conflict between two Yorkshire families from Hanson's own neighborhood, the Elands and the Beaumonts—the first a prose narrative (ff. 12–18v) and the second a long ballad (ff. 33–42).[1] The former, either by design or accidentally, creates the (false) impression that the latter literary treatment of the feud is consistent with the historical record, or at least with the historical memory of those living in the area in which the original events of the story took place. These accounts of the Eland-Beaumont feud in prose and verse comprise a unique combination of materials from what might be termed "folk history." Every episode narrated in the ballad could have been drawn

1. In the text discussion we cite the prose narrative by folio number and the ballad by stanza and line numbers.

from the prose version, which is ultimately independent of the ballad since its last part covers events omitted from the poem: the subsequent careers and deaths of the avengers who brought the Eland family line to an end. Whether or not the balladeer made immediate use of the prose narrative, Hanson's anthology preserves the only known sixteenth-century combination of a contemporary and unpublished prose parallel with its companion text, a "popular" or "folk" ballad.

The basic story is one of crime, revenge, and vengeful overreaching in mid-fourteenth-century southwest Yorkshire, extending from one generation to the next, with consequences for a third. It begins, shockingly, with the account of how a local sheriff, Sir John Eland, and his men murdered Hugh Quermby and William Lockwood, friends and supporters of Sir Robert Beaumont, before invading the moated manor house of Beaumont himself and murdering him in the sight of his family. Beaumont's son Adam and the sons of the murdered Quermby and Lockwood and the Beaumont kinsman Thomas Lacy[2] were taken to Lancashire, where they grew to manhood and resolved to take revenge on Eland. The second part of the story begins with the now-grown Adam Beaumont, Quermby, Lockwood, and Lacy returning to their home territory to ambush and slay Sir John Eland before retreating to safety in Lancashire. The third part of the story portrays the avengers' overreaching in their ambushing of Sir John Eland's son and grandson (thus destroying the patrilineage of the Elands), then fleeing the neighborhood pursued by local Eland supporters. The pursuers seriously wound and then callously kill Quermby, whom, after an emotional parting, his friends had been compelled to leave as they fled. The ballad ends with this slaying of Quermby by Eland's men, while the prose account extends the story further, adding an episode in which Lockwood is betrayed to his enemies by his lover and concluding with a brief account of the subsequent histories of Lacy and Beaumont.[3]

---

2. From the time of the Norman Conquest, the Lacy (or de Lacy) family was prominent in Yorkshire. See W. E. Wightman, *The Lacy Family in England and Normandy 1066–1194* (Oxford: Clarendon Press, 1966).

3. Since there is, however, some information in the ballad not found in the prose history, such as the names of Sir John Eland's four dependents, it is obvious that the poetic account had another source or other sources as well.

Differences between the Prose and Ballad Versions of the Eland-Beaumont Conflict

The prose narrative of the Eland-Beaumont conflict and the ballad version of the events differ somewhat in both details and emphasis. The prose narrative begins in medias res with Sir John Eland getting right to the planning of the attack on Sir Robert Beaumont: "It happened in the monthe of maye that sir John Eland forcasted the waye and whan to betray Sir Robert Beaumont" (f. 12). The ballad, by contrast, starts with general moral reflections on the dangers of pride, ambition, and social rivalry, before presenting Eland as a prideful villain ready to assault Sir Robert. The ballad gestures toward a possible context for the antagonism in alluding to oral history:

> Some saye that Eland sheryff was
> by bea[m]ount Dysobeyed
> whiche myght hym make for such trespase
> wyth hym the worse appeyd
>
> (f. 33v, st. 14)

The precise historical circumstances of the feud, however, are occluded in both narratives.[4]

While the prose version mentions that Eland gathered "agreat number of mene" (f. 12), the ballad is more specific in identifying them as "frendes and tennantes all" (15.2) who were selected because they were "stowt sturdye mene and taulle" (15.4)—that is, thugs. In the prose version, Eland and his men slay Quermby and Lockwood because "Eland suspected [they] wolde stand in armes agaynst hym in behalf of theyr kynsman Sir Robert" (f. 12). In the ballad, the two victims are called "Syr Robartes [*sic*] beamount ayde" (18.2), but their murders are presented first without justification. In the prose version, the moat around Sir Robert Beaumont's house is not specifically mentioned, though it is in the ballad, and the drawbridge figures

4. The relevant historical documents dealing with the feud and its surrounding events are discussed in J. M. Kaye, "The Eland Murders, 1350–51: A Study of the Legend of the Eland Feud," *Yorkshire Archaeological Journal* 51 (1979): 61–79.

in both accounts, for the home invasion takes place after "a mayde of the howse" (f. 12) lets down the bridge in the early morning. The prose version notes that the "famylye [was] in bedde no thynge syspectyng the mater" (f. 12v), while the ballad cuts right to the invasion into the "knyghtes chamber" (21.2). In the prose account Sir Robert gets up suddenly and, with his family members, fights the attackers, forcing them to retreat. In the ballad, Sir Robert "fought agenst theym manfullye" (22.3) though he was "unarmed" (22.4), and only then "hys servantes Rose and styll wythestood / and stroke wythe myght and mayne / in hys defence" (23.2–4)—in vain. In the ballad, though not in the prose account, Lady Beaumont "cryed and skyrked wythall / from hyr than whan they ledde / hyr Deare husband into the haule / and there storke [*sic*] of hys heade" (24.1–4)—a detail missing from the prose but amplified emotionally and interpreted morally in the subsequent ballad stanzas.

In the prose narrative, the death of Sir Robert Beaumont takes place in the context of armed struggle, and the death of Beaumont's brother William is mentioned, as well as the killing of someone named Exley. The latter is identified as a relative who "aforetyme slewe sir John Eland brotheres sonne for the Which to agrement he gave acertan peece of land to the Elandes yet after the agrement made Sir John Eland sought to have slayne hym and therefore Exle was constrayned to flee unto thafforsayd sir Robert Beaumont for ayde who bycause he was hys kynsman Rescued hym whiche partlye was the occasyon of the great malice that was betwyxt the sayd sir Robert Beaumont and sir John Eland" (ff. 12v–13). At the point in the story at which Beaumont dies, a context that might explain Eland's own wish for revenge is provided (instead of being presented at the start), information that is missing from the more simplified circumstances of the ballad, except possibly in the vague reference in stanza 14 to an act of disobedience on Beaumont's part when Eland was sheriff.

The prose narrative and the ballad differ in their presentation of the involvement of Beaumont's Lancashire relatives, to whom the family appeals for rescue. In the midst of the prose account of Eland's attack, we are told that "one of Sir Roberte kynsmen and a frend of hys went to lancashyer to geyt knowledge [of the attack] unto Sir John brewerton and Syr John Towneley" and, in response, "they assented to come over wythe Dyverse gentlymen and otheres well armed to Rescue Syr Robert beamount" (f. 12v). On the way, a messenger informs them of the death of Sir Robert and they return to their home county, sending later for Sir Robert's surviving children and those of Quermby, Lockwood, and Lacy to put them under their protection. In the ballad, the help of the Lancashire relatives is sought after Sir Robert's death, and because they were Lady Beaumont's relatives, after she has fled they take the widow and the children into their protection in Lancashire at Bruerton (Brereton) and Townley Hall.

Both the prose text and the ballad include a scene in which Eland and the home invaders force the Beaumont family to sit down to breakfast with them after they have killed Sir Robert. In the prose account this happens (improbably) after the Lancashire relatives are assured of the safety of the family and return home; in the ballad the Lancashire relatives are not involved at this point. In the prose text, Eland calls Beaumont's children before him and offers them bread, "whiche they Receyved but adam Beamount theldest after he hade taken yt, he wythe dysdeignne threwe yt at hym agayne, which Eland perceyvynge sayd that he would wede owt thofspring of his blood as they wede the weedes owt of corne" (f. 13r–v), but Eland does not kill the children, allowing them to go to Lancashire. In the ballad, there is less detail about the incident: after slaying Sir Robert, the murderers sit down to eat before the rest of the family, and after Eland ordered Sir Robert's sons to dine with him, one of them, Adam, "wold nether eite nor Drynke" (30.4), at which point Eland foresees the child's growing up to avenge his father's death and threatens to kill him if he sees him "wax wilde" (32.1). Though at this point the prose narrative continues uninterruptedly, the ballad here marks the end of the "fyrst fraye" (33.1).

The next part of the story deals with the relocation of the Beaumont, Quermby, and Lockwood children, along with Thomas Lacy, to the houses of Lady Beaumont's Lancashire kinsmen. The prose account does not mention Lady Beaumont, though the ballad has her fleeing her home territory with her children. In the prose version the next stage of the story abruptly begins by noting that the sojourn in Lancashire lasted until "they" (the children) were "xx yeires of age" and "weare strong and of good audacitye and well cowlde handyll theyr weapons," at which point they "Remembred the traytoures Done unto theyr parentes by sir John Eland" (f. 13v) and resolved to pursue revenge. In the ballad, the young men are trained in "Feates of fence" for "fyften yeires" (42.3), at which point Lockwood proposes the vengeance on both Sir John Eland Sr. and his son ("Caines sede," 44.4). In marked contrast to the prose account, the ballad emotionally heightens the scene and also has the narrator sympathize with the young men in their desire for revenge by lamenting the murders of their fathers:

> oh Lord this was a wicked dede
> who cowlde theyr handes Refrayne
> for to wede owt suche wicked menne
> Though yt were to theyr payne
>
> (f. 36, st. 46)

In recounting the preparation for the ambush of Sir John Eland, the prose version sticks to the main facts, but the ballad gives some emotional texture to the scene and more detail about the setting, though both versions mention Sir John's doffing his cap to the young men in "curtesye" (f. 14)—a gesture that causes them to announce their intention of avenging the deaths of their fathers. Both versions sketch out the fight that took place, though the ballad adds the detail that they killed Eland "at the Lanes end" (61.2) after separating him from his companions. The prose account moves immediately to relating that the killers returned to "Fournyshe Felles"[5] (f. 14v), but to conclude this section of the story, the ballad offers four stanzas of moral reflections on what had just happened (62–65), contrasting a Christian ethic of forgiveness with the behavior of the natural man who pursues rough justice. This anticipates the moral conclusion drawn at the end of the ballad—an ethical context missing in the prose narrative.

The next section of the story, introduced by a brief summary of the action in the prose account, deals with the second wave of vengeance, the killing of Sir John Eland Jr. and his son. The prose narrative, after mentioning the avengers' stay in Lancashire, moves right to their coming back to their home country to pursue their purpose ruthlessly. The ballad, on the other hand, gives a moral context to their actions in the narrator's assertion that the young men had corrupted consciences and were being boastful and villainously calculating. The narrator makes a point here of noting that "in Eland paryshe" (73.2) there also dwelt another gentleman, "savile" (73.3), who spent half the year living elsewhere and who, in any

5. A range of hills west of Lake Windermere.

case, "kept hym selfe from suche debate" (74.1). Neither here nor at the end of story, however, does the prose narrative mention the Savile family.

Before the ambushing of Sir John Eland Jr. there is a comic digressive episode at the mill where the avengers hide themselves before attacking him. They capture the miller's wife when she comes to the mill, and when her angry husband comes to fetch her and punish her for her tardiness, the young men bind him and lay him beside his wife. Although the events are presented in a similar fashion in both the prose and poetic versions of the story, in the prose account the weapon the miller seizes to "chastize" his wife is called a "staple"[6] (f. 15), and in the ballad it is, perhaps for metrical reasons, "a good staffe" (80.3). The premonitory dream Sir John Eland Jr. has the night before he is killed figures also in both accounts, as does his wife's making light of it.

The avengers' attack on Sir John and his retinue is similar in both versions, as is his scornful defiance after they fail to pierce his armor with their arrows. In the ballad, however, Lockwood tells Adam Beaumont that he "shott awydde" (88.4) before he himself shoots Sir John in the head. Before dealing with the flight of the avengers from the roused citizenry, the prose account mentions the heiress sister of Sir John Eland Jr. and her marriage to Savile, as does the ballad, but the ballad moralizes the disruption of the lineage.[7]

The characterization of the pursuers differs somewhat in the two versions. The ballad gives more details, not only naming four men who were Sir John Eland's dependents but also attributing good motives to the commoners joining the pursuit: "all sortes of mene shewed theyr good wylles" (104.1). The parishioners coming to church who willingly participate are "hardye men" who "stand all same / in sight nowe weare they bown" (105.3–4). The ballad portrays the whole local population rising up in moral outrage and loyalty to their fallen feudal lord.

Because the Hanson manuscript is missing a folio, for which a tipped-in leaf in a later hand has been added (see figure 1), there is a problem of discontinuity in this part of the prose account: there is some narrative overlap between folios 15v and 16 and the text differs in some details, particularly

6. The *OED*, definition 1.a has a "post, pillar, column (of wood, stone, metal), *obs*."

7. We discuss this topic below. The prose account refers to "A full sister who inherited his lands & was married to Savill in Edward the 3ds time" (f. 15).

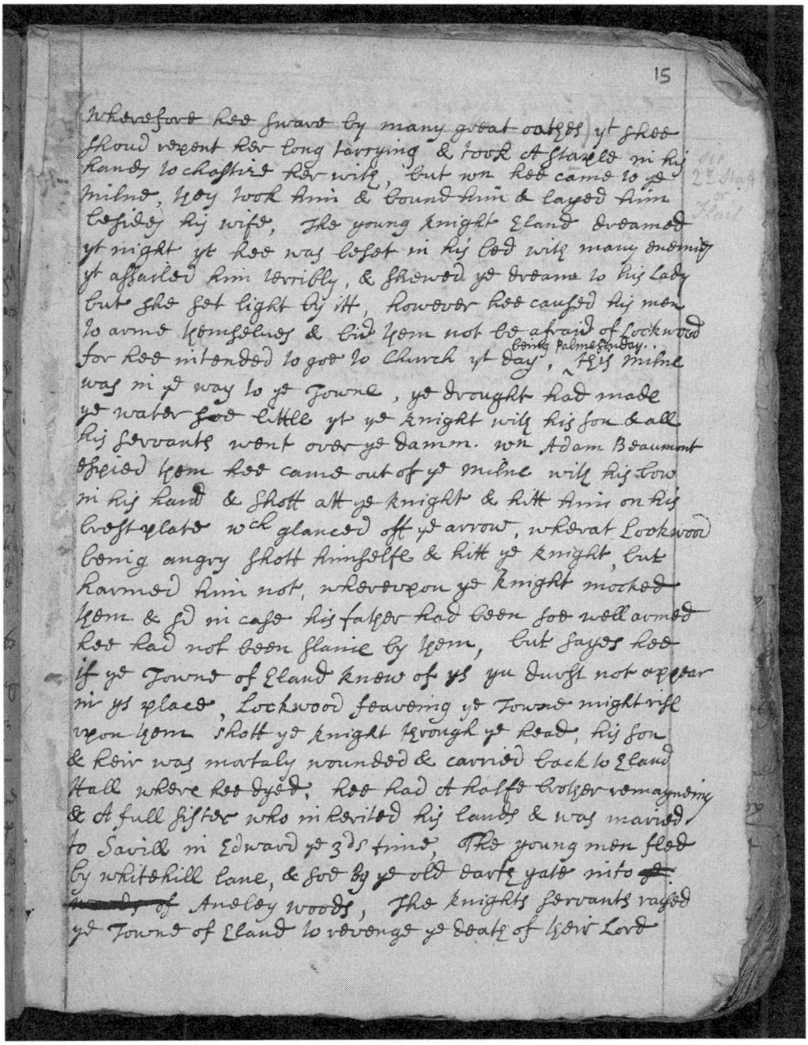
15

Wherefore hee swore by many great oathes yt shee should repent her long tarrying & took A stacke in his hands to chastise her with, but wn hee came to ye milne, they took him & bound him & layed him beside his wife, The young knight Eland dreamed yt night yt hee was beset in his bed with many enemies yt assailed him terribly, & shewed ye dreame to his Lady but she set light by itt, however hee caused his men to arme themselves & bid them not be afraid of Lockwood for hee intended to goe to Church yt day, being Palme Sunday. this milne was in ye way to ye Towne, ye drought had made ye water soe little yt ye knight with his son & all his servants went over ye damm. wn Adam Beaumont espied them hee came out of ye milne with his bow in his hand & shott att ye knight & hitt him on his brest plate wch glanced off ye arrow, whereat Lockwood being angry shott himselfe & hitt ye knight, but harmed him not, whereupon ye knight mocked them & sd in case his father had been soe well armed hee had not been slaine by them, but sayes hee if ye Towne of Eland know of ys you durst not appear in ys place, Lockwood feareing ye Towne might rise upon them shott ye knight through ye head, his son & heir was mortaly wounded & carried back to Eland Hall where hee dyed; hee had A halfe brother remayning & A full sister who inherited his lands & was maried to Savill in Edward ye 3ds time, The young men fled by whitehill lane, & soe by ye old dartsyate into ~~ye~~ ~~[illegible]~~ of Anley woods, The knights servants raysed ye Towne of Eland to revenge ye death of their Lord

Figure 1. BL Add. MS 82370, f. 15. Tipped-in folio to replace lost sheet of prose account of Eland-Beaumont feud. Reproduced by permission of The British Library Board.

with regard to the fate of the wounded Quermby, whom his companions hide in Aynley woods before they leave and who is eventually discovered and cruelly killed by the pursuers. The emotional content of the parting is more developed in the ballad than it is in the prose narration: Quermby, wounded and dying, gives his gold to his friends, stating "my frendes welfare ys my Riches / and cheife felycytye" (111.3–4) as he bids them a noble farewell:

> Gyve place wythe spede and fare yowe well
> Chryst shelde yowe from myschaunce
> In case yt otherwyse befell
> yt wold be my grevance
>
> (f. 41, st. 112)

Quermby's subsequent treatment by his enemies, who "hym slewe quyte owt of hand" (116.1), is vicious and ruthless.

The escape of the other avengers and the death of Quermby complete the narrative of the ballad, followed by the didactic conclusion. The prose version, however, adds another story to the main one, a tale of love and betrayal: "how Lockwood was anamored on a woman Dwellyng at Cannellhaule and howe he was betrayed and slayn" (f. 16v). To conclude this narrative, information is provided about the subsequent fates of Lacy and Beaumont. The new material about Lockwood and his traitorous love, whom he calls "whore" (f. 18) because she betrayed him by cutting his bowstring during his fight with his attackers, involves yet another armed conflict and another unchivalric killing—here by men who first promised Lockwood their "frendshippe" and then "slewe hym verey cruellye" (f. 18). This makes Lockwood's death as ignominious as Quermby's. Beaumont's flight to foreign parts, where he somewhat redeems himself by chivalric service as a crusader (finally dying in Hungary), is explained in relation to the London authorities' sending "Dyverse processes Dyrected to the shiryffe and dyverse other noble menne for to attache him" (f. 18v): what is introduced here is the national legal context that calls attention to the conflict between the primitive revenge ethic of provincial locals and the more civilized forces of law and order. This conclusion asserts the historical veracity of the main events of the story and their aftermath.

The Eland-Beaumont Ballad

The literary significance of this neglected ballad is difficult to establish in context because we lack widely accepted definitions of the "folk" ballad, "popular" ballad, and "art" or "literate" ballad. These categories are beset by complicated questions about the content, origins, performance, and textual transmission of such poems. Must a ballad be primarily a narrative, and if so, can it include a burden (the hallmark of the carol) or a refrain (more typical of purely lyric verse)? Can a folk or popular ballad be composed by a professional minstrel or must it be the work of an anonymous, preferably rural and illiterate, swain (or swains)? Were minstrels musicians who merely recited or chanted the texts to musical accompaniment, as the many references to "talking," and "now let us talk" suggest,[8] and if so can poems that were not sung be considered ballads? Must an authentic folk ballad be taken down from performance? Can it be copied out as well from an old manuscript or even transcribed from a printed text?

Strangely, this generic confusion was unaffected when Francis James Child published his five-volume *English and Scottish Popular Ballads* (1882–98), which has governed virtually all later studies of the subject.[9] This is because Child struggled throughout his career to make final distinctions among types of ballads. Nor have his successors established workable definitions of the ballad genre or its types. Some clarity has been achieved in the course of breaking down the received dichotomy of oral versus scribal and print culture. Adam Fox's important study of this interface is particularly relevant to the ballad. Fox concludes with regard to the discursive mechanisms tying oral folk culture to the written word that the two media were thoroughly intertwined by the late Middle Ages. Scribal culture, he notes, was a pervasive cultural force that was centuries old by 1800, while cheap printed texts were readily available from the early Tudor period onward.[10] Thus, while pockets of strictly oral culture may have existed in early medieval England, they were soon infiltrated by scribal culture, followed by print culture, beginning late in the fifteenth century.

8. David C. Fowler, *A Literary History of the Popular Ballad* (Durham, NC: Duke University Press, 1968), 105, 119, 163.

9. Child, *English and Scottish Popular Ballads*, 5 vols. (1884–98; repr., New York: Dover Publications, 1965). Mary Ellen Brown notes that Child's definition of authentic popular ballads as unwritten, memorized works transmitted orally disqualifies many of the ballads he edited in his landmark anthology. "The Popular Ballad and Oral Tradition," *Oral Tradition* 18 (2003): 176–77. George Shuffelton summarizes the debate over ballad origins as the work of skilled minstrels rather than ignorant amateurs in "Is There a Minstrel in the House? Domestic Entertainment in Late Medieval England," *Philological Quarterly* 87 (2008): 51–76. In "The Folk-Ballad: The Illegitimate Child of the Popular Ballad," *Journal of Folklore Research* 33 (1996): 221–26, Sigrid Rieuwerts reviews Child's efforts to distinguish the popular from the folk ballad.

10. Fox, *Oral and Literate Culture in England 1500–1700* (Oxford: Oxford University Press, 2000), 7–9.

In his influential *The Ballad and the Folk* (1972), David Buchan proposes an exception to this rule in the ballad-rich region of northeast Scotland around Aberdeen. Buchan argues that this area remained largely illiterate until the late eighteenth century, so that its numerous ballads, about one third of Child's total corpus, testify to a wholly oral tradition. Buchan acknowledges the problem of defining the ballad, working sensibly from a general definition that it is a "'folksong that tells a story.'"[11] The methodological problem remains, however, because all the texts he cites date from the eighteenth century at the earliest, and any speculation as to their origins, nature, or form before that time is necessarily guesswork.

In his authoritative study of the ballad, David C. Fowler concluded that poets combined folksong with medieval romance in the second half of the fifteenth century to create the English and Scottish ballad tradition. Fowler brushed off the romantic notion that these poems were products of oral folk transmission from time immemorial with the dictum "A given ballad took the particular shape it has about the same time it was written down, unless there is specific evidence to the contrary."[12] Accordingly, the ballad as a literary type emerged only in the late fifteenth century and as a very fluid genre. Fowler argues, for example, that the "The Battle of Otterburn," based in part on printed sources, was adapted from "Chevy Chase," as revealed by its inclusion of several stanzas from the older ballad.[13] Suppose, however, that some ballads, at least, originated as songs composed and sung by unlettered cottagers—what many consider "genuine" folk ballads. A literate participant in this tradition, minstrel or other, might eventually write out a text for sale to a printer, with whatever editorial and creative changes he saw fit. The resulting publication, perhaps subject to further editing, might then in some sense be considered a "literate/art" ballad, even if it largely reproduced the original folk text. As its dissemination in print inspired readers to sing it anew, it would revert to its communal life as a folk or popular ballad until (and perhaps after many alterations) a later singer or member of his audience prepared it again for the press to continue the cycle. The multiple editions of individual ballads preserved from the seventeenth century onward as represented in such collections as

11. Buchan, *The Ballad and the Folk* (1972; repr., East Linton, Scot.: Tuckwell Press, 1997), 1, 4–5.
12. Fowler, *Literary History*, 18, 5.
13. Ibid., 109.

the Pepys, Roxburghe, and Bagford ballads bear witness to this process. As a variation on it, a literate performer of the song or member of his audience might copy it into a surviving manuscript, giving us a version of the text as presented at that moment in time.[14] John Hanson's copy of the Eland feud ballad is apparently this kind of text.

There is yet another common and perplexing path in the transmission of ballad texts that helps to explain why workable definitions of the genre are lacking. What status shall we assign to at least some of the works of such professional Elizabethan balladeers as William Elderton, Thomas Deloney, John Barker, William Birch, and their fellows who wrote for the commercial broadside market? Some of their art ballads became popular hits; as Autolycus brags of one in his pack, "There's scarce a maid westward but she sings it."[15] Such popular songs, derived from the printed work of professional poets, were necessarily generic hybrids, being simultaneously literate/art ballads in origin but folk/popular ballads in performance and subsequent oral transmission. As evidence of this commingling of ballad types, Fox notes that at least ninety-one supposed folksongs current in the nineteenth century are traceable to broadside ballads printed before 1700.[16] Had the original broadside ballads on the celebration of the Armada defeat copied by Hanson (ff. 19–26v) become popular songs, as was invited by the refrain to one of them, they might have followed this path of popular ballad dissemination. Despite Child's career-long effort to edit popular ballads, the great majority of his ballads are set forth from just such printed broadsides. Only a small minority reflect actual performance or are extant in manuscripts demonstrably earlier than the prints.

---

14. Tessa Watt distinguishes broadside ballads from "traditional" ballads restricted to oral culture, noting that the printed versions tended to lose their literary trappings as they entered popular, oral culture. *Cheap Print and Popular Piety 1550–1640* (Cambridge: Cambridge University Press, 1991), 37, citing Tristram P. Coffin, "The Folk Ballad and the Literary Ballad: An Essay in Classification," *Midwest Folklore* 9 (1959): 5–18. Coffin espouses the romantic view of ballad production "as a product of untrained genius working sporadically, at different times in history, without conscious literary aims" (5).

15. *The Winter's Tale*, 4.4.289–90, from *The Riverside Shakespeare*, ed. G. Blakemore Evans (Boston: Houghton Mifflin, 1974). More convincing, perhaps, is the testimony of Izaac Walton's rural "Maudlin" in *The Compleat Angler* (1653), that she "shal sit by and sing you the good old Song of the *Hunting in Chevy Chase*, or some other good Ballad, for she hath good store of them" (sig. O6).

16. Fox, *Oral and Literate Culture*, 9.

Ballads routinely defy definition because of their protean tendency to migrate from popular performance to the press and back to the people, or from broadside to popular performance and back to the press. The well-known ballad of the "Hunting of the Cheviot" ("Chevy Chase") apparently originated in some form in the fifteenth century, perhaps in the pre-Caxton era. It then, however, made its way through the folk-to-print-to-folk cycle for centuries.[17] Accordingly, ballads can seldom if ever be defined in terms other than those that describe the stage in this cycle of transmission represented by a given text. By this criterion, it is not clear that the popular or folk ballad, composed by ordinary, nonprofessional poets, is an identifiable genre. These works may have existed, yet evidence of their genuine popular origins would be very difficult to document, especially within the corpus of Renaissance texts.

We thus know the Renaissance ballad, whether preserved in manuscript or print, as it survived in only two generic forms, granted that the distinctions between them may be imperceptible on a case-by-case basis. Both are literate/art ballads, produced by professional poets, the only difference being to what end. First, and closest to the romantic view of ballad origins, is the ballad composed by a local minstrel who will chant or sing it to audiences for his livelihood? Second, is the ballad composed, again, by a professional poet, for sale to a printer rather than for first-hand performance? Both the minstrel and the broadside balladeers wrote out their texts, and so the minstrel could become a broadside balladeer simply by offering his work to a printer.[18]

17. The earliest extant printed text is *STC* 5129.5 (c. 1625), entitled *A Memorable song made vpon the vnhappy hunting in Chevy Chase*. At least seven further reprints of this broadside appeared at regular intervals to the end of the century. A chapbook edition with a prose introduction to the ballad was published in 1690 (Wing F359A, reprinted in 1700, Wing F360). *EEBO* records eighteenth-century broadside editions published c. 1709, 1710, 1720, and 1760.

18. In "Bodleian MS Ashmole 48 and the Ballad Press," *English Manuscript Studies 1100–1700* 14 (2008): 219–43, Andrew Taylor argues that Richard Sheale, probable compiler of much of MS Ashmole 48, was both a minstrel who composed and sang ballads and someone who collected his own and others' ballads for sale to the broadside press. In another article, however, "The Myth of the Minstrel Manuscript," *Speculum* 66, no. 1 (January 1991): 43–73, Taylor dispels the "myth" that there are many surviving "minstrel manuscripts," arguing instead that most documents offered as evidence are literary compilations associated with abbeys, monasteries, other ecclesiastical venues, literate aristocratic households, and commercial production of texts for a literary market in "the age of the [manuscript] library book" (54). These earlier studies are now part of Taylor's book *The Songs and Travels of a Tudor Minstrel: Richard Sheale of Tamworth* (York, UK: University of York, 2012).

These ballads are similar in technical form and style. As Fowler notes, in the four-line stanzas, whether rhymed as fourteener couplets (with lines 2 and 4 rhyming *aa*) or as genuine quatrains with cross rhyme (*abab*), the second line is often a "filler" that conveys little or no new information but gives the performer time to compose the last two lines of the stanza. A few such filler lines occur in the Eland-Beaumont ballad: Beaumont's servants resist the ambush, for example, "and stroke wythe myght and mayne" (23.1). In 2.2 we learn only that "in dede the storye telles." The poet certainly does not depend on this device to frame his stanzas. The phrase "had cryed wythe myght & mayne" (101.2) is again used to set up the final rhyme of the stanza in which it appears, but the line "With myght and mayne to save his lyffe" also occurs at 60.3, where it is not in rhyming position.

The Eland-Beaumont ballad also shares many motifs with other ballads. Using the master list provided by Natascha Würzbach and Simone M. Salz, we see that it combines the following familiar elements: accusation (of murder), anger, combat (between enemies as well as between citizens and outlaws), a family feud, flight, murder of a father's murderer, murder by ambush, outlaws, premonition, pursuit, and revenge.[19] The influence of these generic expectations and elements, which intensify the emotional impact of the story, is actually stronger than the historical realities alluded to in the ballad in shaping the way the narrative is presented.

Historical Ballads

Including the prose account of the Eland-Beaumont story in his manuscript, John Hanson underscored the historicity of the ballad, its rootedness in the collective memory of his provincial society. The text of the ballad Hanson copied belongs to a group of seven ballads extant by the sixteenth century that share similar characteristics. Child published five of these poems: "Chevy Chase" (no. 162), "The Battle of Otterburn" (no. 161), "Sir Andrew Barton" (no. 167), "Flodden Field" (no. 168), and

19. Würzbach and Salz, *Motif Index of the Child Corpus: The English and Scottish Popular Ballad*, trans. Gayna Walls (Berlin: Walter de Gruyter, 1995).

"Captain Car" (no. 178).[20] He overlooked the Eland-Beaumont feud ballad, despite its survival in multiple manuscripts and print publication in at least six editions between 1775 and 1890. Furthermore, he set forth the text of "Chevy Chase" in Bodelian Ashmole MS 48 but ignored the ballad of "Lewes West" in the same manuscript, which bears a number of affinities with the seven ballads cited above.[21] All seven works are verse narratives based on actual events that took place in northern England or Scotland or, in the case of "Sir Andrew Barton," had a Scottish connection. They use first-person speech and dialogue to add a sense of immediacy to the narration but develop their plots with an episodic complexity that distances them from the lyric. All seven were designed for public performance, to be chanted or sung. In addition to their entertainment value, positive characterization of some of the historical figures involved in these ballads would have encouraged a favorable reception by their descendants: the balladeers may have composed these works with an eye toward eliciting patronage from a specific audience.

With regard to historicity, Hanson's ballad (as noted below) narrates an actual feud that played out in Yorkshire and Lancashire in the second quarter of the fourteenth century. The conflict celebrated in this ballad is thus some decades earlier than that of the Battle of Otterburn (1388), subject of the ballad of the same name, and of the related and more famous "Hunting of the Cheviot" ("Chevy Chase").[22] The three remaining Child

20. Fowler, *Literary History*, 95, 115–20, includes number 167, "Sir Andrew Barton," on the basis of a sixteenth-century manuscript in the York Minster Library unknown to Child. Fowler did not identify this document, however, and a search of the library's manuscripts failed to bring it to light. We are grateful to Jessica Edmondes for locating an edition of this text, "The Sonnge of Sir Andraye Barton, Knight," in *A Volume of English Miscellanies Illustrating the History and Language of the Northern Counties of England*, Surtees Society, vol. 85, ed. James Raine (Durham, UK: Surtees Society, 1890), 64–75.

21. The ballad is transcribed on ff. 31–35v. It was edited from this manuscript in R. H. Evans, *Old Ballads, Historical and Narrative, With Some of Modern Date; Collected from Rare Copies and MSS. By Thomas Evans. A New Edition; Revised and Considerably Enlarged . . . by his Son*, 4 vols. (London: W. Bulmer, 1810), 4:16–25. Thomas Wright published a second edition of the Ashmole text in *Songs and Ballads with Other Short Poems, Chiefly of the Reign of Philip and Mary* (1860; repr., New York: B. Franklin, 1970), 46–54. Andrew Taylor notes that among the seventy-seven poems in the Ashmole anthology, aside from Richard Sheale's lament, only "Chevy Chase" and "Lewes West" are set forth with "sustained narrative." "Bodleian MS Ashmole 48 and the Ballad Press," 221.

22. For a discussion of these two ballads in their northern English context, see Taylor, *Songs and Travels*, 117–35.

ballads recount sixteenth-century events. "Sir Andrew Barton" tells how Lord Thomas Howard pursued and killed a notorious Scottish pirate in 1511.[23] "Flodden Field" concerns the English victory over the Scots on 9 September 1513, although the action is restricted to events surrounding news of the battle brought to Henry VIII, then in France. "Lewes West" recounts the stalking, ambush, and slaughter of the West brothers on the road outside Rotherham, Yorkshire, by John and George Darcy in 1556.[24] "Captain Car" deals with a massacre that took place in Scotland in 1571. Although historical fact is significantly distorted in all six ballads, two of them assure their audiences that they are hearing the truth. The Eland feud poet states that Elland was a market town in Sir John Eland's day, adding, "The patent hathe bene sene" (11.2). He later emphasizes the validity of his research on the subject by affirming, "Yet have I rede most certanlye" of Sir Robert Beaumont's resistance to the men who invaded his home (22.1). A similar emphasis on historicity occurs in "The Battle of Otterburn," with an assurance regarding the number of the dead that "The cronykle wyll not layne [lie]" (Child, no. 161A, st. 35.2). Again, the pervasive interface between oral and written culture is undeniable.

Direct speech and dialogue enhance the aesthetic effect in each of these works. A majority of the lines in "Flodden Field" and "Captain Car" are direct discourse (about 68% and 58%, respectively). These ballads could easily be adapted as playlets. In the ballad of "Sir Andrew Barton," the dying pirate's last words are perhaps the most memorable of the entire poem. As he lies on the deck of his ship with an arrow in his heart, Barton nevertheless cries out to his crew,

"Feight, Maisters! . . .
I'se a lettle hurt, but I ame not slayne,

23. In "The Sonnge" text, as in Percy's *Folio Manuscript*, he has been anachronistically rechristened "Lord Charls Howwarde" (st. 4, p. 65). Queen Elizabeth appointed Lord Charles Howard her Lord Admiral in 1585. He gained little fame from this post before being credited with defeat of the Spanish Armada in 1588. Thus the York Minster Library text dates from quite late in the sixteenth century at the earliest.

24. Joseph Hunter recounted the historical feud between the Wests and Darcys and its aftermath in *South Yorkshire*, 2 vols. (1828–31; repr., Sheffield: E. F. Publishing, 1974), 2:173–76. Of the poem he wrote, "which ballad well deserves to be more generally known, as a favourable specimen of the simple narrative ballad of those times" (2:173).

Ile lie me downe and bleede a whill,
Ile risse and feight with yowe agayne."[25]

In "Chevy Chase," James, second Earl of Douglas, challenges Lord Percy to single combat in order to avoid a bloodbath:

But, Perse, thowe art a lord of lande,
    I am a yerle callyd within my contre,
Let all our men uppone a parti stande,
    and do the battell off the° and of me. °*thee*

(Child, no. 162A , st. 19)

During their combat, Douglas demands that Percy surrender, and is refused, and when the Scot dies of an arrow wound, Percy laments: "Wo ys me for the! / To have savyde thy lyffe, I wolde have partyde with / my landes for years thre" (Child no. 162A, st. 38.4–39.2).

Lewes West, outnumbered by the Darcys' retainers at least four to one, replies to John Darcy's challenge with an invitation to single combat that recalls Douglas's challenge to Percy:

A jentyllemane I knowe youe be,
    And so youe wate° ame I; °*wot, know*
With shame therefor mordare not me,
    But thus the mattare trye.
Cum youe and foware off your best men
    At ons and fyght withe me

(Wright, p. 51)

In "Otterburn," Douglas challenges Percy to gather his forces and meet him in battle. The most dramatic speech in this ballad reveals the intensity of Percy's determination to answer the challenge. When a messenger brings him word that his father asks him to delay the battle until he can bring reinforcements, Percy replies, "Wende to my lodre by father agayne, / And saye thow sawe me not wyth yee [eye]. / My trowth ys plyght to yonne Skottysh knyght, / It nedes me not to layne [hide]" (Child no. 161A, st. 39.3–40.2).

25. "The Sonnge," st. 34, p. 73.

When the young avengers in the Eland ballad confront Sir John, he at first doffs his hat to them, whereupon Adam Beaumont makes clear their intentions:

Thy curtsye vayles the nought sir knyght,
Thowe slewe my father Deare,
Somtyme syr Roberte beamount knyght,
And slayne shalt thowe be heare.

(f. 37, st. 58)

In their ambush of Eland's son, Beaumont fails to bring down the sheriff with his first arrow, whereat "Wilkyn of Lockewodd wrothe therat / Sayd, cossen yowe shott awydde," and manages to shoot Eland through the head (88.3–4). As the avengers flee the townsmen who have risen in Eland's defense, the wounded Quermby must be left behind. His farewell to Lockwood includes this bequest:

"Take here the gold to yowe" sayd he,
"And to my cossynes here,
And in yowre myrthe Remember me
Yet whan yowe make good cheare."

(f. 41, st. 110)

Telling use of first-person speech and dialogue heightens characterization and the dramatic impact of many scenes in all these ballads.

While direct discourse creates a personal lyricism that is the hallmark of such later ballads as "Sir Patrick Spens" (Child, no. 58) and "Bonny Barbara Allan" (Child, no. 84), the "historical" ballads retain their primarily narrative identity. Their plots develop with at least a degree of episodic complexity rather than a direct narrative path to the denouement. Narrative detail produces a sense of significant action, what in Aristotelian criticism is termed "magnitude."[26] "Captain Car" is the least well-developed of the group by this criterion, yet it still maintains some complication of plot: Car (Ker) marches to the castle, interviews Lady

26. *Poetics* 1.6, and see Elder Olson, *Tragedy and the Theory of Drama* (Detroit, MI: Wayne State University Press, 1966), 41, 57–59.

Forbes, treacherously murders her son, then burns the hold and its occupants. In the concluding stanzas her husband expresses his outrage at the massacre. The four remaining Child ballads tend to be structured as two or three major actions. "Flodden Field" presents a balanced three-part structure. In part 1, the Earl of Derby is disgraced by the Earl of Surrey's false message to the king, who is told that Derby's retainers, the men of Lancashire and Cheshire, fled the battlefield. Derby's lament and the king's reaction are followed in part 2 by the arrival of a message from Queen Katherine with a true account of the battle in which Derby's retainers are credited with the victory. Part 3 has Derby forgiving Surrey's offense and the king parceling out rewards. "The Battle of Otterburn" and "Chevy Chase" have rather opposite two-part structures. In "Otterburn," Douglas invades England and challenges Percy, who then assembles his army, meets and kills the Scot, and is ransomed home. Percy, however, initiates the plot of "Chevy Chase" by invading the marches, where he meets and kills Douglas at the cost of his own life. In part 2, Henry IV avenges his death at the battle of Homildon. "Sir Andrew Barton" offers the most intricately developed plot of the five. When Henry VIII asks for volunteers to stop Barton's preying on English shipping, Lord Howard volunteers. He selects his crew, then meets at sea with the merchant Henry Hunt, one of Barton's recent victims. Hunt shows Howard where to find the pirate, and together they defeat his ships, kill Barton, and bring his flagship back to London.

The Eland-Beaumont feud ballad sets forth an even more elaborately developed plot, the most complex of the seven works in question. The poet skillfully manipulates the ballad's three-part structure to heighten the work's emotional impact. First, Sir John Eland assaults Quermby, Lockwood, and Beaumont in their homes and kills them. Second, upon reaching maturity, his victims' sons kill Sir John, bringing the action to a satisfactory resolution in which the audience feels that Eland has been justly punished for his crimes. In part 3, however, the avengers ambush Eland's son and grandson, killing them both and bringing the family line to an end.

The "Lewes West" ballad begins with eleven stanzas of philosophical musings about legendary victims of envy. These resemble the seven stanzas against pride that open the Eland-Beaumont feud. The "Lewes West" poet recounts the Darcy brothers' two failed attempts to ambush and kill West before describing in detail the final encounter. There is no mention of prosecution or punishment of the brothers for their crime,[27] but in a final episode a piper who accompanied them exclaims after the killings, "'[A]las! / This ys to great a shame.'" Far from repenting their actions, one of the brothers "Persyde hime throrowe with his sworde" for expressing his disapproval (Wright, p. 53).

Although its 126 stanzas make it the longest of these seven ballads,[28] the ballad of the Eland-Beaumont feud was clearly written to be sung by a minstrel. At 12.1 the poet exclaims, "But nowe I dowte to synge for drede." His song is divided not into "fits" but according to the three "frays" that create a narrative structure of three roughly equal parts. These mark the three central conflicts in the plot: the massacre of Sir Robert Beaumont and his friends, the revenge on Sir John Eland, and the final massacre of Sir John's son and grandson and its aftermath. At stanza 33 the minstrel informs his audience, "The fyrst fraye here nowe have ye herd / The secund shall ensue." He expands this formula at stanza 66:

> The secund fraye[29] nowe heare ye have
> The thyrd nowe shall yowe heare
> of yowre kyndenes no more I crave
> But onelye to gyve eare.
>
> (f. 38, st. 66)

27. Hunter records that John agreed to a settlement of five hundred marks, while George "took sanctuary at Westminster, and . . . was whipped, wearing a white sheet," as an act of public penance. *South Yorkshire*, 2:176.

28. Comparison of lengths is complicated by the different technical forms of these works. Although Child edits all five in short-line stanzas with rough 4.3.4.3 meters, they are written predominantly in seven-stress couplets. Moreover, four triplets in "The Hunting" produce four six-line stanzas in Child's artificial rendering of the MS Ashmole 48 text (no. 161A). In "Flodden Field," Child's stanzas 7, 58, 59, 85, 87, 94, 103 are likewise triplets, the equivalent of three and a half additonal quatrains. Assessing the correct length of "Captain Car" is further complicated by its refrain, couched in the same seven-stress couplets as its narrative.

When all five Child ballads are reduced to the quatrain equivalent of Hanson's 126-stanza text, their relative lengths are "Otterburn" and "Chevy Chase," 70 stanzas each; "Captain Car," 60 stanzas (counting the 30 refrains that would have been repeated in performance); "Barton," 82 stanzas; and "Flodden Field," 106.5 stanzas. The "West" ballad by this tally comprises 55 stanzas. The first three ballads and this last one are short enough for one-sheet broadside publication, while "Flodden Field" and the Eland-Beaumont feud would have required a pamphlet format.

29. The *OED* defines "fraye" as "2. assault; 3a. a disturbance, esp. one caused by fighting; a noisy quarrel, a brawl; a fight, skirmish, conflict."

Three of the five Child ballads include similar passages testifying to their performance by a professional minstrel. The audience is directly addressed in "Chevy Chase":

> That day, that day, that dredfull day!
> the first fit here I fynde;
> and youe wyll here any more a the hountynge a the Chyviat,
> yet ys ther more behynde
>
> (Child, no. 162A, st. 24)

Even so, and despite the popularity of its tune in the seventeenth century, the earliest text of "Chevy Chase" does not clearly indicate that it was sung. Although the oldest text of "Sir Andrew Barton" is termed a "Sonnge," it was likewise written for recitation before an audience, as confirmed by the first line of stanza 19: "Nowe will we leave talkinge of Harry Hunt" ("The Sonnge," p. 69). The opening line of "Flodden Field" shows that it, too, was meant to be recited, not sung, by a professional entertainer: "Now let us talke of [the] Mount of Flodden" (Child, no. 168). The "Lewes West" balladeer explains, "Off Lawncelate and stronge Trystram / I cannote speke this howre," indicating that it was also a recitation piece. The refrain after every stanza of "Captain Car" shows that it was written to be sung, but the audience is not addressed outright in this ballad. Only the Eland-Beaumont ballad explicitly testifies to its public performance as song.

Another trait common to these ballads is their suitability for eliciting patronage from aristocratic or noble patrons. Although Fowler interprets "Otterburn" as pro-English and "Chevy Chase" as pro-Scottish, both were written in English and could have been sung to the greater glory of the house of Percy. "Chevy Chase," apparently the oldest of the five Child ballads, leaves both Percy and Douglas dead on the field. However, in the reactions of their two kings to losing such warriors (stanzas 59–64), a clear English bias emerges. Henry IV vows to avenge Percy's death and does so in the historical victory over the Scots at Homildon (1402).[30] In "The Battle

30. Fowler, *Literary History*, reads a Scottish bias into "Chevy Chase" by arguing that its blatantly pro-English passage concerning the reaction of the two kings is a later insertion marked by the cessation of stanzas rhyming abab (114). Yet well over half the poem's seventy stanzas rhyme

of Otterburn," Percy kills Douglas but is led away captive at the end of the poem. However, the Scots make no effort to exact revenge. Percy is ransomed in a prisoner exchange, and the ballad ends with a prayer for Percy, "a gentyll knyght" (Child, no. 161A, st. 70.4). Lord Thomas Howard is rewarded by Henry VIII for defeating Barton; the ballad is a tribute to the Howard earls of Surrey, dukes of Norfolk, and in its earliest extant form, to Charles Howard, Earl of Nottingham. Ironically, "Flodden Field" denigrates Thomas Howard's father, the then Earl of Surrey who commanded the English army in its victory over the Scots. This ballad instead makes Thomas, Earl of Derby, its protagonist and the focus of its praise. "Lewes West" concludes with four stanzas of benediction of the West family and condemnation of the Darcys. They begin:

God sende them well to lyve and fare,
And eas off all thear smarttes,
And for the othare sorte prepare,
That whiche ys thear desarttes

(Wright, p. 53)

The English text of "Captain Car," as set forth in the Cotton manuscript, has the least apparent utility as a patronage piece. The ballad's heroine is Lady Forbes, who died with her children when Captain Thomas Ker burned Towie Castle, due east of Aberdeen. A Scots version of the ballad might have strongly appealed to the clan of Forbes, but there is no trace of any such text. In contrast, the Eland-Beaumont ballad is an explicit patronage piece. It narrates in detail the otherwise irrelevant fact that Eland manor became the property of the Savile family as a result of the feud. The poet then concludes his narrative by addressing its moral to this family: "Learne saviles here I yow beseke" (125.1).

These seven history-based ballads share other characteristics of technical form and style, but are especially significant as among the oldest surviving

only as long-line couplets, while one of the rhyming quatrains occurs within the "two kings" passage (stanza 64). Ruth Perry, following Child, agrees that "Chevy Chase" is the pro-English version. "War and the Media in Border Minstrelsy: The Ballad of Chevy Chase," in *Ballads and Broadsides in Britain, 1500–1800*, ed. Patricia Fumerton, Anita Guerrini, and Kris McAbee (Farnham, UK: Ashgate, 2010), 255.

popular ballads. Fowler classified the five Child historical ballads (among Child's total of 305) as the oldest representatives of the type. That is, they are the only ones that survive in texts datable as far back as the sixteenth century.[31] The Eland-Beaumont ballad and "Lewes West" obviously share this distinction. However, we disagree with Fowler's exclusion of a number of other fifteenth- and sixteenth-century ballads, especially those about Robin Hood and Adam Bell, on grounds that they were not sung.[32] In form, style, and emphasis upon narrative these works are comparable to the seven works we have analyzed but differ from them in their lack of historicity. Granted, the "historical" ballads distort the historical record, often significantly (as we can see in some detail in the case of the Eland-Beaumont ballad). Yet they are grounded on actual events that can be independently verified. This is not true for any of the earlier ballads so far as we can determine. They are fictional narratives with no further historical roots than their alleged occurrence during the reigns of various English kings.[33] Thus, the seven ballads isolated here as based on historical fact comprise the earliest known examples of this distinctive subset of the popular ballad.

The Historical Contexts of the Ballad

Three historical contexts are relevant to our analysis of the Eland-Beaumont ballad (and prose narrative): that of the mid-fourteenth-century historical

31. Child, nos. 161, 162, 167, 168, and 178. Fowler excludes the important earlier corpus of Robin Hood ballads on grounds that they were recited rather than sung. *Literary History*, 10. This subgenre's questionable historicity could also be objected.

32. Fowler insists that genuine popular ballads be sung to melodies—that is, "rounded tunes." *Literary History*, 94. However, he identified and accepted as our earliest popular ballads the five works from Child considered here because they were all eventually sung to named tunes. As we have shown, three of them were explicitly written to be recited or chanted. *The Index of Middle English Verse*, ed. Carleton Brown and Rossell Hope Robbins (New York: Modern Language Association, 1943), cites, for example, three Robin Hood ballads in fifteenth-century manuscripts (BR 1915, 1533, and 1534; Child, nos. 117, 121, 119). *STC* lists three editions of the "Adam Bell, Clim of the Clough, and William of Cloudesly" ballad published between c. 1505 and c. 1565 (*STC* 1805.7, 1806, and 1807; Child, no. 116).

33. J. C. Holt concludes that though some episodes of the Robin Hood legend can be aligned with historical events, "none of the rest gets beyond the guesswork or coincidence of name or circumstance." In contrast, the events narrated in "genuinely historical ballads" can be independently corroborated. *Robin Hood* (London: Thames and Hudson, 1982), 61.

events that were loosely fictionalized in the story, that of the time of the ballad's composition in the latter part of Henry VIII's reign, and that of the ballad's transcription in the Hanson manuscript in the late sixteenth century. The first makes clear the radical historical revisionism in both the ballad and the prose narrative; the second highlights the possible purpose of the ballad's narrative in relation to a contemporary early sixteenth-century Yorkshire feud; and the third relates to the main manuscript scribe's interest in both local history and legend, partly because of the material's connection to the contemporary Savile family, to whom he was related by marriage.

The Fourteenth-Century Events and Their Later Historical Representations

In his study of the recoverable historical facts of the Eland-Beaumont conflict, J.M. Kaye has demonstrated the way the ballad and prose narrative highly distort and selectively use the details of the events they claim to represent faithfully.[34] Kaye has found no substantiation of the supposed outrageous murders that Sir John Eland committed in the dramatic opening episode of the story: in fact, Sir Robert Beaumont had died in 1330, eleven years before Eland was sheriff, and his son Adam would have been between twenty-nine and thirty-two, not a twenty-year-old, at the time of the killing of Sir John Eland.[35] Instead of being the prideful rival of the Beaumonts, the actual Sir John Eland Sr. appears to have been a conscientious justice of the peace who was frustrated in his attempts to enforce the law against criminals in his jurisdiction. The paterfamilias of the Beaumont family has little visibility in the historical record, but it is fictionally convenient to portray him as the unjustly assaulted defender of house and home. His son, Sir John Beaumont (with whom the ballad may be confusing him), was a member of a gang of what Kaye calls "criminal knights" escaping the reach of the authorities for some time, guilty of thefts and

34. Kaye, "The Eland Murders." For an account of the feud and its historical context that mixes the factual with the fictional, see A. M. W. Stirling, *Annals of a Yorkshire House: From the Papers of a Macaroni & His Kindred*, 2 vols. (London: John Lane, 1911), 1:7–18. See also John Crabtree, *A Concise History of the Parish and Vicarage of Halifax* (Halifax: Hartley and Walker, 1836), 439–52, which bases its historical narrative largely on the ballad and the prose version of the story.

35. Kaye, "The Eland Murders," 71.

murders.[36] Kaye points out that the murder of Sir John Eland Jr. followed the indictment on 9 April 1351 of those responsible for his father's death and that the conspirators may have been retaliating against him for this prosecution.[37]

The historical realities of the Eland-Beaumont feud are either distorted or erased in the ballad. Early in the story the narrator notes that "Some saye that Eland sheryff was / by bea[m]ont Dysobeyed" (14.1–2): this may refer to the unsubstantiated story mentioned in the prose account and rehearsed by early commentators on the ballad—Sir Robert Beaumont's supposed harboring of a man named Exley who had killed Sir John Eland's relative (either a nephew or a more distant relation), the compensation for which crime Eland had originally accepted in the form of property before deciding on a course of personal revenge.[38] Eland's status as sheriff complicated the matter. Was he seeking a fugitive from the law or seeking private satisfaction? In any event, behind this private issue of crime and revenge early commentators have claimed there was also a baronial conflict, between John Warrene, Earl of Surrey (d. 1347), and Thomas, Earl of Lancaster, to which the title of the prose narrative alludes: "The Dyscourse of the slaghteres of Eland Beamoun[t] Lockwod Quermby &c how Sir John Eland of Eland haule and Sir Robert Beamount of Croslandhaull had batteled thon agenst thother in the behalfe of theyr maisteres whom they weare faythfull unto whyche was a destruction unto theym bothe" (f. 12) (see figure 2).[39]

One of the obvious things to conclude about the disparity between the ballad and prose narratives of the Eland-Beaumont feud, on the one hand, and the historical events they portray, on the other, is that the former obscure or eliminate most of the legal realities of the situation—most notably, the lawlessness of various characters, their indictments and outlawing,

36. Ibid., 75. Such characters were familiar enough for Shakespeare to portray them comically in the figure of Falstaff and his henchmen in his second historical tetralogy.

37. Ibid., 64–65.

38. The prose text refers to "one Exley whyche aforetyme slewe sir John Eland brotheres sonne for the Whiche to agrement he gave acertan peece of land to the Elandes yet after the agrement made Sir John Eland sought to have slayn hym and therfore Exle was constrayned to flee unto thafforsayd sir Robert Beamount for ayde who bycause he was hys kynsman Rescued hym which partlye was the occasyon of the great malice that was betwyxt the sayd sir Robert Beamount and sir John Eland" (ff. 12v–13).

39. The baronial context of the story is discussed in Stirling, *Annals of a Yorkshire House*, 7–10.

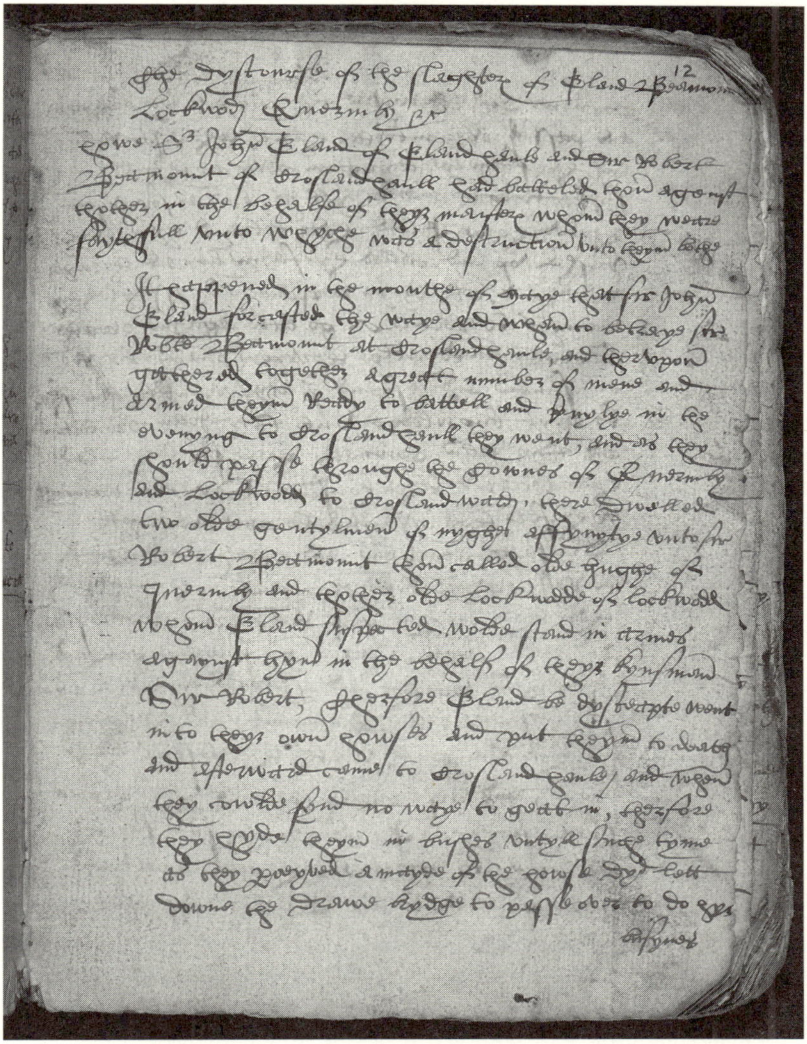

Figure 2. BL Add. MS 82370, f. 12. Beginning of prose account of Eland-Beaumont feud. Reproduced by permission of The British Library Board.

and the ineffectiveness of policing and the judicial system: it was hard to arrest criminals and even harder to convict them, especially if they were of high social status. An adventure story of righteous revenge, which concludes in the prose version with an exemplary misogynistic tale of romantic betrayal,[40] is more literarily satisfying than the realities of the events it fictionalizes. The past to which the ballad looks was one of out-of-control gang violence and thievery with which both national and provincial authorities could not cope well. Converting a beleaguered sheriff into a cold-blooded killer and the wronged descendants of his alleged victims into morally sanctioned avengers (who, of course, fail finally to control their own violence) distorts the less heroic story of criminality and law enforcement. A relatively lawless fourteenth-century Yorkshire is made the setting for an exciting tale of bloodlust, revenge, and overreaching—a narrative that is more interesting than the historical realities of crimes, prosecution, and the authorities' attempts to uphold the law and maintain public order. The historical distance of the ballad from the events it narrates allows for some political/legal perspective. It is clear that, in mid-fourteenth-century Yorkshire, there was a primitive system of social controls but that these could conflict with a more modern and centralized political/legal system.[41]

The traditional antiquarian accounts and historical narratives of the Eland-Beaumont feud uncritically accept the story told in the ballad and the prose account. The earliest of these (undated), "[Roger]'s Note of the Feud between Elland and Beaumont" (Bodleian MS Dodsworth 145), states:

> Sir John Elland was High Steward to Earl of Warren of the manor of Wakefield, lord of Elland, Tankersley, Fulridge, Hinchfield, and Ratchdale. Slew Robert Beaumont at his house, Crossland Hall, 24 Edward III [1350]—163—Beaumont's sons killed him, and then his son and heir on Palm Sunday morning: "this appeareth by evidence and pedigree in the keeping of John Armitage, Esq.: and they have a Play and Song thereof in the country still. The quarrel was about the Earl of Lancaster and the Earl of Warren that took away the said Earl of Lancaster's wife, there being a man slain of the Earl Warren's party in a hurly-burly betwixt the said

40. In the prose account, the betrayed Lockwood says to his lover after she has cut his bowstring: "[F]ye on the whore that ever thowe were ordeyned to be the Destructyon of menes bloode for by the and such lyke maye all menne take an example" (f. 18).

41. Concentrating on the Tudor and early Stuart periods, Mervyn James, *Society, Politics and Culture: Studies in Early Modern England* (Cambridge: Cambridge University Press, 1986), examines the transition in early modern England from a feudal "honor society" to a law-governed civil society.

> Lords. . . . Elland came to search for the murderer in the said Beaumont's house, who belonged to the Earl of Lancaster, and slew him in his own hall. . . ." This in Mr. Armitage of Kirkley's evidences, 1621. (f. 107)[42]

The eighteenth-century antiquarian John Watson, who apparently thought he was presenting an accurate historical account, printed a version of the ballad and appended to it his "Observations on the above POEM." He first opined that the ballad "was wrote by some bard, for the use of the minstrels, to be sung to the gentlemen of these parts, at their public entertainments, and divided, for that reason, into parts, between each of which there was always a considerable interval allowed, either to indulge variety, or that the company might the better make their remarks on the performance, and the uncommon facts therein recorded."[43] After noting that the "manner of executing private revenge was brought from Normandy to England," he offers a tentative explanation of the origin of the Eland-Beaumont feud:

> I have read in other Mss. that one Exley had killed the brother's son of sir John Eland, and that sir Robert Beaumont screened him from the resentment of sir John, also that the affair was, in some measure, made up, sir John Eland having accepted of a compensation in lieu of justice being done upon the murdered, but that he afterwards violated the agreement in the manner above related [in the ballad]. It seems not unlikely that some fresh provocation was given, from what is said in verse 17, Lockwood, of Lockwood, being there charged with something of the sort, when he is called "a wiley wight," and said to have "stirred the strife anew." He appears, indeed, to have been a person of a bad character, for in the court rolls at Wakefield, 35 Edw. I. [1306/07] John de Lockwood was presented, and afterwards found guilty, of having forcibly ejected one Matthew de Linthwaite from his free tenament, and when the earl's grave and bailiff came to take possession thereof, he made an attempt, with others unknown, to have slain them, for that they barely escaped with their lives.[44]

---

42. The antiquarian Roger Dodsworth's account cited in Joseph Hunter, "Antiquarian Notices of Clay House, in Greteland, in the Parish of Halifax, and County of York," ed. Thomas James, *Yorkshire Archaeological and Topographical Journal* 2 (1871): 163. Since Dodsworth died in 1654, his narrative was written some time earlier.

43. John Watson, *The History and Antiquities of the Parish of Halifax, in Yorkshire* (1775; repr., Manchester: Morten Publishers, 1973), 176.

44. Ibid., 177.

Watson then refers to another manuscript

> which saies, that Exley . . . was a relation of sir Robert Beaumont's, and that he happened to kill a sister's (not brother's) son of sir John Eland's, for which Exley gave to the Elands a piece of land for satisfaction, yet notwithstanding sir John sought to slay him, and he fled thereupon to sir Robert Beaumont for protection; on which sir John got together a considerable number of armed men, and in one night, in the month of May, put to death the said sir Robert, and two old gentlemen, his near relations, sir Hugh de Quarmby and old Lockwood.[45]

Watson refers for confirmation to the manuscripts of the Yorkshire antiquarian John Hopkinson, which note that both Exley and Sir Robert Beaumont's brother William were also slain.

Watson comments on some relevant aspects of the Eland and Beaumont genealogies, dating the age of Adam Beaumont at five at the time of his father's murder and twenty at the time of his revenge on Sir John Eland. He notes that Lacy was not a victim of Eland's violence but that he became involved in the revenge plans. Finally, he retells the story of Lockwood's fatal romance and of Adam Beaumont's subsequent history (probably deriving its details from the prose version of these events). Clearly the fictional and the historical are muddled in Watson's account, which was also affected by the eighteenth-century romantic understanding of late medieval culture.

In a separate section with its own title page in *Halifax. And Its Gibbet-Law Placed in a true Light* (1708), William Bentley offers a sensationalized version of the prose narrative: "Revenge upon Revenge: or, an Historical Narrative, &c.," followed by "A Short but full Account of the Lives and Deaths of Wilkin Lockwood, and Adam Beaumont, Esqrs. and what Travels and Adventures happened unto them after the Battle with *Eland* Men in *Anely* Wood, as the same is Recorded in a very Ancient Manuscript, in the Custody of a very worthy Gentleman, kindly communicated for Public Satisfaction."[46] In *The Elland Tragedies* (1890), J. Horsfall Turner edited a 124-stanza version of the ballad, interspersed with a 110-stanza version

45. Ibid., 177–78.

46. This text was reprinted in 1712 and 1761. It was also reproduced, along with two versions of the ballad in J. Horsfall Turner, ed., *The Elland Tragedies* (Bingley, UK: T. Harrison & Sons, 1890).

(see the discussion of textual matters below). To the ballads he appended one page of historical background dealing with legal processes connected to the feud and the malefactors.[47] Turner sets the story in the context of baronial feuding and provides several genealogies, but he makes no real attempt at documentary history. In his account we are still very close to the romantic distortions of oral history and folklore.

The Eland-Beaumont Feud from a Sixteenth-Century Perspective

In a sixteenth-century context, the ballad and prose narrative had several functions: (1) to affirm local identity and give historical depth to regional topography, (2) to express a nostalgia for and to romanticize some aspects of an earlier era, (3) to moralize history, and (4) to relate older events to the kinship relations of the sixteenth-century Saviles of Yorkshire and to that family's conflict and local power struggle with Sir Richard Tempest.

(1) The Eland-Beaumont feud ballad is based on local tradition and its transformations of historical events in oral history. Like other ballads from the North and from Scotland, it connects local sites to notable events and confirms regional identity. It was probably sung and/or recited by the kinds of minstrels who were patronized by the local gentry and yeomanry.[48] In his study of oral tradition in early modern England, D. R. Woolf observes,

> Oral cultures have little sense of a relative past and either do not assign dates to events in their tradition or forget large parts of the past; the transmitters of such traditions thereby "telescope" their own history and provide a chronology which, though it is comprehensible to the members of their group,

47. Ibid., 83.

48. C. H. Firth, "The Ballad History of the Reigns of Henry VII. and Henry VIII," *Transactions of the Royal Historical Society*, 3rd ser., 2 (1908): 22, states that "[a]t the time when Henry VII. ascended the throne the men who wrote the ballads were either the minstrels who sang them or dependents of the great families whose deeds they celebrated." Firth, *Ballad History*, names the Percys, the Howards, and the Stanleys, in particular, as patrons of ballad production. Taylor, *Songs and Travels*, 13–81, discusses Richard Sheale's relationship to the Stanley family. Upper-class attitudes toward ballads and other elements of popular culture became progressively negative in the sixteenth century, as Peter Burke, *Popular Culture in Early Modern Europe* (New York: New York University Press, 1978), 270, has argued. He writes, "In Elizabeth's reign the references made by educated men to minstrels and their ballads became more and more patronising as the literary ideals of the Renaissance made their impact" (277), cited in Eric Nebeker, "Broadside Ballads, Miscellanies, and the Lyric in Print," *ELH* 76, no. 4 (Winter 2009): 1009.

> will mislead outside observers conditioned to dealing in firm dates. What is true of the formal tribal narrative holds *a fortiori* for rural early modern England, where the sense of the past was focused less on time than on space, less on dates than on locations.[49]

In his study of orality and print, Adam Fox remarks:

> Many traditions served an aetiological function, purporting to explain the origin of local place names or account for the evolution of the topographical landmarks which provided people with their mental reference points. Indeed, the landscape all around was a vast repository of memory. Memories of the past comprised part of that local knowledge from which people derived a sense of identity and pride based upon place. They provided an imagined heritage which helped to underscore the emotional solidarity of the community and they were expressed in the "common voice," "common fame," or "common report" of the inhabitants which antiquaries and travellers frequently encountered as they toured the country.[50]

In the Eland-Beaumont ballad, local place names firmly ground the story in west Yorkshire, in the very territory in which the Hanson and Stanhope families lived. Beyond his alliance with the Savile family, John Hanson would naturally have taken a personal interest in the feud story in both its versions as a relic of ongoing family history and tradition even though none of his ancestors is mentioned in it. Both stories were brought to life daily for Hanson and his neighbors through local place names and surnames in their immediate vicinity. Locations connected with the Elands and their supporters—including Elland, Cannelhall (Cannon Hall, later residence of the Stanhopes), Cawthorn, Emley Park, and Emley Hall—are all within roughly a ten-mile radius of Rastrick, as are Crossland Hall, Huddersfield, Honley, Holmefirth, Meltham, Lepton, and Whitley, places associated with Beaumont, Quermby, Lockwood, and Lacy. Sir John Eland was ambushed after he presided at the Brighouse turn, a court at which Hanson served on juries on several occasions (nor did he travel far to do so, for Brighouse is located just across the River Calder from

---

49. D. R. Woolf, "The 'Common Voice': History, Folklore, and Oral Tradition in Early Modern England," *Past and Present*, no. 120 (August 1988): 31.

50. Fox, *Oral and Literate Culture*, 215.

Figure 3. Detail of map of the West Riding of Yorkshire from John Speed, *[Theatre of the Empire of Great Britaine. Latin] Theatrum imperii Magnae Britanniae . . . Map of West Riding, Yorkshire* (London, 1616; *STC* 23044), between pp. 79 and 80. Reproduction by permission of the Folger Shakespeare Library, Washington, DC.

Rastrick—see figure 3).[51] In 1513 Hanson's grandfather provided timber to repair the bridge there, and Hanson continued the tradition by leaving one pound for its repair in his will.[52] As Daniel Woolf has noted, "Very old man-made structures . . . acted as focal points for local traditions and legends, lightning rods which inspired the popular imagination."[53] This was doubtless the case in the connection between surviving local structures and the Eland-Beaumont narrative.

Every significant character in the feud narrative except for Quermby had a namesake, presumably a descendant or collateral relative, living in Hanson's immediate neighborhood. Hanson's uncle, Henry Savile, was

51. He served, e.g., in 1557, 1562, 1567, and 1579. Turner, *The Elland Tragedies*, 149, 151, 154.

52. J. Horsfall Turner, *History of Brighouse, Rastrick, and Hipperholme* (Bingley, UK: T. Harrison and Sons, 1893), 211; ***CP*** 27, f. 671.

53. Daniel Woolf, *The Social Circulation of the Past: English Historical Culture 1500–1730* (Oxford: Oxford University Press, 2003), 30.

buried at Elland church in 1566; it was the parish church for both families, and many other Hanson and Savile family members are listed in its records. The revengers' good friends, Dawson, Haigh, and Dyson, are represented by multiple entries in the Elland parish register between, for example, 1569 and 1587. Children of William Lacy and John Lacy were baptized at Elland during the same period. Henry Lockwood's daughter was buried there in 1564, while George Lockwood married Agnes Hurst in the church in 1567; she was apparently the "Agnes Lockwod vidue de Rastrick" buried in the church in 1587. Three children of John Beaumont were baptized there between 1576 and 1583, while another John Beaumont married Agnes Preistlay in the church 13 February 1585/86.[54] Hanson's business dealings also brought him into constant contact with persons whose surnames occur in the feud narratives. Both James Dyson and William Dawson, for instance, are named in the grant of 1562 in which Hanson identified himself as the scribe. In 1574 Hanson drew up an indenture witnessed by John and Thomas Hagh; the latter also witnessed, with Hanson, a release of 1581.[55] The feud's social and cultural context simply extended through time to become the milieu in which Hanson and his neighbors lived their daily lives.

Only in the last part of the story as recounted in the prose version is the geographical focus broadened to northern England and to continental Europe, moving the tale finally from its provincial confines onto a world stage. The story of the Eland-Beaumont feud in both its poetic and prose forms, then, is one that served the purpose of affirming local (west Yorkshire) identity—both for the original audiences, which might have been socially diverse,[56] and later for the main compiler of the Hanson manuscript. Such an affirmation might be understood as a form of resistance to the politically centralizing forces operating in sixteenth-century England.[57]

54. John William Clay, ed., *The Registers of Elland, Co. Yorkshire*, vol. 1 (Leeds, U.K.: J. Whitehead and Son, n.d.), 17, 13, 19, 94, 11, 88, 48, 56, and 75.

55. WYAS, Calderdale, KM: 255; KM 370; KM 428*.

56. Itinerant minstrels could perform in alehouses and taverns, marketplaces, and the houses of the yeomanry, gentry, and aristocracy. See Taylor, *Songs and Travels*, 13–39, for a discussion of Richard Sheale and his audiences.

57. Woolf, *Social Circulation*, 304, observes, "Locality . . . was a potent force behind the creation of new historical traditions and the preservation of some older ones throughout the sixteenth and seventeenth centuries, even at a time of increasing cultural pressure from the centre."

(2) One of the puzzles about the historical revisionism of the ballad is why the author vilifies Sir John Eland Sr. with the opening story of vicious home invasion and murder. Kaye suggests that the motive might have been to "whitewash" the Beaumont family, "which in his day, had become respectable and influential in the county," but it is also possible, Kaye claims, that the ballad-author "was influenced by the outlaw-ballads, especially the 'Gest of Robyn Hode' which had been printed shortly before the Eland ballad's probable date of composition. From this source he may have drawn the idea that the forces of law and order in the Middle Ages were invariably oppressive and treacherous, and that those who opposed them always had moral right on their side." Kaye suggests that the portrayal of the flight of Adam Beaumont and his friends might have been influenced by that of Robin Hood and the Sheriff of Nottingham. In addition, the episode in the ballad dealing with the miller and his wife might have had a source in popular literature and "Eland's siege of, and entry into, Crosland Hall . . . may owe something to the late-fifteenth-century ballad about the murder of Sir John Butler, of Bewsey."[58] Generic conventions and literary influences, as well as local social conditions in the West Riding in the early sixteenth century would thus have been a stronger force than the historical facts of the original events, which would themselves have been either inaccessible or distorted in oral tradition and historical memory.

One of the interesting features of the ballad that relates to the question of both medieval and early modern outlaw behavior is the importance of the longbow as a weapon. It figures in the slaying of Sir John Eland Jr., who is shot in the head with an arrow. In the prose narrative it is crucial to the downfall of Lockwood, whose bowstring was cut by his betraying lover when he was defending himself from attack by his enemies. C.H. Firth notes that, although archery was declining in importance during Henry VIII's reign, "just at the moment when this process of decay was beginning, the ballads in which the bow was glorified found their way into print."[59] Child's ballad no.116 celebrates the northern outlaws Adam Bell,

58. Kaye, "The Eland Murders," 76.

59. Firth, "Ballad History," 31. In the mid-Tudor period, the decline in the number of sturdy men able to pull the longbow was perceived as a serious problem. See Jeremy Goring, "Social Change and Military Decline in Mid-Tudor England," *History* 60 (1975): 185–97. Goring, 193, cites a 1549 sermon of Bishop Latimer before King Edward VI that praised archery as "a gift of God that He hath given us to excel all other nations withal" but that was now neglected.

Clym of the Cloughe, and William of Cloudesly, who regularly poached the king's deer and later killed the local sheriff, the justice of the peace, the mayor of Carlisle, and many others. These criminals are pardoned by the king after the queen's intercession and after William successfully (like William Tell) cleaves an apple on his son's head with an arrow shot from a great distance. The king is so impressed by the outlaws' skill with the longbow that he employs them finally as part of the royal household.[60] Robin Hood ballads, of course, are prime examples of texts that glorify proficiency with the longbow, and much is made in "Chevy Chase" and "The Hunting of the Cheviot" of the contrast between the 1,500 English bowmen and 2,000 Scottish spearmen.[61] In an era in which guns were starting to become important as weapons, the romanticizing of the longbow was an act of nostalgia. Having the longbow as the main weapon of the impassioned avengers associates the narrative with romantic outlaw ballads.

(3) Even more than the prose narrative, the ballad lays heavy emphasis on the ethical coordinates of the story, offering moral comments on the incidents and drawing moral conclusions at the end. The tone is set in the first seven stanzas, which offer general observations about the dangers of social ambition, pride, and the kind of intense envy that can lead to violence and murder. This is the ethical context of Sir John Eland's wickedly prideful attack on Lockwood, Quermby, and Beaumont. This initial episode portrays him as a dastardly assassin of a "kynde and curtyse

60. See the text of this ballad and discussion of it in Stephen Knight and Thomas Ohlgren, eds., *Robin Hood and Other Outlaw Tales* (Kalamazoo, MI: Medieval Institute Publications for TEAMS [The Consortium for Teaching the Middle Ages] in association with the University of Rochester, 2000), 235–67. This ballad survives in a three-signature quarto published in 1565 by William Copland (*STC* 1807). Fragments of 1505? and 1536 editions also survive (*STC* 1805.7 and 1806). There were also several seventeenth-century printings of the piece. There is another ballad reproduced in James Kinsley, ed.,*The Oxford Book of Ballads* (Oxford: Clarendon Press, 1969), no. 97, pp. 363–74, that tells how "outlaw Murray" came to terms with the Scottish king, who gave him local authority as a sheriff and free possession of his lands. Child, no. 117, "A Gest of Robyn Hood," also has a situation of outlaws' being taken (temporarily) into the king's service. For a discussion of such ballads in relation to actual late medieval outlaws, see Barbara A. Hannawalt, "Ballads and Bandits: Fourteenth-Century Outlaws and the Robin Hood Poems," in *Robin Hood: An Anthology of Scholarship and Criticism*, ed. Stephen Knight (Cambridge: D. S. Brewer, 1999), 263–84.

61. It is interesting that the Eland-Beaumont feud is used to illustrate the importance of the longbow in George Agar Hansard, *The Book of Archery, Being the Complete History and Practice of the Art, Ancient and Modern* (London: Henry G. Bohn, 1851), 44–51.

knyght" (9.2), Sir Robert Beaumont, who, though unarmed, fights "manfullye" (22.3) against the attackers who invade his bedchamber. Eland violates *both* the chivalric honor code and Christian morality. He uses "crafte myscheff & crueltye" (25.3), moved by "the verye devyll of hell" (26.4) to do his deeds, which culminate in his beheading the knight (a detail missing in the prose account). At this point the narrator moralizes:

> Se herin what uncertantye
> this wretched world ys ledde
> at nyght in his prosperytye
> at morowe slayne & Dead
>
> (f. 34v, st. 28)

Notably, at the stage in the story in which the younger members of the Beaumont, Lockwood, and Quermby families exact revenge for the murder of their fathers, the conflict between a revenge ethic and Christian morality is highlighted, as the roles of victim and assassin get reversed—Beaumont, Lockwood, Quermby, and Lacy now ambushing Sir John Eland. The narrator pauses for a moral assessment of the situation after the revenge has been enacted: in stanzas 63–65 he portrays the death of Eland as a consequence of his actions, but does not refrain from criticizing Beaumont and his accomplices for their unchristian behavior, arguing that natural urges ("kynd," 65.1), rather than Christian conscience, controlled their behavior. In the aftermath of this "second fraye" (66.1), the avengers plan their next action, but it is one motivated by "cruel mars" (68.1), naked aggression. Their consciences are "corrupt" (69.1).

The killers of Sir John Eland go about "bostyng of theyr mysdede," "more myscheiff contryvyng" (71.2–3) as they prepare to reinvade Eland territory and kill Sir John's son. The narrator sets up the situation of this second ambush by noting that Sir John Eland Jr. is on his way to church "to heare the servyce songe and Redde" (84.4): "To serve god thys present Daye / The knyght than made hym bowne" (85.1–2) to observe the Palm Sunday feast. The victim is identified not only as an observant Christian but as a "knyght," just as Sir Robert was earlier. He faces his attackers courageously, but after his armor initially protects him against the first arrows shot by Beaumont and Lockwood, the latter "shott the knyght quyte through the head / and slewe hym than wythe sped" (93.3–4). The narrator inserts a moral reflection on the subsequent undoing of the killers, emphasizing that, rather than imitating their behavior, people should adhere to "symple vertue," which is "the beste / and cheife felycytye" (97.3–4). The "Lordes servantes throughowt the towne," "gentyll yeomen" (101.3) who pursue the assassins, do so out of loyalty, but their outrage is presented as justified, with the narrator noting that "the paryshe . . . Joyned theym wythe the towne" (105.1–2).

One more moral volte-face, however, takes place in relation to the wounding and death of Quermby. Quermby dies the death of a generous, chivalric hero, not that of an ambusher/assassin. He is the gentleman victim of a mob of vulgar attackers. After describing his death, the narrator turns to a general moralizing he applies to the whole narrative: he concludes that a "bretche of charytye" (117.1), that central Christian virtue, caused the tragedy, and he urges his genteel audience to "Love one another" (121.1) as well as those socially beneath them ("the yeomanrye," 121.2) so that they themselves will merit God's approval and the reward of heaven. The poem ends as a sermon might, drawing moral lessons from an arresting narrative. Analogously, at the end of "The Hunting of the Cheviot" the narrator turns from the quasi-heroic mode of the feudal conflict to moralize about the social danger of aristocratic bellicosity:

> God save our king, and blesse this land
> with plentye, joy, and peace.
> And grant hencforth that foule debate
> twixt noble men may ceaze![62]

Narrative tales about feuding and revenge were the stock-in-trade of medieval preachers, who used them to illustrate the importance of overcoming anger and exercising Christian charity in forgiving one's enemy. One such story, drawn from Robert Manning's *Handlyng Synne*, is found in a poetic version in Bodleian MS Ashmole 61.[63] It is a tale of two knights

62. Child's version of the poem cited in Perry, "War and the Media in Border Minstrelsy," 270.

63. George Shuffleton, ed., *Codex Ashmole 61: A Compilation of Popular Middle English Verse* (Kalamazoo, MI: Medieval Institute Publications, 2008), 81–83. See also the commentary on pp. 463–65. Shuffleton points out that "the story existed in several Middle English prose versions and one other verse rendition. In the prose versions that appear in both Latin and Middle English handbooks for preachers, the story is told tersely, presumably so that a preacher could tell it quickly and efficiently in the course of a long sermon" (463).

from a foreign country who were feuding and one slew the other. The child of the slain knight "toke him to rede / For to venge his fader dede" (ll. 8–9) and besieged the murderer's castle for twelve months, not allowing his enemy to issue forth to attend Mass or do other religious duties. On Good Friday, "When men schuld leve wreth and pride" (l. 20), the knight sees his besiegers going to church barefoot "To aske mersy for there mysded" (l. 26) and goes himself to church with the same purpose. Captured by the vengeful son, he pleads for mercy in the name of Christ and the Virgin Mary, and elicits the following response from him:

"Seth thou haste me besought
For Jhesu love that dere us bought,
And for his moder love so dere,
For them I grante thee my powere."

(ll. 55–58)

The knights kiss one another and become friends "In gowd love and perfyte charyté" (l. 63). They enter the church to kiss the cross, according to custom, but when the younger man starts to do so, "the crucyfyx hym kyste" (l. 85), a "merakyll" (l. 88), witnessed and approved by the congregation. The preachers thereafter

can spell,
So that every man in that contré
Lyve well the more in charité,
And all men the soner forgave
Ther wreth that thei to other have.

(ll. 98–102)

The story teaches that God loves those who overcome wrath and forgive their enemies and that it is best for people to live in peace and Christian charity.

As noted above, in Bodleian MS Ashmole 48 there is a ballad describing events in Yorkshire that have some similarities to the feud between the Elands and Beaumonts.[64] This is the poem we identify above as the seventh

64. We cite Wright's unlineated edition (poem 17 in *Songs and Ballads*, 1860) parenthetically by page number. For a discussion of the sources of the poems in this manuscript, see Hyder Rollins, "Concerning Ms. Ashmole 48," *Modern Language Notes* 34, no. 6 (June 1919): 340-51. Rollins, 349, claims that this manuscript "was copied during 1557–65" and that printed broadsides were the source of most of its items.

of only seven historical ballads datable as early as the sixteenth century. It tells the story of the hostility of the sons of "the lord Darsé" (p. 49), Johan and Jorge, toward Lewes West, "[a] goodly jentill mane and squyare" (p. 48), whom they first try to surprise at home and then later attack on the road, killing him in an act of gang violence in a situation in which they and their accomplices greatly outnumber him and his party. The attempted home invasion resembles that by Sir John Eland Sr. The encounter on the road is similar to that of Eland with Adam Beaumont and his friends as well as to the later encounter of the avengers with Sir John Eland Jr. and his young son. Johan and Jorge, "whos hartes iere [ire] dyde flame, / Voyd of all grace or marcye," with their henchmen "Assawghtyde hyme to have hime slayne / At his owene howse at Walyllys" (p. 48). They fail in their attempt, but several weeks later, even after Lord Darcy himself tries to make peace, they attack West and his brother, refusing first West's offer to depart without violence and then his gentlemanly proposal of single or even-number combat, slaying him and his brother shamefully. They also kill a piper in their own company, who remarks "how great a shame" their actions were. The narrator wishes on the attackers

> condyne ponishmente,
> And dethe for theare offence;
> And gyve them grace for to repente,
> Or there departure hence.
> A shamfull thing it ys to kenne,
> And also moste unfite,
> That ever any jentill men
> Such evell shulde commyte.
> A warning, Lorde, grawnte this to be,
> For them to fle such mys,
> Even thowe that dyede uppone a tre,
> To brynge us to the blys.
>
> (pp. 53–54)

The ballad ends with an evocation of Christian morality, but the actions are portrayed in the narrative as fundamentally a violation of community standards of gentlemanly behavior. The same clash between pacific, gentle behavior and unreasoning naked aggression is portrayed in the confrontation and fight between Tybalt and Romeo in Shakespeare's *Romeo and*

Juliet, a play that was written at a time when feuds between "gentle" families were still a social problem.[65]

To some extent, the Eland-Beaumont ballad affirms the importance of Christian charity in a world in which violence was sanctioned as a response to personal injury, but there is no real forgiveness on anyone's part. The Easter season figures in the narrative in the scene in which Sir John Eland's son is ambushed on his way to church, but there are no miracles or signs from God to approve of the characters' behavior, since they all act mercilessly and in an unchristian fashion. The narrator's plea for Christian charity is addressed to the ballad's primary audience, which, in its original performance situation,[66] was probably the Saviles, who had been feuding with another family.

Three systems of social control coexisted within both the original circumstances of the Eland-Beaumont feud and those of the ballad's composition and circulation: a traditional feudal practice of private justice and revenge, a personal and social ethic of Christian charity, and a civil legal and judicial system. From the perspective of a late medieval provincial set of events, the sixteenth-century ballad emphasizes the first two, but it is clear that the third context is very important—especially since, in a period of the centralizing of monarchical and legal authority associated with the nascent modern nation-state, feuds and the pursuit of blood revenge look like the kinds of traditional behaviors that the civilized rule of law needed to control. In the ballad, the judicial system is on the periphery of the local—not only in a part of Yorkshire somewhat distant from the events recounted in the ballad proper but also as far away as London. Even for an audience with local loyalties and a provincial identity, the message was that private feuding and the pursuit of revenge were practices that should not be tolerated in the new order—not only because they violated norms

65. M. C. Bradbrook suggests a particular connection of the play with the Earl of Southampton and his "concealing a friend who had just killed his foe in a feud. Two brothers, Sir Charles and Sir Henry Danvers, were involved in a quarrel with the family of Sir Walter Long; in a fight at an inn, Henry Long had wounded Sir Charles with his sword, whereupon Sir Henry Danvers shot Long dead. Both fled to the Earl of Southampton who concealed them." Cited in *The Arden Edition of the Works of William Shakespeare: Romeo and Juliet*, ed. Brian Gibbons (London: Methuen, 1980], 3n2.

66. At one point in the ballad, the narrator asks his audience to "gyve eare" (66.4) to what he is about to relate.

of Christian charity but also because they posed the kind of threat to public order the judicial system and national authorities could not condone.

The local was a potential site of religio-political nonconformity or resistance, particularly in the case of Yorkshire in both the later Henrician period in which the Catholic rebellion called the Pilgrimage of Grace took place (1536) and the early Elizabethan moment of Northern Rebellion (1569–70), when adherents to the "old religion" and discontented nobles resentful of the rise of "new men" in political and economic power tried to overthrow the Queen and replace her with the Catholic Mary, Queen of Scots.[67] The larger cultural context, however, was more than religious: it involved, as it did in other European countries, a transition from a system of feudal baronies and decentralized power to a newly centralized national polity that monarchs wanted to be legally, religiously, and culturally unified.[68] Richard Helgerson has demonstrated how chorography, involving an emphasis on the local and its historical groundedness, could be a political counterweight to a London-based centralized monarchical power. Christopher Marlowe dramatized this resistance in *Edward II*, where medieval barons assert their power and authority against the king, and William Shakespeare, in his second historical tetralogy, portrayed it in the troublesome relationship of nobles who had home country power bases to whoever was on the throne.[69]

Underscoring the importance of local, especially folk, history could be interpreted as an affirmation of sources of identity and power outside the official ones of the nation-state. This is easy to perceive in the tradition of the Robin Hood ballads, which celebrate opposition to the Crown and its local agents. The Eland-Beaumont narrative is centered on local place names, and it names local families whose presence in west Yorkshire spans the period from the time of the mid-fourteenth-century feud to that

67. See K. J. Kesserlring, *The Northern Rebellion of 1569: Faith, Politics, and Protest in Elizabethan England* (Houndmills, UK: Palgrave Macmillan, 2007).

68. In his recent repositioning of the boundary between medieval and early modern English culture, James Simpson, *Reform and Cultural Revolution*, The Oxford English Literary History, vol. 2, 1350–1547 (Oxford: Oxford University Press, 2002), 1, argues that "in the first half of the sixteenth century, a culture that simplified and centralized jurisdiction aggressively displaced a culture of jurisdictional heterogeneity." This is generally true, but allowances need to be made for the slower rate of change in outlying areas such as the North of England.

69. Richard Helgerson, *Forms of Nationhood: The Elizabethan Writing of England* (Chicago: University of Chicago Press, 1992), 105–47.

of the ballad's probable composition in the 1530s and its transcription in the last part of the sixteenth century. It is topographically myopic, except for brief glances at a national legal order and, in the case of the prose narrative, an international context. As far as this narrative is concerned "all politics are local." But local culture—whether it be Irish, Scottish, Cornish, Welsh, or, in this case, Yorkshire in character—could be perceived as, paradoxically, that which was being preserved and reaffirmed at the same time as being identified as retrograde and in need of civilizing within a new order.[70]

(4) What follows in the Hanson manuscript after the "finis" that marks the conclusion of the narrative and its moralization are three additional stanzas, the first of which refers to the marriage of someone who is described as Sir John Eland Jr.'s surviving sister to a male member of the Savile family (st. 124). In British Library MS Additional 56076, f. 3, this stanza appears in the main narrative, after the one that begins "A full sister forsooth had he [Sir John Eland Jr.]" (stanza 95 in the Hanson manuscript). It makes no sense to have this where it is in the Hanson version, except that the next two stanzas (125 and 126) seem to apply the moral of the story directly to the contemporary Savile family and might have served as an epilogue used in a performance venue in which Savile family members were present.

In the conclusion of the Eland-Beaumont ballad and in the rest of the narrative, the Eland-Savile connection is given more attention than it is in the prose tale. It is first noted in the description of the town of Eland toward which the avengers move in order to ambush their victim. Only one other gentry family is mentioned as residing there, though not full-time:

> mo gentlylmen then was ^not^ there ~~non~~
> in Eland paryshe Dweld

70. Some recent studies of local history have pointed out the cultural variety and heterogeneity of early modern England and the discontinuities between local cultures and a national ideology and system. See, for example, Eamon Duffy, *The Voices of Morebath: Reformation & Rebellion in an English Village* (New Haven: Yale University Press, 2001), and Robert W. Barrett, Jr., *Against All England: Regional Identity and Cheshire Writing, 1195–1656* (Notre Dame, IN: University of Notre Dame Press, 2009). For a useful discussion of microhistory as a historiographical practice, see John Brewer, "Microhistory and the Histories of Everyday Life," *Cultural and Social History* 7, no. 1 (2010): 87–109.

save savile half parte of the yeire
hys howse at Ry*she*w*orth* held
he kept hym selfe from suche debate
Removynge thence wythaull
twyse in the yeire by saviles gate
unto the bothom halle

(f. 38v, st. 73–74)

In the Hanson manuscript there is a manicule next to the line referring to Rishworth (or Rushworth), a property owned by the sixteenth-century Saviles: both it and the name "savile" are underlined. Here, the separateness of the Elands and Saviles is noted in the context of the personal (as well as moral) distance of the Saviles from the feud. In any case, according to the ballad, the Savile family is morally innocent in relation to the bloody acts recounted in the story.

In the ballad, as in the prose account, the diversion of the Eland family inheritance is mentioned as a consequence of the slaying of Sir John Eland Jr. After mentioning that his wounded son died after having been taken back to Eland Hall, the narrator observes that because no male in the line of direct descent survived, a "full syster heire must be" (95.3), so "from Eland Elandes name / Dysplaced was" (96.2–3) and "Elandes land came to saviles name / In Edwardes Dayes the thyrd" (98.3–4). The family and community ties between the mid-fourteenth century and the sixteenth-century time of the work's composition are emphasized. In fact, early in the ballad, the narrator expresses fear that there might be contemporary local thugs ("Caynes sede," 12.3) that might be displeased by his story and resort to violence.

This fear, we believe, relates to the contemporary feud between the Savile and Tempest families. Kaye notes that this struggle for dominance in the Yorkshire locale that was also the setting of the Eland-Beaumont feud narrative

> arose out of a conflict of interests in the lands in Stainland, Barkisland, Rishworth . . . and other places within the honour of Wakefield which had once belonged to Sir John Eland and which, by the sixteenth century, were in the hands of the Saviles. . . . Savile claimed a meane lordship in these lands and hence the right to compel tenants to make suit at his courts, and to pay heriots, wards, reliefs and other dues in addition to whatever dues and services

> they rendered to the honour courts. Tempest, who was seneschal of Wakefield under the king, resisted these claims.[71]

In Henrician England there supposedly were stronger forces of law and order than in the era of warlord feudalism, but in the context of a live feud between the Saviles and Sir Richard Tempest, the danger posed by those willing to resort to Cain-like violence was palpable. Kaye suggests that "Tempest, in the eyes of the Savile faction, was a man rather like Sir John Eland in the ballad portrayal: a local magnate able, by virtue of his official position, to terrorise a whole district—the same district in each case—and to commit murders with impunity."[72] Instead of attacking the family into which the Saviles had married, then, the poem takes as its target the contemporary enemy of the Saviles, while warning them to avoid criminality and cruelty. "Caines sede" (44.4), then, is not biologically rooted in the Eland lineage but rather is morally transmitted to a new, unrelated figure whose deeds make him a moral monster.[73]

In the original circumstances of its composition, then, the ballad apparently had a contemporary relevance to the legal disputes and struggles for local dominance in which the Saviles were involved with the Tempest family,[74] and it offered advice about peacemaking. Kaye summarizes the purpose of the ballad in its original circumstances of composition:

> The Eland ballad was composed not solely for the entertainment of the Yorkshire gentry, as has usually been supposed, but as a warning to them, and in particular to Sir Henry Savile, that persistence in criminal courses was likely to lead to death and disinheritance. The ballad was probably written in the 1530s, before the feud between Savile and Sir Richard Tempest was brought to an end by the latter's death, and while the outrages perpetrated by or attributed to the two men and their adherents were fresh in mind. The fate of Sir John Eland was exhibited as an example to prove the point. The narrative is almost entirely fictitious, for Sir John, a blameless,

71. Kaye, "The Eland Murders," 78.

72. Ibid.

73. Kaye, ibid., 76, suggests that, in addition to projecting Sir Richard Tempest's behavior back onto Sir John Eland Sr., the ballad composer might have confused Sir John Eland Sr. with the criminal Sir Hugh Eland of Doncaster.

74. See the discussion of this ibid., 77–78. See also R. B. Smith, *Land and Politics in the England of Henry VIII, The West Riding of Yorkshire: 1530–46* (Oxford: Clarendon Press, 1970), 147–50.

> hard-working and highly respected minister, ironically lost his life in striving to combat the very kinds of lawless conduct which the ballad maker found objectionable in his own times. . . . No harm could come of denigrating Eland: his family was extinct, and all men would join in reviling a sheriff.[75]

R. B. Smith summarizes the legal charges and countercharges between Savile and Tempest, suggesting that both were guilty of real crimes. Tempest accused Savile of falsely claiming "mesne lordship of Stansfield, Wadsworth, Barkisland and . . . other townships within the lordships of Wakefield and Sowerbyshire" as well as of entering another township, Holmfirth, and driving off "the cattle of the King's copyholders there." He also accused him of protecting from justice a murderer and a counterfeiter, maintaining men after they had murdered the deputy bailiff of Halifax, stealing plate and money from Sir Thomas Tempest, and hunting the king's deer in Wakefield New Park.[76] Savile countered with his own set of charges against Tempest, accusing him of "abusing his authority as steward" in taking illegal fines for new enclosures; embezzling money for soldiers he never led to Scotland; and sheltering five murderers (some of whom he might have hired as assassins).[77] The abuse of power, the maintenance of armed thugs, the sheltering of murderers all resonate with the Eland-Beaumont narrative.

At the time of the probable composition of the poetic and prose versions of the Yorkshire feud, the Savile family, as the one that "displaced" the Eland name, would have had a special interest in the story as part of their family history. Portraying Sir John Eland Sr. as a ruthless assassin whose crimes resulted ultimately in the alienation of his property might have helped to justify the Saviles' inheritance. Several decades later, in the context of the Hanson manuscript, the text served the compiler's need to maintain good relations with the Savile family, as it affirmed the perennial value of Christian charity and neighborliness, joining other items in the collection that embodied traditional moral standards, such as the versified Decalogue. Local history, even when radically distorted and fictionalized,

75. Kaye, "The Eland Murders," 78–79.
76. Smith, *Land and Politics*, 148–49.
77. Ibid., 149.

could affirm both shared social identity and shared moral ideals. The relationship of the ballad to the Savile-Tempest dispute suggests a date of composition in the 1530s preceding the Pilgrimage of Grace (1536–37) and Tempest's unwise siding with the rebels, a fact that led to Sir Richard's downfall and the final victory of the Saviles. Certainly, by the time of the transcription of the ballad in the Hanson manuscript, the social and economic success of the Saviles in the county would have been quite evident and the family connection between the Hansons and the Saviles a crucial one. The Hanson-Savile relationship is also emphasized by the juxtaposition of two memorial poems for deceased Saviles that immediately follow the ballad version of the story. [78]

The Prose History of the Eland-Beaumont Feud

f. 12] *The Dyscourse of the slaghteres of Eland Beamoun[t]*
Lockwod Quermby &c

how Sir John Eland of Eland haule and Sir Robert
Beamount of Croslandhaull had battleled thon° agenst °*the one*
thother in the behalfe of theyr maisteres whom they weare
faythfull unto whyche was a destruction unto theym bothe

It happened in the monthe of maye that sir John
Eland forcasted the waye and whan to betraye sir
Roberte Beamount at Croslandhaule, and therupon
gathered together a great number of mene and
armed theym Ready to battell and privylye in the

78. These two poems that are transcribed together in the manuscript (discussed in the next chapter) refer to two different men named Henry Savile, Sir Henry Savile of Thornhill (1499–1558) and Henry Savile, Esq., of Thornhill (1517/18–1569) and of Lupset. The former was the one involved in a feud with Sir Richard Tempest—therefore the Savile addressed in the moral conclusion of the Eland-Beaumont ballad. It alludes to his support of Henry VIII at the time of the Pilgrimage of Grace (while Tempest supported the rebel side), as well as to his stewardship of Pontefract Castle, membership in the Council of the North, and two terms as sheriff in Yorkshire. The second Savile served as sheriff in Yorkshire (1567–68), held the lordship of Wakefield and the stewardship of Hatfield, and was a member of the Council of the North. For both Saviles, and for other members of the Savile family, see the *ODNB* article by Joan Kirby, http://www.oxforddnb.com/view/printable/71873.

evenyng to Croslandhaull they went, and as they
should passe throughe the Townes of Quermby
and Lockwodd to Croslandward, there Dwelled
two olde gentylmen of nyghe affynytye unto sir
Robert Beamount thon called olde hughe of
quermby and thother old Lockwodde of lockwodd
whom Eland suspected wolde stand in armes
agaynst hym in the behalf of theyr kynsman
Sir Robert, Therfore Eland be° dysceapte went °*by*
into theyr own howses and put theym to death
and afterward came to Croslandhaule/ and when
they cowlde fynd no waye to geat in, therfore
they hyde theym in bushes untyll suche tyme
as they perceyved a mayde of the howse Dyd lett
downe the Drawe brydge to passe over to do hyr
busynes[79]

f. 12v] busynes and therwythe they came to the brydge
and passed over into the haule where sir Roberte
and hys famylye beyng in bedde no thynge
suspectyng the matter, yet as sone as sir Roberte
perceved howe Eland hade betrayed hym sodenlye
Rushed up and called hys famylie/ and therwyth
unarmed toke theyr weapones and assayled theyr
enymyes to Recule° or go bake agayn over the °*gather together*
bridge/ immedyatlye therupon one of [Si]r[80] Roberte
kynsmen and a frend of hys went to lancashyer
to geyt knowledge unto Sir John brewerton
and Syr John Towneley howe sir John eland
hade betrayed theyr kynsman Sir Robert beamount
wherfore they assented to come over wythe
Dyverse gentylmen and otheres well armed
to Rescue Syr Roberte beamount who conjectured
that the more parte of Sir Roberte mene weare slayn
and made away, therfore he sodenlye gathered
hys menne together and assayled by battell and
slewe sir Robert Beamount, and hys brother
William beamount, wythe the Rest of hys

79. Catchword.

80. "Rr" for "Sr" in MS.

menne, and also one Exley whyche aforetyme
slewe sir John Eland brotheres sonne for the
Whiche to agrement he gave acertan
pece of land to the Elandes yet after the

f. 13] agrement made Sir John Eland sought to have slayn
hym and therfore Exle was constrayned to flee unto
thafforsayd sir Robert Beamount for ayde/ who
bycause he was hys kynsman Rescued hym whiche
partlye was the occasyon of the great Malice that was
betwyxt the sayd sir Roberte Beamount and sir John
Eland and as they weare in battyll sir John bruerton
and sir John Towneley wythe Dyverse gentylmen
and otheres well armed weare commyng owt of la[n]cashyer
to Rescue theyr kynsman sir Roberte Beamount, and
in theyr commyng betwyxt puell and the standyng
stone, to Crosland ward/ they mett a messenger
sent unto theym, advertysynge° theym of the Deathe °*informing*
of sir Robert and his brother william and the
Reste as ys aforsayd/ Then they enquyred what
was become of his wyffe and children/ who answered
for the savegard of theyr lyves they weare con[v]eyed[81]
into a secret place amongest theyr frendes/ after
this the knyghtes Returned into Lancashyer withe
theyr companye But sir John Eland[82] that sir
Roberte his children shoulde be brought before hym
and whan they weare come he profered theym breade
whiche they Receyved/ but adam Beamount
theldest after he hade taken yt, he wythe dysdeignne
threwe yt at hym agayne, whiche Eland perceyvynge
sayd that he woulde wede owt thofspryng of his blood

f. 13v] as they wede the weedes owt of corne, Immedyatlye
after thys Sir John Brewarton and syr John
Townley sent for syr Robert hys chyldren to be
brought into Lancashyer, and wythe theym
went thether the chyldren of Querneby and
Lockwodd/ and also one Lacye beyng of neighe

81. The MS reads "conbeyed."

82. Other texts insert "caused" or "commanded" at this point.

affynytye thon to thother as brotheres and
systeres chyldren and so they contynued there
unto° they weare xx yeires of age, at the °*until*
which age they weare stronge and of good
audacytye and well cowlde handyll theyr weapons
they Remembred the traytoures° Done unto theyr °*treasons, betrayals*
parentes by sir John Eland for the whyche
Lockwodd the eldest of theym sayd that yt
weare great shame unto theym to contynue
amongest theyr frendes, and not to Revenge
the Deathes of theyr parentes and otheres theyr
kinsmen In thuse° of thys communycacion yt °*the course*
chaunced that thre honest mene of theyr
kinred one called Dysowne/ an other haighe
the thyrd Dawson whiche came into lancashyer
to vysyt theym, to whom they opened theyr
communicacion before hade/ wherunto they
Answered that sir John Eland had appoy[n]ted

f. 14] Acertan Daye to kepe the shirif Returne° at Bridghowse °*sheriff's court*
wherof they shoulde have knowledge/ and agaynst° that °*in preparation for*
Daye accordynge to promyse they hade, wherfore they
came over and leye in cromblebothom woddes/ and waytyng
for Sir John Eland hys commyng from the shiriffes Returne
they appoynted aspye to gyve theym knowledge
Whiche the spye Dyd accordynge to theyr commande
ment, then they prepared theym selves Ready/ and
upon the water betwyxt the bridge Foote and
Brydghowse they mett sir John wythall his
Companye/ who hade no lyttyll marvell what
yonge gentylmen they should be/ and at theyr
approchyng neighe hym, he moved his cappe unto
theym, whiche adam Beamount perceyvyng sayd
knyght thy curtesye prevaylethe the° nought °*thee*
because thowe hast slayne sir Robert beamount
my father, lykewyse sayd lockwood/ and quermby
thowe hast slayne owre fatheres two, therfore on
the and thyne wyll we be Revenged/ and then
they battelled thon wythe the other verey fercely
this battell conntynued Longe, but ever yt was

to the Destructyon of the knyght great proues° °*prowess*
and valyantnes herin was shaped,[83] But at the
last they Redowbled theyr strokes agenst sir John
and hys menne, and therby they vanqueste the knyght
and put hym to Deathe and after Returnyed to[84]

f. 14v] Fournyshe Felles wheare they contynued amongest
theyr frendes Declarynge what they had Done
in the Revengyng of the Deathes of theyr paren[tes]

howe adam Beamount lockwood Quermby
and lacye had battellyng agenst sir John
Eland his sonne, and howe they vanquyshed
hym and put hym to Deathe and afterward
slewe hys sonne

When adam Beamount Lockwodd Querneby
and lacy had contynued even untyll palmes
sondaye followynge amongest theyr frendes
at Fourny Felles from whence they came over
to Eland, and that nyght they Lodged there
in the mylnes howse° wheare they herd say tha[t] °*mill house*
sir John Eland his sonne was and kept howse
yt chaunced as that nyght the myller
commaunded hys wyfe to Repeyre° to the myllne °*go*
to fetche home certan corne, she fulfyllyng
hyr husbands commaundement went thether
the yong gentlemen percyvyng hyr,
suffered hyr to com in, and so toke hyr and
tyed hyr faste and leyd hyr asyde, the por
Miller musyng not alytyll what yt should
be that caused his wyffe tary so longe
wherefore he sware by many greate othes[85]

f. 15][86] (<u>Wherefore hee sware by many great oathes</u>) that shee
shoud repent her long tarrying & took A staple° in his °*stake, rod*

83. The *OED* has several obsolete meanings of the verb "to shape" that may explain its use here: "5.a To fashion an image of, portray; 5.b To present, set (an example); 5.c To depict, describe."

84. In the left margin (probably in Hand D): "21 E 3," that is, 1347/48, the twenty-first year of the reign of Edward III.

85. * in left margin by later scribe to note beginning of transcription of missing page.

86. This folio is a tipped-in new leaf in a later hand (Hand E) providing missing text.

hands to chastize her with, but when hee came to the
Milne, they took him & bound him & layed him
besides his wife, The young knight Eland dreamed
that night that hee was beset in his bed with many enemies
that assailed him terribly, & shewed the dreame to his Lady
but she set light by itt, however hee caused his men
to arme themselves & bid them not be afraid of Lockwood
for hee intended to goe to Church that Day ^being Palmesonday^
this milne
was in the way to the Towne, the drought had made
the water soe little that the knight with his son & all
his servants went over the damm. when Adam Beaumont
espied them hee came out of the Milne with his bow
in his hand & shott att the knight & hitt him on his
brestplate which glanced off° the arrow, wherat Lookwood °*turned aside*
being angry shott himselfe & hitt the knight, but
harmed him not, whereupon the knight mocked
them and said in case his father had been soe well armed
hee had not been slaine by them, but sayes hee
if the Towne of Eland knew of this thou durst not appear
in this place, Lockwood feareing the Towne might rise
upon them shott the knight through the head, his son
& heir was mortaly wounded & carried back to Eland
Hall where hee dyed, hee had A halfe brother remayneing
& A full sister who inherited his lands & was maried
to Savill in Edward the 3ds time, The young men fled
by Whitehill lane, & soe by the old earth [g]ate° into ~~the~~ °*dirt road*
~~woods of~~ Aneley woods, The knights servants raised
the Towne of Eland to revenge the death of their Lord

f. 15v] Whithill Smith Wilkinson & Bury with many others being
furiousely enraged pursued their Lords enemies, with bows
clubs & rusty bills,° & were assisted by many of the
Parishione[r]s °*halberds*
that were goeing to church, Beamount Lockwood &
Quernby resisted them as long as they had any arrows
remaineing & then betooke themselves to flight
Querneby the hardiest of them was mortaly wounded
but Lookwood bare him on his back & hid him
in the wood, hee gave Lockwood all his gold & bid

them make merry with itt, here they left Quernby
& fled away towards Huddersfield &c.[87]

f. 16][88] and bare hym on hys backe wyllyng hys
cosynge Adam beamount to shoote in hys
Rome,° whyche he Dyd and so Defended theym °*room, place*
from theyr enemyes untyll Quermbye was
brought to Aynley woodes[89] wheare for the
savegard of hys lyfe they hyd hym in an yvye
tree bycause the countrye came so faste abowt
theym/ yett Quermeby bycause he shoulde be
hade in Remembrance not onelye for that they
weare brotheres and systeres children/ or in the
tyme of theyr myrthe and Dysporte but
also for theyr valyant actes and enterprises[90]
Done Dyd gyve unto theym hys purse
full of golde and sylver to be Devyded amongst
theym, And after thys they passed from hym
not alytyll thankyng hym for hys gyfte and
good wyll, The contrye styll followed them unty[l]
they approched neighe hudder Feild at whyche
tyme they weare owt of theyr Daunger/ And
so they passed to Crosland honley holmefirth
And meltam, The contrye then Retyred and
went backe marveylynge what they had done
wythe Quermby, and in theyr Returnyng they
harde the chatteryng of crowes and pyes abowt
the Ivye tree, wherein he leye hyd, they partlye
suspectyng

f. 16v] the matter went thyther and found querneby
hyd whom they slewe most cruellye
howe Lockwood was anamored on a
woman Dwellyng at Cannellhaule
and howe he was betrayed and slayn

87. The bottom two-thirds of this page is blank. This appears to be a gap caused by a missing folio or folios. The new scribe is condensing material that is elaborated below.

88. There is a symbol in the left margin at the start of this page.

89. This underlining is in darker ink.

90. "Amen" is written sideways in the margin.

After all thies thynges yt chaunced that
Lockwood was anamored on a woman
Dwellyng at Cannellhaulle neighe Cawthorn
and accordyng to theyr appoyntment mette
often tymes in Emleye parke at a great
holowe oke whiche the keper seyng betrayed
or opened theyr Doynges yet notwithstandyng
yt chaunced that lockwood after he had bene
absent from hys woman awhile at Feney
bridge as he was Repeyryng to hyr agayn
mett wythe two maydes of hys kynred
commyng from Lepton or whytley whiche
sayd unto hym coosyn we mervell not alytyll
that yowe are absent from yowre cossen
Adam Beamount bycause that we her° saye *°hear*
ye are sought fore by the shiryffe and[91]

f. 17] And otheres to be attached/° and also the places and *°arrested*
standes that ye Repayre unto are well known
Therfore yt weare yowre beste° to be at crosland *°best for you*
honley and holmefirth huntynge the Reade dere
wythe adam Beamount, then to be imprisoned
and in Danger of yowre lyfe wythowt any
myrth at all (except ye here nowe and then
the pypyng° of the myse in some corner[)] *°peeping, squeaking*
Therfore procede no further to yowre woman
by whom yowe shalbe betrayed. But Returne
wythe us to adam Beamount Then he
promissed to be wythe theym before he Dyd
eyther eyte or Drynke, and after this he departed
from theym and passed throughe the woddes to
Emleyhaule wheare hys woman was, and before
hys commyng thyther Boswell who than was
under shiryffe/, and also owner of the sayd
[H]aule mynaced° his tennante that he wold put *°threatened*
hym from hys fermolde[92] (except by some

91. An *m* is written at the bottom of the page, probably by Hand D.

92. This appears to be a variation of the term "freehold," which the *OED* defines as "permanent and absolute tenure of land or property with freedom to dispose of it at will." Hanson's text omits a necessary part of Boswell's bargain after "he wold," that his tenant "deliver Lockwood into his hands, & if he did doe it." WYAS, Bradford, 32D86/12, f. 44.

devyce or meanes he wold not only permytt
hym to be his tennant but also woulde gyve[93]

f. 17v] hym manye great gyftes[94] and upon this condicion
hys tennant graunted hym to do hys endevor
therin/ and Immedyatlye therupon yt chansed
that lockwood cam to cannellhaule, and hys
tennant privelye gave hym knowledge therof
than Boswell gathered agreat companye
of mene together and cam to cannellhaule and
besett yt Rownde abowt and asked for
Lockwood/ who perceyved howe he was
betrayed/ yet not wythstandying lookwod
boldlye answered and sayd I ame here, then
he wythe otheres commaunded hym to yeld
hym self into theyr handes whiche lockwood
Refused to do so longe as he had lyffe
and therwythe he bent hys bowe and
manfullye Defended hym selfe agenst
theym all a longe tyme Boswell and
hys companye perceyvyng that they cowld
not have theyr wylles on hym they
threatned hym to burne the howse over

f. 18] hys heade/ whiche Lockwoodd no thyng feared
hys woman perceyvyng hym most busye in the
Defence of hym self, In whom he had most
truste She sodenlye louped° unto hym and ° *leaped (Scot.)*
wythe hyr knyfe she cutt hys bowestrynge and
than she Ranne fast from hym/ whan Lockwood
perceyved thys in hys woman he sayd fye on
the° whore/ that ever thowe were ordeyned to °*thee*
be the Destructyon of menes bloode for by the
and suche lyke maye all menne take an
example/ After thys yt chaunced that boswell
and hys companye promessed hym verey muche
frendshippe in case he would yelde hym self

93. At bottom of page, "1579," probably by Hand D.

94. Hanson omits closing the parenthesis here.

into theyr handes/ which at the last throughe
theyr feyre and pleasant communicacion and upon
hope of theyr promese yelded hym self to
theym, and then he Delyvered theym hys
weapones yet further they Requested hym
to permytt theym to bynde his handes which
he suffered theym to do, and then they slewe
hym verey cruellye But when adam beamount
Dyd understand of the Deathe of hys coosyng[95]

f. 18v] he was therfore not alytyll sorye, and also
for the Departyng of hys coosyn lacye/ who
was gone into the northe, and therby he was
constrayned to wander all alone wherby
he was half Descomforted/ and at the last
partlye for that cause, and partlye for asmuche
as there cam Downe from London Dyverse
pr[o]ceses° Dyrecte[d] to the shiryff and dyverse °*writs, orders*
other noble menne for to attache hym, and he
was owt of quyetnes of hym self and his
frendes/ he was constayned to flye into
Forane Realmes./ and so contynued amongst
the knyghtes of the Rodes and hungarye/ wheare
hys valyant actes weare hade in estymacion
and so he was appoynted to fyght agenst the
heathen from whence he Dyrected his lettres
into yorkeshyer to aspecyall frend of hys
called Jenkyn Dyson Dwellyng at the
holehowse wythin the paryshe of almonburye
And afterwardes adam beamount had his abydyng
somtymes at the Rodes and somtyme at
hungarye where he ended his lyffe.//

Textual Analysis

Textual Sources:

A BL MS Add. 82370, ff. 12–18v
A26 BL MS Add. 26739, ff. 102v–106

95. There are minims at the bottom of the page.

H	WYAS, Bradford, 32D86/12, ff. 41–45v, a genealogical collection compiled c. 1660–80 by John Hopkinson[96]
H46	BL MS Harley 4630, ff. 89–91
Sp	WYAS, Bradford, SpSt/6/3/15, pp. 101–4
T2	J. Horsfall Turner, ed., *The Elland Tragedies* (Bingley, UK.: T. Harrison and Sons, 1890), 52–58, from "Mr. Barber's [H. J. Barber's] MS. copy" (p. 59)

The earliest printed account we have found of the Eland-Beaumont feud occurs in William Bentley's *Hallifax, And Its Gibbet-Law . . . To which are added, The Unparallel'd Tragedie committed by Sir John Eland, of Eland, and his Grand Antagonists* (Hallifax, 1708, with later editions in 1712, 1761, and 1789). Bentley's prose account is an example of the florid, late-Stuart high style at its grandest. The appended narrative is based on both the verse and prose versions of the story, although Bentley's heightened paraphrase is textually useless. The first part, ending with the retreat to safety of Beaumont and Lockwood after they have extinguished the Eland line, is based primarily on the ballad, for Bentley refers several times to "the Poet." The last part is entitled "A short but full Account of the Lives and Deaths of Wilkin Lockwood, and Adam Beamont . . . as the same is recorded in a very Ancient Manuscript, in the Custody of a worthy Gentleman, kindly communicated for Publick Satisfaction" (154). This portion of the narrative derives from H. J. Barber's manuscript as cited by Turner (*T2*) or a closely related text. Although many details and much of the phrasing in Bentley's account match *T2* and *A* equally, several errors mark *T2* as his source. Both his account and the manuscript employed by Turner fail to mention Sir Robert Beaumont's brother, William, who died with him (an incident also mentioned in *A26* and *H46*). At the end, Bentley describes Adam Beaumont fleeing "into a foreign country . . . [and] after a few nights and days he was safely landed within in the realm of France" (edition of 1789, p. 54). This follows the *T2* error, "he was constrained to Flye into france Realmes" (58), whereas *A* reads, "he was constrayned to flye into Forane Realmes" (f. 18v).

John Watson included the ballad of the feud in his *History and Antiquities of the Parish of Halifax, in Yorkshire*, followed by a prose account of the further adventures of Lockwood and Beaumont "as the same is recorded

96. This appears to be MS 12.

in a very antient manuscript."[97] The quotation from Bentley's title shows that Watson drew upon this source. He continues with a succinct paraphrase of Bentley's narrative in which Adam Beaumont, upon leaving England, lands "safe in France" (182). Again, Watson's version sheds no light on the original textual state of the prose narrative. However, his analysis of the texts was based on multiple sources. In his coverage of the feud's historical background he refers at several points to "Hopkinson's Mss." (179, 180), and with regard to stanza 76, to the reading "in some copies, 'Cromwelbottom hall,' instead of 'wood'" (179). As we shall see, *A* and two other substantive manuscripts contain the reading "hall" at 76.1, while only the Hopkinson transcript of the ballad reads "wood." Thus Watson had access to original and as yet unidentified sources for both the ballad and prose accounts of the feud.

The six substantive textual sources are therefore the five manuscripts cited above plus Turner's transcription of the Barber manuscript. *H46, A26, Sp*, and *H* agree in error when they confuse Sir John Eland Jr.'s son with Sir John in the attack at the mill. The contradictory account after Lockwood shoots at Sir John reads in *H46*: "[H]e suddainly fell downe & there they slew him, afterwards he was carried to Eland-Hall & soe knowne to be alive after the death of his father" (f. 90v). *A, T2* (and Bentley) specify that both Sir John and his son die in the battle at the mill. In *A*, Lockwood "shott the knight through the head, his son & heir was mortaly wounded & carried back to Eland Hall, where hee dyed" (f. 15). *T2* drops the word "back" but otherwise preserves this passage exactly. Thus *H46, A26, Sp*, and *H* descend from a common ancestor that erased Sir John's son and heir from the narrative at that point. They may also agree in error in their reference to Lockwood's "arrowe headed with Peacocks feathers" (*H46*, f. 90v). In other details and wording, these versions closely resemble each other but conflict with *A* and *T2*.

Further evidence that *H46, A26, Sp*, and *H* are collateral with *A-T2* occurs in the narrative where these four sources retain a passage in which Boswell seeks a means to capture and kill Lockwood. In *H46* this reads, "[H]e would by some device or means deliver Lockwood into his hands" (f. 91). Eye skip caused a version of the text ancestral to *A* to jumble this into "by some Devyce or meanes he wold not only permytt hym to be his

97. Watson, *History and Antiquities*, 180.

tennant." (f. 17). *T2* omits even more of this passage, thus confirming its relationship with *A*. These two sources agree against the other manuscripts in several other errors and details. They name Sir Robert Beaumont's Lancashire kinsman Sir John Brewerton, for example, whereas he is Sir Robert Brearton in *H46, A26, Sp*, and *H*. While it is unclear which of the two names is correct, *A* and *T2* are certainly in error at this point when they attribute the death of Sir Robert Beaumont to their relatives and would-be rescuers, Brerton and Townley. In *A* the passage reads, "[T]hey assented to come over wythe Dyverse gentylmen and otheres well armed to Rescue Syr Roberte beamount who conjectured that the more parte of Sir Roberte mene weare slayn and made away, therfore he sodenlye gathered hys menne together and assayled by battell and slewe sir Robert Beamount, and hys brother william beamount, wythe the Rest of hys menne, and also one Exley" (f. 12v). *T2* reads "Sr Roberts men" and, as we have seen, omits the brother, William Beaumont, but otherwise preserves this passage verbatim (p. 53). The other manuscripts correctly attribute these deaths to Eland: "But Sir. Jno Eland suddenly gathered and called together his Men and Slew Sir Robert Beaumont, his Brother William Beaumont with the rest of his Kinsmen and one Exley" (*Sp*, p. 101).

Two additional mistakes confirm the descent of *A* and *T2* from a common ancestor. Both refer to "the traytoures Done unto theyr parentes by Sir John Eland," where the other sources read "the Traiterous Acts." As the young men plan their revenge in Lancashire, *H46, A26, Sp*, and *H* state that Dyson, Haigh, and Dawson visit them "In the time of this their communication" (*H46*, f. 89v). *A* transforms this into "In thuse [the use] of thys communycacion," further corrupted by *T2* as "In th'use of this communion." Bentley drew on *T2* (or a nearly derived descendant) for his sequel to the events narrated in the ballad, while Watson relied on Bentley for his prose summary of these events. *T2* introduces so many errors not found in *A* that it could not have been Hanson's source. But could *T2* have been copied from *A*? Turner's old-spelling text differs radically from the orthography of *A* yet preserves most of its unusual linguistic features.[98]

98. Turner, *The Elland Tragedies*, dated the handwriting of the *T2* manuscript "to about 1600–80," adding that it was "evidently copied from an older manuscript" (58). Indeed, *T2* retains many of the archaic or dialect words and spellings found in *A*, such as "louped" for "leaped" (f. 18/p. 57) and "coosyng" for "cousin" (f. 18/p. 58). The *OED* recognizes the spelling of this word with a final *g* only in Middle English through the fifteenth century.

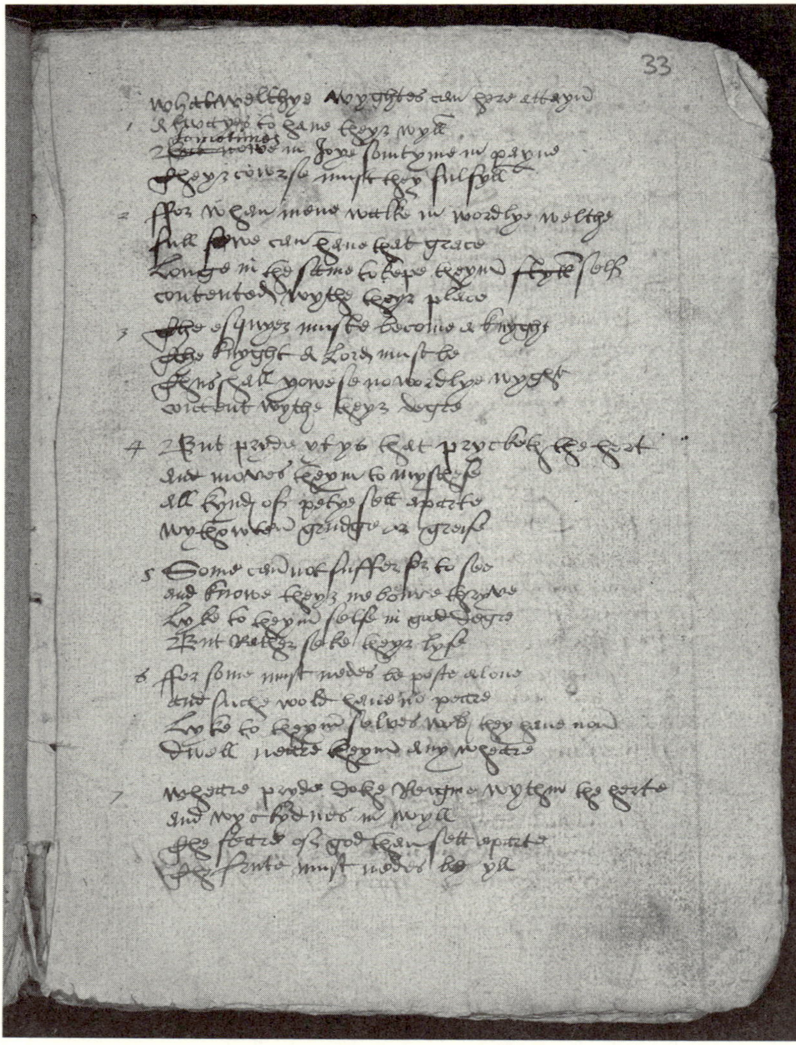

Figure 4. BL Add. MS 82370, f. 33. Start of ballad about Eland-Beaumont feud. Reproduced by permission of The British Library Board.

T2 does, however, correct two faulty readings in *A*. First, on folio 12v, Hanson's text states that when "sir Roberte perceved howe Eland hade betrayed hym sodenlye Rushed up and called hys famylie." *T2* corrects this ellipitical description by supplying a clear subject for "rushed": when

"Sir. Robert perceived how Eland had betray'd him he suddenly rushed" (p. 52). Second, on folio 13, *A* omits a much-needed verb: "But sir John Eland that sir Roberte his children shoulde be brought before hym." *T2* clarifies Eland's demand with, "But Sr John Eland caused that Sir Roberts children should be brought before him" (p. 53). Both mistakes in *A* might reasonably have been corrected by the scribe of *T2*, a possibility reinforced by the fact that in place of "caused" supplied in the second example, *H46, A26*, and *Sp* read "commanded," while *H* has "bade."

We thus conclude that the prose narrative of the Eland-Beaumont feud followed two main lines of descent from the archetype, with *A* and *T2* probably dependent on a lost version that transmitted the errors listed above, or, almost as likely, that *T2* was copied directly from *A*. A second hypothetical source was ancestral to *H46, A26, Sp*, and *H*. It failed to mention the death of the junior Sir John Eland's heir but included the arrow "headed" not with (armor-piercing) steel but peacock feathers.

The Ballad

f. 33] 1[99] what welthye wyghtes° can here attayn °*persons*
Alwayes to have theyr wyll
~~But nowe~~ ^sometimes^ in Joye somtyme in payne
Theyr cowrse must they fulfyll

2 For whan mene walke in wordlye° welthe °*alt. spelling of worldly*
full fewe can have that grace
Longe in the same to kepe theym ~~styll~~ self
contented wythe theyr place

3 The esquyer muste become a knyght
The knyght a Lord must be
Thus shall yowe se no wordlye wyght
content wyth theyr Degre

99. The stanza numbers in the margins for the first 34 stanzas of the poem are transcribed in a different hand from that of the main text. This scribe, however, makes several mistakes: he or she uses the number "12" for stanza 20; places "27" in the margin between "26" and "28" without any poetic text next to it; and consequently misnumbers stanzas 27 through 34 (with numerous deletions) before leaving off the task of numbering stanzas. We include the correct numbers in brackets for these stanzas and provide stanza numbers in brackets for the rest of the 126-stanza poem's unnumbered stanzas.

4 But pryde yt ys that prycketh the hert
and moves theym to myschefe
all kynd of petye° sett aparte °pity
wythowten grudge or greife

5[100] Some can not suffer for to see
and knowe theyr neboure thryve
Lyke to theym selfe in good Degre
But Rather seke theyr lyfe

6 For some must nedes be poste° alone °placed, stationed
and suche wold have no peare
Lyke to theym selves wold they have non
dwell neare theym any wheare

7 wheare pryde Dothe Reigne wythin the herte
and wyckydnes in wyll
The feare of god then sett aparte
The frute must nedes be yll

f. 33v] 8 wythe such Lyke falte was foule infecte
one Syr John Eland knyght
his Doynges makith hym sore suspecte
in thys to have Delyght

9 Somtyme there Dwelt at Croslandhaulle
A kynde and curtyse knyght
yt was well known that he wythall
Sir Robart beamount hyght° °was named

10 At Eland Sir John Eland Dwelt
Wythin the maner haulle
The Towne hys owne, the paryshe held
most parte upon hym all

11 The market towne was Eland than
The patent hathe bene sene
Under kynge Edward Seale certayn
The fyrst Edward I wene/° °think, believe

100. Stanzas 5 and 6 come after 7 in the 1860 print version.

12 But nowe I dowte° to synge for drede °*fear*
to knowe myn owne contrye
so stowtlye stored wythe Caynes sede
there spryngyng plentuouslye

13 halas suche store of wyttye menne
as there are nowe thies Dayes
was bothe unborne and gotten then
to staye° such wycked wayes °*prevent*

14 Some saye that Eland sheryff was
by bea[m]ount Dysobeyed
whiche myght hym make for such trespase
wythe hym the worse appeyd° °*satisfied, contented, pleased*

f. 34] 15 he[101] Rasyd the contrye Round abowte
hys frendes and tennantes all
Mene for that purpose pyked owt
stowt sturdye mene and taulle

16 To Querneby haule they cam by nyght
and there the Lord they slewe
at that tyme heire of Querneby Ryght
before the contrye knewe

17 To Lockewodd than the selfe same nyght
They cam and there the[y] slewe
Lockewodd of lockewod that herdy wyght
who styrred the stryff anewe

18 whan they hade slayn thus sodenlye
Syr Robartes beamount ayde
They came to Croseland crafteleye
of nought weare they appayd° °*pleased, satisfied*

19 The haule was watered welle abowt
no wyght cowlde com wythin
Tyll tyme the bridge were well leyd owt
They durst not enter in

101. In darker ink in later hand.

12 [20] Before the howse they cowlde invade
in bushement° they Dyd lygge° *°ambushment . . . °did lie*
and watched a wenche wythe wylye trade[102]
tyll she let Downe the brydgge

f. 34v] 21 Than sett they seigge asalt they made
haynouslye to the hawlle
The knyghtes chamber dyd they invade
And toke the knyght wythall

22 Yet have I Rede most certanlye
headed° before he weare *°beheaded*
he fought agenst theym manfullye
unarmed as he weare

23 hys servantes Rose and styll wythestood
and stroke wythe myght and mayne
in hys Defence they shedde theyr bloode
but all that was in vayne

24 The ladye cryed and skryked wythall
from hyr than whan they ledde
hyr Deare husband into the haule
and there storke[103] of hys heade

25 But all in vayne the more petye
for petye/ hade no place
for craftte myscheff & crueltye
thies menne Dyd moste imbrace

26 They hade a guyde that guyded theym
wythin theyr hertes dyd Dwell
The same to this that moved theym
the verye devyll of hell

28 [27] Se herin what uncertantye
this wretched world ys ledde
at nyght in his prosperytye
at morowe slayne & dead

102. The *OED* defines "trade" as a "way or method of attaining an end; a contrivance, expedient, *obs. rare*."

103. Hanson's error for "struck."

f. 35] 2~~8~~9[28] Iwys° a wofull howse there was °*indeed, certainly*
the Lord laye slayne & dead
30 Theyr fooes than eate before theyr face
theyr meate alle wyne & breade

*3~~0~~1[29] To <u>sones</u> ^boyes^[104] sir Roberte beamount [had], they lefte
onely unslayne
Sir John Eland he theym bade, com eyte with hym certayn[105]

32 [30] The one Dyde eite wyth hym trulye
the yonger he was I thynke
Adam the other sturdelye
wold nether eite nor Drynke

~~2~~3[31] Se howe this boye sayd Eland see
his fatheres Deathe can take
yf anye be, yt wylbe he
the same shall venge and wrake° °*wreak*

3~~3~~4[32] But yf that he wax wilde anon
I shall so hym for see° °*anticipate*
and cut theym of by one and onne
as tyme shall serve me[106]

3~~34~~5 [33] The fyrst fraye here nowe have ye herd
The secund shall ensue
And howe muche myscheiff afterward
upon thys murder grewe

34~~5~~6[34] And howe this myscheiff he contryved
his wycked hert wythin
lyght of° hym self shalbe dyscribed °*alighted on*
Marke nowe for I begyn

f. 35v] [35] The same mornyng a messynger
ys sent to Lancashyer
to maister Towneley & bruerton there
theyr helpe for to Requyer

104. "Sones" is underlined, not deleted, with "boyes" written directly above it.
105. This stanza is transcribed as a couplet.
106. This line lacks a syllable.

[36] unto the mount benethe Marsdeyn[107]
to whom they went wythe spede
but hearyng than theyr frend was slayne
Returned agayn in Dede

[37] When Eland wythe his wylfulnes
Thus Beamoundes bloode hade shedde
into the costes[108] of Lancashyer
the ladye Beamount fledde

[38] wythe hyr she toke her children all
At bruerton to Remayn
somtyme also at Towneley haulle
they sogerned° certayn °*sojourned, resided*

[39 Bruerton & Towneley frendes they weare
to hyr and of hyr bloode
as presentlye yt Dyd appeare
They sought to do hyr good

[40] They kept the boyes tyll they increast
in person strenght and age
Theyr fatheres Deathe to have Redrest
Styll kyndled theyr currage

[41] Lacye and lockewodd was wythe theym
brought up at bruerton grene
and Querneby kynseman unto they[m]
at home Durst not be sene/

f. 36] [42] The Feates of fence they practysed
To weald theyr weapon° well °*weapons*
tyll fyften yeires were fynyshed
and than so yt befell

[43] Lockwodd as eldest of theym all
sayd frendes I thynke yt good
we went into owre contrye all
to venge owre fatheres bloode

107. Town southwest of Huddersfield.

108. The *OED* defines "coast" as "6. A tract or region of the earth; a district, place, *obs*."

[44] yf Eland have thys for welledone
he wyll slea° mo in Dedde °*slay*
best weare [it][109] than we slewe hym sone
And cut of Caines sede

[45] I sawe my father lockwodd slayn
And Querneby in the nyght
and last of all they slewe certayn
Sir Roberte beamount knyght

[46] Oh Lord this was a wicked Dede
who cowlde theyr handes Refrayn
for to wede owt suche wicked menne
Thoughe yt were to theyr payne

[47] To thys the Reste then all agreyd
Devysyng Daye by Daye
of thys theyr purpose for to sped° °*accomplish*
what weare the Redyest waye/

f. 36v] [48] Two mene that tyme from Querneby came
dawson and haghe, in Dede
whom they consulted for the same
in thys howe to procede

[49 Those contrye menne of cowrse onelye
sayd Eland kept alwaye
The turne[110] at bryghouse certaynlye
and yowe shall knowe the Daye

[50] By Cromwelbothom must he comme
in woddes lye yowe in wayte
So maye yowe slea theym all and somme
And take theym at astrayte° °*a narrow place*

[51] The Daye was sett, the Turne was kept
At Brighouse by Sir John
lyttyll wyst° he, he was besett °*knew, suspected*
than at hys commyng home/

109. Hanson wrote "in" for "it."

110. The *OED* defines "tourn" as the "tour, turn, or circuit formerly made by the sheriff of a county twice in the year, in which he presided at the hundred-court in each hundred of the county; the great court leet of the county, held by him on these occasions; it was a court of record."

[52] Dawson and hagh hade pleyd theyr partes
and brought from bruerton grene
yonge gentylmen wythe hardy hartes
as well were known and sene

[53] Adam of Beamount there was layde
Lacye wythe hym also
and Lockwodd who was nought affrayd
To fyght agenst hys foo

f. 37][111] [54] in Cromwelbothom woddes they leye
A nomber wythe theym mo
armed they weare in good araye
a spye they hade also

[55] To spye the tyme whan Eland came
from Bryghowse [t]urne[112] that Daye
who played hys parte and shewed the same
to theym whearas they laye

[56] Beneth broukefotte a hyll ther ys
to Bryghowse in the waye
forthe cam they to the toppe of thys
there spying for theyr praye/

[57] From the lane end cam Eland than
and spyed thies gentylmen
sore wondred he who weare those men
and vayled hys bonet than

[58] Thy curtsye vayles° the nought sir knyght ° *avails, benefits*
thowe slewe my father Deare
Somtyme syr Roberte beamount knyght
and slayne shalt thowe be heare

[59] Sayd adam Beamount wythe the Rest
owre fatheres hast thowe slaynne
Whose Deathes we mynde shalbe Redrest
of the and thyne agayn

111. There is a one-leaf stub between folios 36v and 37, with writing on both sides.

112. Hanson wrote "gurne" for "turne."

f. 37v] [60] To stryke at hym styll Dyd they stryffe° °*strive*
But Eland styll wythstod
Wythe myght and mayne to save hys lyffe
but styll they shed his bloode

[61] They cut him from hys companye
belyke° at the Lanes end °*in all likelihood, probably*
and so they slewe hym certanlye
and thus he made hys ende

[62][113] Marke here the ende of crueltye
suche fyne° hathe fa[l]shood loo[114] °*end, conclusion, obs.*
Such ende hym selff lo heare hath he
as he brought other° to °*others*

[63] But Beamount yet was muche to blame
Thoughe heare he played the manne
that parte he playd not in the same[115]
of a Ryght chrysten manne

[64] A pure consyence cowlde never fynde
an harte to do thys Dede
Thoughe thys Day shoulde be assynde
hys own herte bloode to blede

[65] But kynd° in thies yonge gentylmen °*nature*
crept wheare yt cowlde not goo[116]
and in suche sorte inforced theym
theyr fatheres bane to sloo° °*slay*

f. 38] [66] The secund fraye° nowe heare ye have °*battle, attack*
The thyrd nowe shall yowe heare
of yowre kyndenes no more I crave
But onelye to gyve eare/

[67] Whan Sir John Eland thus was slayne
in dede the storye telles

113. There is a cross in the left margin next to this stanza, perhaps to mark the moral lesson being drawn at this point in the narrative.

114. This is another example of double *o* as long *o*.

115. This might be a mistranscription of "fame."

116. Crept where it could not walk; proverbial.

both Beamount and his feares° certan °*companions*
fledde all to Fournes Felles

[68] Oh cruell mars whye weare thou nought
contented yett wythe thys
to sheade more bloode but styll thou sought
for suche thy nature ys

[69] The yonge consyence corrupt° by the °*corrupted*
in Dede cowlde never staye
tyll unto extreme myserye
yt Ranne the Redye waye

[70] For Caynes sede on every syde
wythe wicked hartes dysgraste
whiche to shewe mercy have Denyed
must nedes be nowe Dysplaste° °*displaced*

[71] In Fo^u^rnes Felles Longe tyme they weare
bostyng of theyr mysdede
In more myscheiff contryvyng there
howe yet they myght procede

[72] They hade theyr spyes in thys contrye
neighe Eland than who Dwelde
wheare sir John eland Dwelt trulye
and there his howse he held

f. 38v] [73] mo gentlymen then was ^not^ there ~~non~~
in Eland paryshe Dweld
{save savile half parte of the yeire
{ hys howse at Rysheworth held[117]

[74] he kept hym selfe from suche debate
Removynge thence wythaull
twyse in the yeire by saviles gate° °*way, road*
unto the bothom halle

[75] Adam of beamount than trulye
Lacy and Lockewodd eke° °*also*

117. A manicule is drawn in the left margin next to the bracketed last two lines of the stanza. Both "savile" and "Ryshworth" are underlined.

and querneby cam to thys contrye
theyr purpose for to seke/

[76] To Cromwelbothom haule they cam
there kept theym secretlye
by fonde° deceipt there Dyd they frame °*foolish*
theyr craftye crueltye

[77] Thys was the ende the sothe to saye
on palmesoneven at nyght
to Eland Myllne[118] they toke the waye
abowt the marke mydnyght

[78] Into the Myllne howse there they brake
and kept theym craftelye
Thus by Deceipt there dyd they seke
The yonge knyght for to slowe° °*slay*

[79] The mornyng came the Mylner sent
hys wyfe for corne° wythe ~~sped with~~ haste °*wheat*
the gentylmen in handes hyr hent° °*seized, arch.*
and bound hyr hard and faste

f. 39] [80] The Mylner swore she should Repent
She taryed there so Longe
a good staffe in his handes he hent
to chastyce hyr wythe wronge° °*unjustly*

[81] Wythe haste into the Myllne Ranne he
and ment wythe hyr to stryve
But they hym bound Immedyatlye
and layd hym by his wyfe

[82] The yonge knyght Dreamed the self same nyght
Wythe fooes he was bestedd° °*beset*
that feyrslye fetled° theym to fyght °*made themselves ready*
agenst hym in hys bedde

[83] he shewed his ladye soonne of thys
but as athyng most vayne

118. The *OED* indicates that this is a pre-seventeenth-century form of "mill."

she wayed the same & sayd I wys° *°iwis, certainly*
that Dreames are ofte most vayne[119]

[84] he sayd arme yow welle my merye menne
and of lockwodd be ye noght adrede
for to the Churche nowe wyll we goe
to heare the servyce songe and Redde[120]

[85] To serve god thys present Daye
The knyght than made hym bowne° *°ready*
and by the Mylne than leye the waye
that ledde unto the Towne/

[86] The drought hade made the water smale
the stakes appeared Drye
The knyght his sone & servantes all
came Down the Dame therby[121]

f. 39v] [87] When adam beamount thys beheld
forthe of the Myllne came he
hys bowe wythe hym in hand he held
and shott at theym sharplye

[88] he hytt the knyght one the brest platte
wherwythe the shutte Dyd slyde° *°shot did glance*
Wilkyn of Lockewodd wrothe therat
sayd cossen yowe shott awydde° *°widely*

[89] And shott hym selfe & hytt the knyght
but nought was hurtt wythe thys
whereat the knyght hade great Delyght
and sayd to theym I wys

[90] In case my father hade be° cladde *°been*
Wythe suche armare certayn
yowre wycked handes escapte he had
and had not so bene slayne/

[91] Oh Eland towne halas sayd he
yf thowe but knewe of this

119. The last two lines are marked with a half-parenthesis.
120. This tetrameter stanza is an anomaly.
121. There are three minims at the bottom of this page.

thes fooes of myne full faste wold flee
and of theyr purpas mysse

[92] By stelthe to worke nedes must they goo
for yt hade bene to muche
The towne knowyng the Lord to slooe° °*have been slain*
for theym and many suche

[93] Wilkyn of lockwodd was adredde
The towne should Ryse in Dede
he shott the knyght quyte through the head
and slewe hym than wythe sped

f. 40][122] [94] hys sonne and heire was wounded there
but yeat not Dead at all
into the howse conveyd he weare
dyed seised in° Eland haule °*possessed of*

[95] A full syster forsothe hade he
and a half brother also
The full syster hys heire must be
The half brother not so

[96] Se heare the ende of all myscheiff
from Eland Elandes name
dysplaced° was to theyr great greife °*removed*
well worthye of the same/

[97] But as for beamount wythe the Reste
undon weare utterlye
Thus symple vertue ys the beste
and cheife felycytye

[98] what tyme thes menne thes frayes Dyd frame
dedes have [I] Redde & herd
Elandes land came to saviles name
in Edwardes Dayes the thyrd

[99] By whythill lane they made theyr flyght
and so to the old earthyate° °*earthgate, dirt road*

122. Written separately in the right margin of this page, in another hand, are "In the" and "name."

They toke the woddes as than they myght
and spyed a prevye gate

[100] Theym selfes conveying craftelye
to Aneley wodd that waye
The towne of Eland manfully
pursued theym that Daye

f. 40v] [101] The Lordes servantes throughowt the towne
had cryed wythe myght & mayne
up gentyll yeomen make yowe bown° *°ready*
Thys Daye yowre Lord ys slayn

[102] Whithill ~~and~~ Smyth & wilkynson
burye wythe manye mo
as bryme as bores they made theym bown *°fierce, raging, obs.*
theyr Lordes enemyes to sloo

[103] And to be shortte the people Rose
through all the town abowtte
fuerslye° followyng upon theyr fooes *°fiercely*
Wythe hwe & crye and showtte

[104] all sortes of mene shewed theyr good wylles
Some bowes and shaftes Dyd beare
some brought forth clubbes & Rustye bylles° *°halberds*
that sawe no sonne° that yeare *°sun*

[105] To Churche nowe as the paryshe came[123]
they Joyned theym wythe the towne
lyke hardye mene they ~~made them bown~~
stand all sam[e]° *°all together, obs.*
in sight nowe weare they bown

[106] Beamount & lockwodd sawe all this
and Querneby wheare they stoode
they feytled theym° to fyght I wys *°got themselves ready*
and shott as they weare woode° *°mad, crazed*

[107] Tyll tyme that all theyr shaftes weare spent
of force than must they flee

123. To the right of this line is the mark "+".

They had Dyspatched all theyr intent
and loste no victorye/

f. 41] [108] The hardyest mane of theym there was
was Querneby this ys true
for he wolde never turne his face
Tyll Eland mene hym slewe

[109] Lockwodd he bare hym one his backe[124]
hyd hym in Aneley wodd
To whom his purse he Dyd betake
of golde bothe fyne and good

[110] Take here the gold to yowe sayd he
and to my cossynes here
and in yowre myrthe Remember me
yet whan yowe make good cheare

[111] In case my foes should this possesse
yt weare a greiff to me
my frendes welfare ys my Riches
and cheife felycytye

[112] Gyve place wythe spede and fare yowe well
Chryst shelde yowe from myschaunce
In case yt otherwyse befell
yt wold be my grevance

[113] Theyr fooes so fuerslye followed on
yt was no bydyng there
Lockwodd wythe spede he went anon° °*at once*
To his frendes wheare they weare

[114] Wythe hast than towardst hudder Feild
they went the Redye waye
The waye than adam beamount held
to Croseland haule that Daye/

f. 41v] [115] Thus Eland menne Retorned home
by aneley wodd that Daye

124. There is a symbol in the left margin next to this line.

there found they Querneby all leyd alone
Scante deade as some men saye

[116] Wheare they hym slewe quyte owt of hand
dyspatched hym of hys payne
the late death of theyr Lord Eland
Incenssed theym° certayn °*inflamed them with wrath*

[117] Marke heare the bretche° of Charytye °*breach*
howe wretchydlye yt endes
Marke here howe heighe felycytye
on charytye Dependes

[118] Awelthe yt ys to everye weight° °*person*
please god what waye ^theye^ canne
yt geites° alwaye wythe great Delyght °*wins*
the hartes of every mane

[119] Oh wrathfull Ire nowe wo worthe the° °*woe upon thee*
Thowe wrought thys wretchednes
thes gentylme[n] brought thowe onelye
to greife and great Dystresse

[120] wheare charytye wythdrawes the harte
from sorrowe and syghyng depe
Ryght hevye makes thowe many an herte
and manye an one to wepe

[121] yowe gentylmen Love one an other
Love well the yeomanrye
Cownt everye chrysten man yowre brother
and lyve in Charytye

f. 42] [122] So shall yt come to passe trulye
That all mene shall yowe Love
and after Deathe so shall yowe be
in Lyfe wythe god above

[123] To whom alwayes of everye wyght
T[h]roughowt all yeires and Dayes
in heaven and Earth bothe Daye and nyght
be honor laude and prayse.
finis
[Epilogue]

[124] his full syster hys heire she was
and savile wedd the same
Thus Lord of Eland savile was
and styll enjoyes the same

[125] Learne saviles here I yow beseke° °*beseech*
teche yowre posterytye
not to be stowte of mynde but meke
and full of Charytye

[126] for by suche wayes yowre elderes came
To knyghtly Dygnytye
Wheare Eland fyrst forsoke the same
and cam to mysyrye

Textual Analysis

The ballad of the Eland-Beaumont feud is by no means a fugitive text. We have found four manuscripts of the poem, plus a full transcription of a fifth. The poem first reached print in 1775 and was reprinted at least five times by 1890. These sources with their sigla are listed below:

- *A* BL, MS Add. 82370, ff. 33–42
- *A6* BL, MS Add 56076, ff. 1–3v
- *C* John Crabtree, *A Concise History of the Parish and Vicarage of Halifax* (Halifax: Hartley and Walker, 1836), 442–46
- *H* WYAS, Bradford, 32D86/12, ff. 11v–18v. The antiquarian John Hopkinson (1610–80), trancribed this text as "The death of Sr John Ealand of Ealand & his sonne in old rymthe."
- *I* C. J. Davison Ingledew, ed., *The Ballads and Songs of Yorkshire* (London: Bell and Daldy, 1860), 67–86
- *R* *Revenge Upon Revenge*, 1789, from Watson's *Halifax* (abbreviated *W* below)
- *T1* J. Horsfall Turner, *The Elland Tragedies* (Bingley, UK: T. Harrison and Sons, 1890), 59–82. Version 1 from Watson (*W*), described as a "pirated copy."
- *T2* J. Horsfall Turner, *The Elland Tragedies* (Bingley, UK: T. Harrison and Sons, 1890). Version 2's stanzas from H. J. Barber's manuscript are intermixed in order with those of version 1 (*T1*).
- *W* John Watson, *History and Antiquities of the Parish of Halifax* (Halifax, 1775; repr., Manchester, UK: E.J. Morten, 1973), 170–77

Whit	Thomas Dunham Whitaker, *Loidis and Elmete; or, an Attempt to Illustrate the Districts Described in Those Words by Bede* (Halifax: T. Davison, 1816)
Y	Oxford, Bodleian Library, MS Top. Yorks. c. 25, ff. 184–85v. Roger Dodsworth's collection (d. 1654)

Five of these sources are substantive. First, and by far the oldest and most complete text is found in MS Add. 82370 (*A*), which preserves 126 stanzas of the poem transcribed by John Hanson about 1588. Hopkinson's version (*H*) is a mid-seventeenth-century copy of the ballad.[125] Its 120 stanzas occur according to the order found in *A* (taken as lemma throughout the following discussion), 1–6, 8–26, 28–69, 71–83, 85–91, 93–95, 124, 96, 98, 97, 99–116, 125–26, 117–18, 120–23. *H* therefore lacks stanzas 7, 27, 70, 84, 92, and 119. *A6* is a gathering of three folios that presents the ballad text written in two columns in two predominately italic hands of the mid-seventeenth century. The 123 stanzas of this version occur in the order 1–25, 27–30, 26, 31–44, 46–49, 45, 51–83, 85–95, 124, 96–110, 112–16, 125–26, 117–23. *A6* thus omits stanzas 50, 84, and 111. The fourth substantive text is *W*, from Watson's *History and Antiquities of the Parish of Halifax* (1775). *W* prints 124 stanzas: 1–4, 7, 5–6, 8–83, 85–95, 124, 96, 98, 97, 99–116, 125–26, 117–18, 120–23; it lacks only stanzas 84 and 119. Turner published *T2*, the fifth independent version of the ballad, from a manuscript we have not traced, one he described as of "much older date than 1650," owned by H.J. Barber (p. 51). *T2* sets forth 111 stanzas in order: 1–3, 7–11, 14–25, 27–63, 65–67, 71–84, 85–95, 124, 96–117, 121–23. It lacks stanzas 4–6, 12–13, 26, 64, 68–70, 118–20, 125–26.

All these five seminal texts are substantive. They descend from two hypothetical ancestors, *X* and *Z*. *T2* closely follows the wording of *A* and is the only other text that preserves stanza 84, an interpolated passage comprising a single iambic octameter couplet as opposed to the quatrains of the rest of the ballad that are written in cross rhyme in alternating tetrameter and trimeter lines: a8b6a8b6. *T2* also agrees in error with *A* at 17.4, "who"; at 37.1, "wylfulness" for "wilful ire" (rhyming with "Lancashyer"); in the

125. This manuscript is briefly described among the papers of Matthew Wilson, Esq., at Eshton Hall, Yorkshire, in the *Third Report of the Royal Commission on Historical Manuscripts* (London: HMSO, 1872), 295.

faulty duplicate rhyme word "knyght" (for "hight" in *R*) at 58.3; and in the ametrical line 85.1. *A* cannot be ancestral to *T2*, however, for the latter corrects *A*'s ametrical lines at 8.3, 32.4, 77.2, and 84.2, plus further misreadings in *A* at 18.2, "Robartes" for "Robert"; at 24.4, "storke" for "Struck"; at 34.3, "lyght of" for "Light on"; at 44.3, "weare in" for "were it"; and at 55.2, "garne" for "towne." We conclude that these two versions of the ballad descend from a lost manuscript, *X* in the stemma below, the unique source of stanza 84 as well as the four errors shared by *A* and *T2* listed above.

The second main line of transmission, from *Z*, is witnessed by *A6, W*, and *H*. At 51.3, *Z* presented these scribes with a misreading that is grammatically obscure. *A* gives a plausible reading of this stanza:

> The Daye was sett, the Turne was kept
> At Brighouse by Sir John
> lyttyll wyst he, he was besett
> than at hys comyng home.

Each scribe in the *Z* tradition handled the problem of l. 3 differently. The *A6* scribe apparently copied the faulty line verbatim: "at Brighthowse by Sir John / litle wist he was beset." *W* improved the line's rhythm but failed to give "wist" a clear subject: "At Brighouse by sir John; / Full little wist he was beset." The *H* scribe clarified the grammar at the expense of the line's rhythm: "att Brighouse by Sir John / But litle wiste he, how he was besett." In addition, *A6, W*, and *H* break the rhyme with "then" in 57.1 at 57.3, where all three read "be" instead. A third agreement in error occurs at 116.4, where the descendants of *Z* explain that the townsmen slew Quermby because the "late death of their lord Eland / Inforced them certain" (*W*, p. 175). *A* and *T2* preserve the superior reading, "Incenssed theym certayn." These three cruxes establish the descent of *A6, W*, and *H* from a lost common ancestor, *Z*.

In addition, *W* and *H* share an intervening hypothetical ancestor *Φ*, witnessed by four errors they share that were not committed by *A6*. First, *Φ* omits two words in the text that create faulty readings. At 35.3, *W* and *H* end the line with "Brerton," which fails to rhyme with "messenger" in 35.1. *A, T2*, and *A6* complete the rhyme with "Brerton there." At 63.4, "Of a right Christian" rhymes with "Though here he played the man" if "Christian" is pronounced as trisyllabic. *Z* (and *X*) must have preserved the more plausible reading "Of a right Christian man" (granted that this repeats the rhyme word). *Φ* also dropped stanza 119. The fourth misreading transmitted by *Φ* adds a word that renders the line ametrical: "They were undone utterly" (97.2). *A6* has the more likely reading here—"But as for Beaumont & the rest / undone were utterly"—a reading shared with *A* and *T2* (which substitute "with" for "&" in 97.1). *W* could not have been copied from *H*, however, for much of its wording diverges considerably from the manuscript, and it avoids a number of errors in *H*. At 10.4, for example "parish halfe" at the end of the line in *H* fails to rhyme with "dwelt" in 10.2, where *W*, with *A6*, reads "parish held." At 40.1, *H* fails to state that the sons of Sir John Eland's victims took refuge with Bruerton and Townley: "They kept there still they increast." *W* and A6 have the correct reading, "They kept the boys till they increas'd." In stanza 60, *W* and *A6* rhyme "cruelty" with "had he," while the rhyme words in *H* are "mischeife" and "forsooth." In the next stanza, *W* and *A6* have the perfect rhymes "blame" and "same" (61.1, 3), but *H* rhymes "blame" with "part." In these and a number of other readings, *W* and *A6* testify to the readings of *Z* and *Φ*, where *H* deviates from both the extant and hypothetical texts.

Other faulty readings that suggest further textual relationships probably result instead from independent variation. *A6* and *W* agree in error at 56.4, where the young assassins are described "There prying for their prey." *Z* no doubt had "prying" in this line, where *A, T2*, and *H* read "spying." The *H* scribe might easily have made this correction independently. At 82.3, both *H* and *A6* have the foes the younger Sir John Eland dreams about "secretly" preparing to attack him. Here, both scribes may have misconstrued unusual spellings of the correct reading, "fiercely," found in *A, T2*, and the modern-spelling text in *W*. At 82.3 the spelling is, for example, "feyrslye" in *A*, which also spells the word "fuerslye" (103.3, 113.1).[126]

The remaining six texts of the ballad descend from *Z* through *Φ* and either *H* or *W*. Except for *Whit*, which lacks stanza 116, these witnesses transmit the errors of Z and *Φ* at 35.3, 51.3, 57.3, 63.4, 97.2, and 116.4. The text in the Bodleian MS (*Y*) is a careful transcript of *H* in a quite illegible scrawl. The MS Top. Yorks. scribe (possibly Thomas Wilson)[127] refers to

126. *OED* records "furese" as a spelling for "fierce" from medieval times through the fifteenth century but gives neither of these spellings for "furiously," nor is that word recorded before 1555.

127. Jan Broadway, "Hopkinson, John," *ODNB*,http://www.oxforddnb.com/view/article/13757?docPos=1.

"Mr Hopkinson's collections" (f. 13). The copy of a letter dated 31 May 1674, tipped into this manuscript after folio 185, suggests that he copied the ballad during the last quarter of the seventeenth century or later. In addition to having the same stanzas in the same order, *Y* agrees in error with Hopkinson's readings at 36.2, "then were they comed"; 39.1, "Bererton & Townleys frends"; 44.3, "Best where it then"; 68.1, "was thou"; 104.1, "men shows"; and in the metrically deficient first line to stanza 107, "Till all their shafts were spent," a trimeter where a tetrameter is required. *Y* does correct one obvious error in *H*, "Theyr lords" for "They Lords" at 101.1. In addition to lacking six stanzas found in *A, H* and its descendent *Y* differ radically in their wording and ordering of the stanzas.

The 1789 reprint of the ballad in *Revenge Upon revenge* (*R*) follows Watson's text closely, including most accidentals. Although its layout is in a single column rather than double, it produces the same stanzas in the same order. With Watson, it italicizes stanzas 33, 34, and 66, and adds exactly the same footnote to 76.1 "Cromwelbottom wood*," "[*hall]." With *W, R* also preserves the spellings "milne" and "milner" at 78.1, 79.1, 81.1, 84.3, and 86.2, although *W*'s "milner" at 80.1 reads "miller" in *R*. Beyond reasonable doubt, *R* was taken directly from *W*, with some deterioration of the text in the faulty readings at 55.3, "play's" for "play'd"; 67.4, "fell" for "fells"; and 106.3, "sence" for "fence."

In 1816, Thomas Dunham Whitaker published a third text of the ballad in his *Loidis and Elmete* (*Whit*). Although Whitaker affirmed that "The following metrical record . . . was transcribed by Mr. Hopkinson about the year 1650" (p. 395), the text on pages 396–400 departs widely from the readings of *H*. Instead, its 123 stanzas (omitting stanza 116), closely follow the readings of *W*, while avoiding *R*'s errors at 55.3, and 67.4, and compounding that at 106.3 into "settled them to sence." Thus *Whit* derives from *W*.

C, John Crabtree's 124-stanza text in *A Concise History of the Parish and Vicarage of Halifax* (1836), is based on *R*, with some reference to *Whit* and, perhaps, *W*. Crabtree quotes exactly Whitaker's title to the poem and his introduction with its citation of Hopkinson's manuscript. His note to 76.1 expands the bare "*hall" in *W* and *R* to "*Some read hall," echoing Whitaker's "*Instead of 'wood,' some read 'hall.'" However, Crabtree depended primarily on *R*, for he includes stanza 116, while his use of italicized words (e.g., at 38.3, 39.1, 49.3, and 50.1) varies from the pattern in *W* and *Whit* but adheres to the practice in *R*. In addition, Crabtree's usages of "milne/mill," are at odds with both *W* and *Whit* but match *R* exactly. Yet Crabtree does correct *R*'s errors at 55.3, 67.4, and 106.3, presumably with reference to *W* (albeit *Whit* likewise avoids the first two errors).

C. J. Davison Ingledew included another 124-stanza text in *I*, his *Ballads and Songs of Yorkshire* (1860). He does not identify his copy text but does mention "Hopkinson's MSS." in several notes. Ingledew avoids *R*'s errors at 55.3, 67.4, and 106.3, while his use of italics and spellings of "miln/milner" are consistent with *W*. His version is almost certainly based on the original, 1775 print, to which he adds about a half-dozen variants, most of them manifest errors.

The latest consequential text of the ballad to appear in print offers two versions of the poem; this is Turner's *The Elland Tragedies* (1890). Version 1 (*T1*), taken from a "pirated copy" of Watson's text is in fact a careful reprint of *R*. Its 124 stanzas occur in the same order, it follows *R*'s pattern of italicization exactly, and it repeats *R*'s errors at 55.3 ("play's") and 67.4 ("fell"). As we have seen, version 2 (*T2*), from "Mr. Barber's MS. copy," descends with *A* from *X*.

These textual relationships are represented in the stemma below.

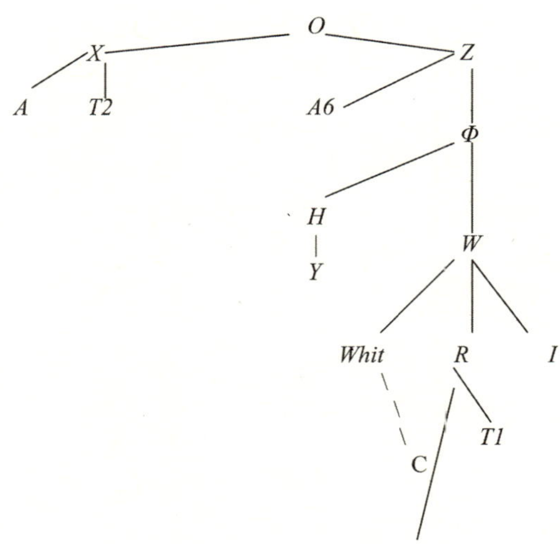

2

Two Lost Ballads of the Armada Thanksgiving Celebration

Menaphon. Your majesty shall shortly have your wish,
And ride in triumph through Persepolis.
Tamburlaine. And ride in triumph through Persepolis!
. . . .
Is it not passing brave to be a king,
And ride in triumph through Persepolis?

Christopher Marlowe, *Tamburlaine*, Part I

The Historical Contexts of the Armada Thanksgiving Ballads

One of the most valuable features of the Hanson manuscript is its unique copies of two ballads depicting Queen Elizabeth's 1588 procession through London to St. Paul's Cathedral to give thanks for the Armada victory. Though printed in their own time, as their registration in the Stationers' Register indicates, they have been lost to literary history, except for the printing of one of them in an obscure Stanhope family history.[1] These are

1. In *Notes and Queries* for 20 February 1909, 147, Mrs. A. M. W. Stirling quoted the first stanza of a ballad describing the 1588 thanksgiving that she had found in a manuscript "Amongst the muniments belonging to my uncle, Sir Walter Spencer Stanhope of Cannon Hall, Yorkshire." This is the first ballad in the Hanson manuscript. Stirling published a text of this ballad in *Life's Little Day, Some Tales and Other Reminiscences* (New York: John Lane, 1924), 277–81. Oddly, Mrs. Stirling made no mention of the second ballad on the same subject. Excerpts from her

important texts celebrating what was patriotically perceived as a providential national deliverance, and they would have interested English citizens both in London and in the provinces. Balladmongers, who traversed the countryside with their wares, would have disseminated them far and wide.[2] In fact, the writer of the second ballad explicitly refers to the larger target audience of his poem when he states at the end, "Thus have I made a symple songe / To synge the contrye folke among / Of all I sawe" (2.206–8).[3] It is no surprise that the poems would have reached John Hanson's neighborhood in Yorkshire. These texts and their multiple local, national, and international contexts are worth our careful examination.

By the first week of August 1588, England had successfully countered the threat posed by the Spanish Armada, although repercussions of the conflict continued for several months and celebrations of victory would have been premature. There were fears that the enemy fleet might still make a hostile surprise landing in England. Coastal defenses remained on alert while the Queen and her Privy Council prepared to reinforce the garrisons in Ireland where a number of the Spanish vessels had been shipwrecked on their way home or had landed to take on supplies. The sense of ongoing emergency is witnessed by the proclamation issued on 14 October 1588 proroguing until 4 February following the Parliament scheduled to open in November.[4] By early November, however, it was clear that both England and Ireland were safe from imminent invasion.[5] The Crown then turned to planning a formal and public thanksgiving for England's deliverance from the Armada, an event it found difficult to orchestrate.

transcription appear in B. M. Ward's *The Seventeenth Earl of Oxford* (London: John Murray, 1928), 293–94, and in Alan H. Nelson's *Monstrous Adversary, The Life of Edward de Vere, 17th Earl of Oxford* (Liverpool: Liverpool University Press, 2003), 318–19.

2. For a discussion of the distribution system for ballads and popular pamphlets, see Margaret Spufford, *Small Books and Pleasant Histories: Popular Fiction and Its Readership in Seventeenth-Century England* (Cambridge: Cambridge University Press, 1985), 111–28. In the case of the two Armada victory celebration ballads, they might have reached John Hanson by way of a family member or friend who brought copies back from a trip to London, but he and others in the provinces would have had easy access to ballad texts through itinerant peddlers.

3. We cite each of the two Armada thanksgiving ballads by ballad number, followed by a line number or numbers.

4. Paul L. Hughes and James F. Larkin, eds., *Tudor Royal Proclamations*, 3 vols. (New Haven: Yale University Press, 1969), 3:27–28.

5. Robert Lemon, ed., *Calendar of State Papers Domestic, 1581–1590* (1865; repr., Nendeln, Liechtenstein: Kraus Reprints, 1967), 557, no. 3.

On 3 November the Council decided that Saturday, 9 November, would be the day of national thanksgiving. Lord Burghley informed the Earl of Shrewsbury that "hir Majesty will oppenly go to Powls or Westminster to gyve publyck thankes to god for his miraculous goodnes in overthrowing of our mortall ennemyes."[6] Rumor had it, however, that the Council then persuaded Elizabeth to forgo such a public procession "for fear that a harquebuss might be fired at her."[7] The Jesuit Henry Garnet's 5 December letter to the Jesuit General in Rome, Claudio Acquaviva, which includes his eyewitness account of the 24 November celebrations, alludes to the fears for the Queen's safety and to the precautions taken:

> This pageant had been long awaited in the city. It had been said that the Queen was afraid to show herself in public—a report confirmed by the order that in every single household along the route no one should be allowed to look out from the windows while she was passing, unless the householder was prepared to stake his life and entire fortune on his trustworthiness.
>
> However . . . there were persons who vouched for me, for they believe I have the Queen's safety more at heart than her own Calvinistic Ministers.[8]

Fears for the Queen's safety, however, were soon overcome, for the celebration was rescheduled for her accession day on Sunday, 17 November. Thomas Cooper, bishop of Winchester, delivered a thanksgiving sermon at Paul's Cross that Sunday, but the Queen failed to attend, probably because it conflicted with the traditional tiltyard ceremonies marking her accession to the throne. Meanwhile, the London guilds were told to prepare to welcome the Queen on the eighteenth as she traveled from Somerset House to St. Paul's to hear a thanksgiving sermon.[9] However, the national day of thanksgiving was postponed until Tuesday, November 19. For this occasion the government issued a special supplement to the liturgy,

---

6. Letter of 4 November 1588, in *Historical Manuscripts Commission, Marquess of Bath, Talbot, Dudley and Devereux Papers 1533–1659*, 5 vols., ed. G. Dyfnallt Owen (London: HMSO, 1980), 5:95.

7. Newsletter from England, 5/15 November 1588, in *Calendar of Letters and State Papers Relating to English Affairs . . . Archives of Simancas*, ed. Martin A. S. Hume (London: HMSO, 1899), 4:480–81.

8. Philip Caraman, *Henry Garnet 1555–1606 and the Gunpowder Plot* (New York: Farrar, Straus, 1964), 83. The original Latin letter is found in the Archivum Historicum Societatis Jesu, Fondo Gesuitico 651, f. 7. During the dangerous 1580s the Queen's progresses were largely restricted to the home counties.

9. John Nichols, *Progresses and Public Processions of Queen Elizabeth*, 3 vols. (1823; repr., New York, AMS Press, n.d.), 2:537–38.

A Psalme and Collect of thankesgiving, not unmeet for this present time: to be said or sung in Churches (see figure 5).[10] There were bonfires and a public procession in London. Stow reports that the livery companies assembled to hear another sermon at Paul's Cross thanking God for the victory.[11] But again the Queen was absent, for she was instead presiding at an unprecedented further celebration of her accession to the throne. The Earl of Essex with other courtiers had resumed the tilting in her honor on grounds that November 19 was St. Elizabeth's Day.[12]

The royal thanksgiving was again postponed until Sunday, November 24, quite possibly to ensure that the French ambassador, Claude, Baron de Châteauneuf, would attend. The crown was naturally anxious to secure the propaganda coup of having the French king's representative participate in this anti-Spanish celebration. Yet the French king, Henry III, was by no means pleased with the English victory, and Châteauneuf had informed him of it with great reluctance. He then protested to the Queen that his instructions did not authorize him to appear at any such celebration. He was at last persuaded to attend when Elizabeth converted the invitation to a service of thanksgiving to God for her thirty-year reign. Even so, Châteauneuf agreed to participate only on the further condition that the thanksgiving be kept separate from the jousting and bonfires that marked the St. Elizabeth's day celebration.[13]

---

10. Liturgies, Church of England, *STC* 16520 (London, 1588). For a discussion of special prayers, fasts, and thanksgivings mandated by the government in Elizabethan England, see Natalie Mears, "Public Worship and Political Participation in Elizabethan England," *Journal of British Studies* 51 (2012): 4–25. Mears argues that these functioned not merely as acts of royal propaganda but also as opportunities for citizens to share their beliefs in both general and special Providence and to demonstrate their own political agency. Mears, 11, notes that the Armada thanksgivings took place around the country as well as officially in London, involving people from all social levels.

11. Hume, *Calendar of Letters and State Papers*, 4:494; John Stow, *The Annales of England* (1592), sig. 4P1-1v. Stow's is the most detailed contemporary printed account we have found of the thanksgiving events; it is reprinted with related documents in Nichols, *Progresses and Public Processions*, 2:538–39.

12. Steven W. May, *The Elizabethan Courtier Poets* (Columbia: University of Missouri Press, 1991), 190–91.

13. Antonio de Vega's report, 8/18 December 1588, in Hume, *Calendar of Letters and State Papers*, 4:494. Anthony Miller, *Roman Triumphs and Early Modern English Culture* (Houndmills, UK: Palgrave, 2001), 12, notes that Renaissance tournaments "opened with a procession often modeled on Roman descriptions of the triumph," so the French ambassador's reluctance to attend the tilting might have been related to his wish to keep a distance from celebrations of military victory.

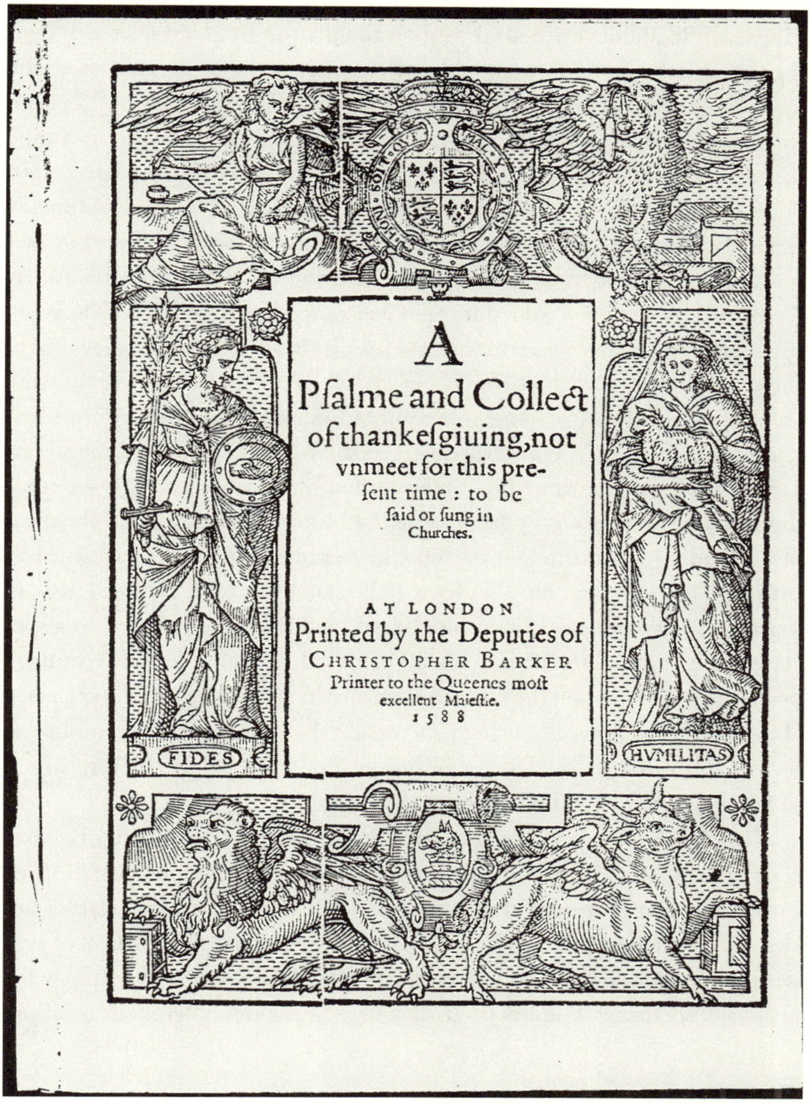
A
Psalme and Collect
of thankesgiuing, not
vnmeet for this pre-
sent time : to be
said or sung in
Churches.

AT LONDON
Printed by the Deputies of
CHRISTOPHER BARKER
Printer to the Queenes most
excellent Maiestie.
1588

Figure 5. Title page of *A Psalme and collect of thankesgiving* (London, 1588; *STC* 16520). Reproduced by permission of The Huntington Library, San Marino, California.

Not until late in the morning on the following Sunday, November 24, did the Queen make her way in triumphant procession from Somerset House to St. Paul's Cathedral to give thanks for England's victory over the Spanish Armada. Contemporary diagrams of the procession show the location of each class of participant in the spectacle (see figure 6).[14] For the third time, the Privy Council instructed the London guilds to assemble in full livery to greet the Queen. According to Stow, she departed from Somerset House in the Strand ensconced "in a Chariot Throne" (*Annales*, sig. 4P1v). She was accompanied by a full entourage of Crown and household officers, along with Châteauneuf and the nobility of the realm. At Temple Bar the mayor and aldermen welcomed her to the city. Observing the scene firsthand, Henry Garnet mentions that an "unceasing uproar of the vast crowds echoed all round her" while all along the way there were "bands of musicians playing in appointed places. Also there were some charming tableaux."[15] Guild members in their livery coats lined the streets as the procession continued on to the cathedral; at its west door a welcoming party of leading clergy headed by the bishop of London and the dean of St. Paul's greeted the Queen, who, in a public gesture of piety, knelt in prayer. They escorted her "under a rich Canapy" down the west aisle to a private, enclosed stall. There she heard the litany, then retired to a specially built "closet" in the north wall of the cathedral. From this vantage point she looked out on the cross in the churchyard where John Piers, royal almoner and bishop of Salisbury, preached the thanksgiving sermon. Afterward, Elizabeth dined at the bishop of London's palace, then returned to Somerset House by torchlight (*Annales*, sig. 4P1v).

The Armada thanksgiving celebrations took place in concentric contexts. Elizabeth's entry into London was part of the complex and historically long relationship of the Crown and the city, which she, unlike her successor, managed well. The city of London, in fact, in the years of war with Spain, had loaned the Queen thirty thousand pounds to help pay for military expenses.[16] The city itself, of course, was a richly symbolic location.

14. At least five manuscript copies of this document are extant: Folger Library, MSS V.a.213, pp. 55–58 and V.b.217, f. 202v; Huntington Library, MS EL 1118, ff. 17–18; British Library, Harleian MS 1877, f. 48r–v; and PRO, SP 12/218/38. The Huntington and Harleian copies are essentially identical in wording and layout.

15. Caraman, *Henry Garnet*, 82.

16. R. B. Wernham, *After the Armada: Elizabethan England and the Struggle for Western Europe 1588–1585* (Oxford: Clarendon Press, 1984), 15.

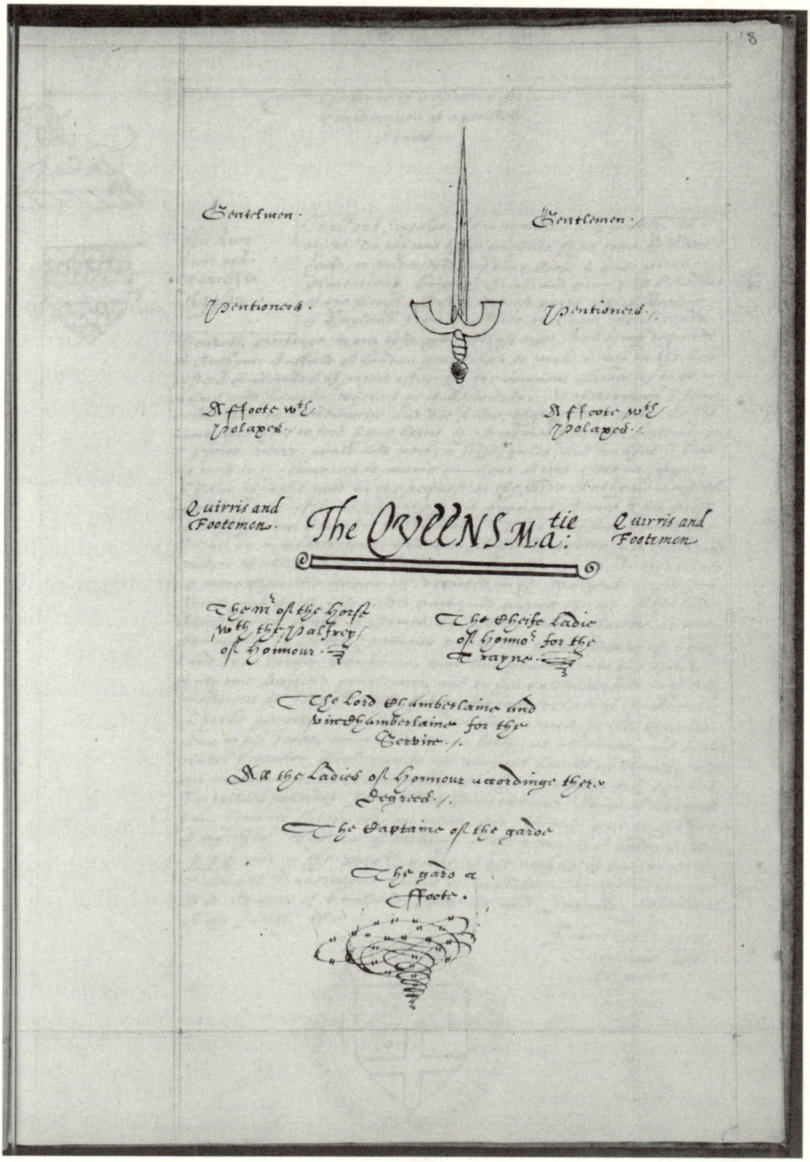

Figure 6. Huntington Library MS EL 1118, f. 18. Reproduced by permission of The Huntington Library, San Marino, California.

As Hester Lees-Jeffries has put it, "London, as it was 'entered' by its prince throughout the medieval and early modern period, was not an empty stage or a blank page, but a palimpsestic conglomeration of landscape and monuments inscribed and re-inscribed with the 'texts' of historical association, communal memory, and accumulated civic pride and idealism."[17] Stow describes a ritual that took place when the Queen was received into the city by the Lord Mayor of London and the aldermen: "[T]he lorde maior and his brethren the aldermen in scarlet, received and welcommed hir majestie to hir citie and chamber, delivering to hir hands the scepter, which after certaine speeches had, hir highnes redelivered to the maior, and he againe taking his horse, bare the same before hir" (*Annales*, sig. 4P1v). Garnet's account differs slightly with regard to the symbolic object presented to the Queen: "[S]he was presented with the sword that is carried before the Lord Mayor only when he is in the presence of the Sovereign."[18]

As we will see from the testimony of the ballads edited below, neither source recounts this transaction accurately. In any event, what took place was simultaneously an acknowledgment of royal sovereignty and of the traditional jurisdictional authority of the Lord Mayor and aldermen. In the ballads, however, the Londoners who, representing the larger English populace, profess their allegiance to their monarch do so in a context where there are long-standing tensions between a centralizing monarchy and the individual and corporate rights of citizens. It is revealing that the first ballad makes a point of repeating the term "Cittizens" (1.43, 45, 51, 63) in referring to the Londoners who have turned out for the celebration: this term, used instead of "subjects," denotes a grounding in traditional laws, liberties, and both local individual and corporate power that could limit, if not conflict with, the powers of the monarch.[19] The second ballad refers

17. Lees-Jeffries, "Location as Metaphor in Queen Elizabeth's Coronation Entry (1559): *Veritas Temporis Filia*," in *The Progresses, Pageants, and Entertainments of Queen Elizabeth I*, ed. Jayne Elizabeth Archer, Elizabeth Goldring, and Sarah Knight (Oxford: Oxford University Press, 2007), 66.

18. Caraman, *Henry Garnet*, 82.

19. For a discussion of the relationship between the terms "subject" and "citizen" see Phil Withington, *The Politics of Commonwealth: Citizens and Freemen in Early Modern England* (Cambridge: Cambridge University Press, 2005), 51–84. For a useful treatment of how dramatic texts, particularly in the Jacobean period, could exploit the tensions between London and the monarchy, see Leah Marcus, *Puzzling Shakespeare: Local Reading and Its Discontents* (Berkeley: University of California Press, 1988), 160–211.

to Queen Elizabeth's "Realme and Cetye of London" (2.205) as though the two jurisdictions could be considered separately. In this case, as in other public stagings of royal authority, there was, as Kevin Sharpe has noted, a negotiation between monarch and subjects meant to achieve a political equilibrium.[20] Official propaganda portrayed harmony where there was potential friction.

The thanksgiving celebrations were also framed by internal English conflicts between Protestants and Catholics, themselves part of international confessional struggles. Although William Cardinal Allen and other exiles hoped that English Catholics would support Spanish invaders and help restore Catholicism in England, the vast majority of Catholic Englishmen were loyal to the Queen before, during, and after the Armada crisis.[21] In any case, the government had taken steps to disarm Catholics and geographically restrict their movements.

Stow's narrative of the events running from the sermon on August 20 through the celebration of November 24 has some revealing juxtapositions. After noting Dean Nowell's August sermon at Paul's Cross "in the presence of the lord maior and alderman in scarlet [and] the companies in their best liveries," he records the judicial condemnation on 26 August of five seminary priests, four laymen who converted to Catholicism, and four priest helpers. Then he devotes a paragraph to the death of the Earl of Leicester (a bête noire for Catholics), before noting another Paul's Cross sermon of thanksgiving

> for the overthrow of our enimies the Spaynyards, and there were shewed 11. ensignes or banners taken in the Spanish ships by our men, these ensignes were set upon the lower battlements of Paules church, before the preacher and the audience, (which was great) all saving one streamer, wherein was an image of our Lady, with hir sonne in hir armes, &c. and this was held in a mans hand over the pulpit. And the same banners were on the next morrow hanged on London bridge towards Southwarke, where then was kept our Lady faire, for all beholders to their great rejoicing. (*Annales*, sigs. 4O8v-4P1)

20. Kevin Sharpe, *Selling the Tudor Monarchy: Authority and Image in Sixteenth-Century England* (New Haven: Yale University Press, 2009), 7.

21. Arnold Pritchard, *Catholic Loyalism in Elizabethan England* (Chapel Hill: University of North Carolina Press, 1979).

The Madonna and child banner was a particular focus for anti-Catholic sentiment. The next paragraph mentions the hanging on 1 October of two priests and a Catholic layman, part of a crackdown on Catholic missionaries and their helpers that took place at the time of the Armada and in its aftermath. In his long doggerel narrative poem, *Elizabetha Triumphans* (1588), James Aske finally urged "English Recusants" to "Despise [the Pope's] deedes . . . And turne your hearts unto your sacred Queene," expressing the hope that they would "Turne to God's word, and shunne the divelish Pope"—that is, convert to Protestantism and commit their allegiance to the Queen.[22] On an earlier occasion, a ballad describing Elizabeth's procession through the city in 1584 emphasized the threat of seditious or traitorous papists, "partakers of the romish rout."[23] In the setting of international relations, the defeat of the Armada, however, did not eliminate the Spanish threat to England, since King Phillip of Spain authorized subsequent Armadas in 1596 and 1597 that failed mainly because they again encountered unfavorable weather conditions. After 1588, however, the position of Henry III in relation to his domestic enemies in the Catholic League and their Spanish backers was stronger,[24] and the Spanish themselves had to pay more attention to the Low Countries, where the Dutch Republic had been given some support by England in its war with Spain.[25] In fact, in the last months of 1588, with the essential help of English forces, the Dutch successfully countered the army of the Duke of Parma, weakening the Spanish hold on the Netherlands.[26]

Locally in London, the message conveyed to the populace was that of harmony between the Crown and London authorities; nationally it was one of unity and loyalty, including English Catholic loyalty to the Queen; internationally it signaled the ascendancy of English naval power and nationalistic resolve (even though the Spanish navy grew in strength and

22. Nichols, *Progresses and Public Processions*, 3:581–82.

23. Richard Harrington, *A famous dittie of the Joyful receaving of the Queens moste excellent majestie, by the worthy Citizens of London the xij day of November, 1584, at her graces comming to Saint James* (London, 1584), *STC* 12798.

24. Henry III died, however, on 1 August 1589, and soon afterward France was bogged down in the struggle over the Protestant Henry of Navarre's ascending the throne as Henry IV.

25. Garrett Mattingly, *The Armada* (1959; repr., Cambridge, MA: Harvard University Press, 1962), 376–86.

26. Wernham, *After the Armada*, 23–47.

England was not a serious military adversary in the event of a full-scale Spanish attack).[27] The triumphalism and chauvinism of the November 24 celebrations rested on an insecure foundation: the Spanish Empire was still much stronger than England and it still represented an imminent threat, while internal religious divisions in England persisted.

Camden's account of the November 24 proceedings includes pointed remarks about the Queen's rewarding those who did her military service: "[S]hee assigned some revenewes unto the Admirall, for the service which hee had performed with so good and happy successe; praised highly her Sea-Captaines, as men borne for the preservation of their Countrey; and as often as shee saw any of the other, called them by their names, to witnesse that shee tooke note of their deserts; which they tooke as sufficient reward for their services: Shee also recompenced the maymed and poorer sort with honourable pensions." But this last statement conflicts with the surviving evidence of ongoing problems with military pay during the late Elizabethan period. In the background, and also among the spectators witnessing the triumphal procession, there were a large number of unpaid or underpaid soldiers and sailors whose experience in the Queen's service was far from satisfying. Basing his remarks on documentary evidence from the period, William Leahy says that the discontented soldiers and sailors who were

> disbanded and present in the streets of London both on the day of the processions and generally around the time of celebration, would not have been able to put aside their anger and hunger. Every attempt they made to alleviate their situation, such as selling their armour or weapons, became criminalised activity and, if caught, they were severely punished. And their number was not few. Furthermore, drawn as they were from the common population it is quite possible that they would have found many of the ordinary people sympathetic to their discontent. The Victory procession needs to be seen in the light of these facts.[28]

Rewarding commanders did little to mitigate the situation. Nevertheless, the official propaganda ignored this (and other contemporary social

---

27. Sharpe, *Selling the Tudor Monarchy*, 436, notes that "after her victory over the Armada in 1588, Elizabeth did not undertake a triumphal progress [into the country]. Persistent rumours of revived Spanish assaults kept her close to London or led her to tours of local fortifications on the south coast."

28. William Leahy, *Elizabethan Triumphal Processions* (Aldershot, UK: Ashgate, 2005), 81.

problems) as it exploited the opportunity for nationalistic celebration both at that moment and later in making the Armada victory an essential part of a British Protestant mythology.[29]

Queen Elizabeth's ritualistic entry into London in 1588 harked back to the other royal entry into London in 1558 for her coronation, which was itself related to the widespread European practice of royal entries and processions, a form with its roots in both traditional religious processions and ancient Roman military triumphal processions. There was also a rich tradition of allegorical and ceremonial representations of triumphs in literature and art. Petrarch's *Trionfi*, a portion of which Queen Elizabeth herself translated, was that author's most popular work in England for most of the sixteenth century.[30] There were many fifteenth- and sixteenth-century visual expressions of the triumphs, including those found in large tapestries at Hampton Court and in other royal palaces.[31] A well-known posthumous portrait of the Queen is related to the allegorical "Triumph of Eternity."[32]

From Thomas More's "Nine Pageauntes" through Sidney's and Spenser's works, as well as in English dramas and masques, English literary works register the impact of the form of the triumph, particularly by way of its elaboration in the visual arts.[33] In the parodic distortion of Elizabethan ceremonialism in the House of Pride in book 1 of Spenser's *The Faerie Queene*, Lucifera is part of a processional display of the seven deadly sins:

So forth she comes, and to her coche does clyme,
    Adorned all with gold, and girlonds gay,
    That seemd as fresh as *Flora* in her prime,
    And strove to match, in royall rich array,

29. David Cressy, *Bonfires and Bells: National Memory and the Protestant Calendar in Elizabethan and Stuart England* (Berkeley: University of California Press, 1989), 122–29.

30. See Robert Coogan, "Petrarch's 'Trionfi' and the English Renaissance," *Studies in Philology* 67, no. 3 (1970): 306–27. Lord Morley, who produced the first full translation of the *Trionfi* into English, did so for Henry VIII: see Henry, *Lord Morley's Tryumphes of Fraunces Petrarcke*, ed. D. D. Carnicelli (Cambridge, MA: Harvard University Press, 1971), 10, and Heather Campbell, "'And in Their Midst a Sun': Petrarch's *Triumphs* and the Elizabethan Icon," in *Goddesses and Queens: The Iconography of Elizabeth I*, ed. Annaliese Connolly and Lisa Hopkins (Manchester: University of Manchester Press, 2007), 83–100.

31. See Morley, *Lord Morley's Tryumphes*, 38–46.

32. The "Triumph of Eternity" portrait (*Queen Elizabeth with Time and Death*) belongs to the Methuen Collection at Corsham Court, Wiltshire.

33. See Morley, *Lord Morley's Tryumphes*, 47–66.

Great *Junoes* golden chaire, the which they say
The Gods stand gazing on, when she does ride
To *Joves* high house through heavens bras-paved way
Drawne of faire Pecocks, that excell in pride,
And full of *Argus* eyes their tailes dispredden wide.[34]

Lucifera's "coche" is drawn by "six unequall beasts / On which her six sage Counsellours did ryde"—six deadly sins other than pride, which was embodied in Lucifera. These beastes (an ass, a swine, a goat, a camel, a wolf, and a lion) contrast with the symbolically pure white steeds pulling Elizabeth's "chariot" in her progress through London.[35]

The ceremony of November 24 staged a basic contradiction between prideful self-assertion in the triumphal procession and the humble stance of thanksgiving: what was being performed in the civic space of the royal entry was at odds with the devout gratitude expressed in the prayers and poems associated with the occasion. Protestants associated processions with Catholic idolatry and superstition.[36] Yet for the thanksgiving extravaganza, the Crown had gone so far as to attire the clergy who greeted the Queen at St. Paul's in leftover Catholic vestments. According to Garnet,

> They looked silly in the eyes of all, dressed up as they were in Catholic copes: copes which heretofore they had burned or cut up in pieces. . . . They had been forced to fetch them, in mutilated condition, from the Queen's chapel or from an old armoury in the Tower. The Dean of St. Paul's, who is considered a very holy man by the heretics, roused some measure of sympathy in a courtier who, as he saw him approaching decked up in cloth of gold, said, "My good man, I am sorry for you. Sir, you are the only man whom this cloth of gold does not puff up with pride."[37]

34. Edmund Spenser, *The Faerie Queene*, bk. 1, canto 4, st. 17, in *The Works of Edmund Spenser, A Variorum Edition*, ed. Edwin Greenlaw et al. (Baltimore: Johns Hopkins University Press, 1932), 1:47.

35. Ibid., st. 18.

36. Not only were religious processions part of the traditional Sunday liturgy, but there were also special processions associated with Candlemas, Corpus Christi, Palm Sunday, and Rogationtide. These were generally suppressed by the English Protestant Church, although the 1547 Edwardine ban on processions was modified by Queen Elizabeth in 1559 to permit Rogationtide processions. See Eamon Duffy, *The Stripping of the Altars: Traditional Religion in England 1400–1580* (New Haven: Yale University Press, 1992), 136–37, 451, 468.

37. Caraman, *Henry Garnet*, 82–83.

Garnet, no doubt, perceived that Queen Elizabeth had, on this occasion and others, appropriated for her own secular purposes the pomp and ceremony of Catholic ritual processions. Kevin Sharpe has observed: "Elizabeth rendered herself the object of a cult. . . . Through rituals, even more than portraits, Elizabeth became an icon, and Catholic processions that fêted the Virgin Mary were appropriated and transmuted into liturgies and paeans to a Protestant Virgin Queen."[38]

The Queen's entrance to London was in form a military triumph in which she took center stage as the conquering hero.[39] Yet all official interpretations of the victory as well as Elizabeth's explicit behavior gave all the credit to God, England's providential rescuer. In both actions and words, the Queen attempted to present herself merely as his humble servant. In her encounter with London's mayor and in her behavior at St. Paul's she sought, with her words and actions, to play down the display of her authority in those very circumstances in which it was visually pronounced. As triumphal queen, she showed herself to her people, as she did on her royal progresses, but, on the ground and in the popular ballads recording the event, she took pains to make a human connection with them rather than to put herself out of reach.

English printers did not shrink from capitalizing on the national emergency. Between June 29 and November 27 they registered twenty-seven ballads dealing with the Armada, only four of which survive in printed form.[40] Thomas Orwyn and John Wolfe entered in the Stationers' Register two of these ballads dealing specifically with the thanksgiving solemnities of November 24.[41] These are the texts preserved in Hanson's manuscript. Thus detailed accounts of events in London, in this case, events with international import, were transmitted through both print and manuscript to

38. Sharpe, *Selling the Tudor Monarchy*, 418.

39. Miller notes that Elizabeth "triumphed not only as head of the nation (like a Roman emperor) but also as a commander in the field (like a republican imperator). In the mythology of the Armada victory, Elizabeth assumed this role on her visit to Tilbury on 8 August. . . . By the time of the queen's visit, the Armada had retreated and the threat of invasion had in fact passed. . . . The timing was exquisitely apt: at the moment of assuming the role of general, Elizabeth assumed also the role of victor." *Roman Triumphs*, 67–68.

40. John J. McAleer, "Ballads on the Spanish Armada," *Texas Studies in Literature and Language* 4, no. 4 (1963): 602–3.

41. Edward Arber, ed., *A Transcript of the Registers of the Company of Stationers of London, 1554–1640*, 5 vols. (London: Private printing, 1875–94), 2:506, 508.

the Queen's subjects in the provinces. Presumably, Hanson borrowed the broadsides to copy into his anthology, as he would have had less reason to do so if he owned the printed copies. In any event, no copies of the printed souvenirs themselves have survived; they are known only from Hanson's transcribed copies.

Ballad 1 is entitled "A Joyfull newe ballad of the Royall entrance of Quene [Elizabeth]" (ff. 19–22). This is undoubtedly the ballad entered to Wolfe on the "Roiall entrance of Quene Elizabeth into her cyty of London the ___ Day of november 1588."[42] The second, untitled, ballad begins,

Gyve eare awhyle good people all,
Bothe yonge and olde yea great and small
And unto yowe Declare I shall
Ryght Joyfull newes from London.

(2.1–4)

This is presumably the ballad registered by Orwyn as "A Joyefull Songe or Sonnett of the royall receavinge of the queenes majestye into the cyttye of London on sondaye the 24th of November 1588. all alonge Flete Streete to the Cathedrall churche of Sainct Paule. &c."[43] The manuscript text is subscribed "finis Richard pygote." We have found no other work attributed to this author.[44]

The first ballad is poetically unremarkable. The scribe presents the text in eight-line stanzas (as set forth below), no doubt reflecting the format of the printed broadside. The poem's technical form, however, is fifty iambic heptameter couplets for a total of one hundred lines of verse. When divided into four-line stanzas, these fourteener couplets and their companion long-line form, poulter's measure (alternating iambic hexameter and heptameter couplet lines), are routinely and ambiguously termed even by specialists "common measure" or "ballad meter." It would be a mistake,

42. Cited in Hyder E. Rollins, *An Analytical Index to the Ballad-Entries (1557–1709) in the Registers of the Company of Stationers of London* (1924; repr., Hatboro, PA: Tradition Press, 1967), no. 2337.

43. Ibid., no. 1330.

44. He is perhaps the Richard Pigot of Buckinghamshire who matriculated from Christ Church, Oxford, on 23 November 1581, at age twelve. Joseph Foster, *Alumni Oxonienses*, 4 vols. (Oxford: Parker and Co., 1891–92), 3:1163.

however, to assume that these old-fashioned forms were designed for the tastes of the lower-class readers who presumably purchased most broadside ballads. It is unlikely that ballad sales targeted a market of the poor and illiterate. In fact, these long-line couplets were regularly employed in such up-market works as William Warner's *Albion's England* and George Chapman's translation of the *Iliad*.

Richard Pygot's celebratory ballad is technically far more ambitious than the first, although no more original in form. It was modeled on William Elderton's 1584 ballad beginning "As I came through the north country."[45] Both are written in complicated twelve-line stanzas rhyming *aaabcccbdddb*; the *b* rhymes are iambic trimeter variable refrains, with the rest in iambic tetrameter. Moreover, the last quatrain in each ballad is itself a refrain, indicated merely by "&c" throughout most of both texts (we exclude these missing refrains from the lineation of ballad 2). Elderton's work is the only other extant Elizabethan poem in this form. Pygot modeled his refrain on its wording as well: Elderton's "to goe to the Cittie of London" and "as it had been at London," for example, are echoed by Pygot's "To everye churche in London" (2.8) and "As order ys in London" (2.92). It may be only coincidence, but Elderton's ballad is a 264-line encomium of the city of York entitled "Yorke, Yorke, for my monie." This raises the possibility that Pygot was from Yorkshire (or at least had Yorkshire connections).

Both ballads provide remarkably detailed eyewitness accounts of the celebration, the second beginning with allusions to the prayers of thanksgiving offered (by royal command) on November 19. They amplify the November 24 spectacle and add incidents that cannot be reconstructed from the chronicle accounts, Garnet's letter, or manuscript diagrams of the event. The ballads thus illustrate how the genre functioned at its best in an age before newspapers and modern electronic media to bring to life contemporary events for remote consumers. Where Stow reports that "[t]he companies of the City in their liveries stoode in their rayles of timber, covered with blewe cloth" (*Annales*, sig. 4P1v), ballad 1 adds that some guild members displayed "streameres" and "Lyttyl flages . . . Wherein

45. *STC* 7559; EV 2688, in Steven W. May and William A. Ringler, Jr., *Elizabethan Poetry: A Bibliography and First-Line Index of English Verse, 1559*–1603, 3 vols. (London: Continuum, 2004), 1:351, and see the index of "Rhyme Schemes and Verse Forms," 3:2164.

theyr armes were Rychelye Drawne" (1.53–55). The ballad adds that each company was represented by "yongmen" (presumably their apprentices) in velvet coats with chains of gold, and that the streets were hung with tapestries. Guildsmen with staves cleared the streets for the royal procession (1.69–72). While Garnet mentions the gray horses that drew the Queen's chariot, Stow describes them as white, noting that the mayor and aldermen were dressed in scarlet.[46] Both ballads mention the Queen's white horses (1.87; 2.45) and add more color to the proceedings. We learn that Elizabeth was "gloryouslye attyred . . . / In clothe of sylver whyte," that the serjeants-at-law and the judges also wore scarlet robes and gold collars, but that the gentlemen attending on the French ambassador were all, no doubt purposely, dressed in black (1.83–84, 105–12, 117–19).

The ballads mention as well a number of incidents omitted from or related in less detail by the other sources we have consulted. Exactly what took place when the mayor and aldermen met the Queen at Temple Bar, for example, seems to have been more accurately recounted in the ballads than by Garnet or Stow. Garnet explains that when the procession reached Temple Bar, Elizabeth "was presented with the sword that is carried before the Lord Mayor only when he is in the presence of the Sovereign." In Stow's account the mayor delivered up a scepter to the Queen, which she "redelivered" to him. He then "bare the same before her" in the procession to St. Paul's.[47] Both ballads confirm the more likely facts of this transaction. The Lord Mayor of London was custodian of both sword and mace as symbols of his authority derived from the Crown[48] but not of the scepter, which was, of course, the badge of royal sovereignty. In royal processions through London, the mayor was on occasion granted the privilege of bearing the scepter before his sovereign.[49] Stow therefore mistook the mayor's

46. Caraman, *Henry Garnet*, 82; Stow, *Annales*, sig. 4P1v.

47. Ibid.

48. In 1600, for instance, the city of Cork, Ireland, petitioned the Privy Council for rights on behalf of its mayor, who, as her officer, carried "her Royall ensignes, as a Hatte of Maintenance, a Sword and Maces." Meeting of 25 May 1600, in *Acts of the Privy Council of England*, vol. 30, *A.D. 1599–1600*, ed. John Roche Dasent (London: HMSO, 1905), 338.

49. Thus Henry Machyn records the mayor's carrying the scepter before Philip and Mary in their procession through London on 22 March 1557. *The Diary of Henry Machyn*, ed. John Gough Nichols (London: Camden Society, 1848), 130. The Garter King at Arms bore the scepter before Elizabeth as she arrived in London as Queen on 28 November 1558. John Stow, *The Chronicles*

presentation of his sword to Elizabeth as delivery of his (nonexistent) scepter. As the ballads correctly state, the Queen "gave the maior a Scepter Rych" that he then carried some distance before her in the procession (1.91–96; 2.69–71). The Huntington diagram also describes the mayor's "bearing a scepter" (f. 17v), while both the ballads and diagrams confirm that the Marquess of Winchester bore the sword immediately before the Queen (not the mayor, as Garnet mistakenly stated). Thus, as she entered London, the Queen received the sword from the Lord Mayor as symbolic authority over the city and in exchange conferred on him her scepter as symbolic authority to act on her behalf during her visit. The first ballad also records that she returned the sword to the mayor upon leaving the city that evening (1.189–90).

The ballads bring other incidents into sharper focus as well. Pygot's account specifies the precedence of the livery companies, headed by the drapers, then the mercers and grocers (2.89–91). Pygot also provides the fullest account of musical accompaniments to the proceedings. He reports that the citizens played music "On Dyverse Instrumentes" during the procession and that the clergymen who met the Queen at the west door of St. Paul's sang the litany as she was escorted to her pew (2.123, 148–49).

The ballads also identify participants in the ceremony or name participants whom the eyewitnesses describe only by title. While all diagrams of the procession depict a sword before the Queen, only the Folger MS V.a.213 and State Papers diagrams identify its bearer as the "Lord Marquesse." The first ballad specifies that this was "The Lord marques of wynchester" (1.121–24), actually the third marquess, William Paulet, premier nobleman of the realm. And only ballad 1 identifies the Lord Great Chamberlain of England:

> The noble earle of oxford then
> Heighe chamberlayn of England
> Rode Ryght before hyr majestye
> Hys bonnet in hys hand.
>
> (1.125–28)

---

of England (1580), *STC* 23333, sig. 3Z8. At Henry VII's funeral procession in 1509, however, the mayor bore the mace before the hearse, as he did at Mary I's coronation 1 October 1553. BL MS Harl. 3504, f. 264v; SP 11/1 f.26.

Edward de Vere, seventeenth Earl of Oxford, held the office of Great Chamberlain of England on ceremonial occasions. The diagrams refer to "the Lord great Chamberlaine Duringe the Service" but show the sword intervening between him and Elizabeth, then show him riding behind the Queen with the vice chamberlain "for the Service" (Huntington Library, MS EL 1118, ff. 17v–18). In addition, Oxford reappears in ballad 1 just after the Queen hears the sermon in an incident not mentioned by any other source:

> The Ear[l] of oxford openyng then
> The wyndowes for hyr grace
> The Chyldren of the hospytall
> She sawe before hyr [f]ace.
>
> (1.173–76)

The identity of these children is uncertain, as is the purpose of their sudden confrontation with the Queen. The children readiest to hand were, of course, the boys of St. Paul's. Originally, the cathedral had nurtured children in a grammar school, a song school, and a hospital or almonry for the poor supervised by an almoner. From at least the thirteenth century the almoner of St. Paul's was responsible for these "charity boys" or "almonry boys." Cathedral statutes of 1263 state that the almoner was to supervise "'eight boys fit for the service of the Church whom he is to have instructed either by himself or by another master in matters pertaining to the service of the Church and in literature,'" that is, Latin grammar.[50] By Elizabeth's reign, these *pueri elemosinarii*, now ten in number, had long "formed the nucleus of the boys of the song school."[51] It was doubly appropriate for Oxford to introduce them to the Queen. As Lord Great Chamberlain on state occasions he could claim some responsibility for ceremony and entertainment, as did the Lord Chamberlain of the royal household on a regular basis. Moreover, under the earl's patronage, Paul's Boys had joined with Oxford's boys to perform John Lyly's plays at court during the Christmas seasons of 1583–84 and 1584–85.

50. A. F. Leach, "St. Paul's School before Colet," *Archaeologia*, 2nd ser., 62 (1910): 196–97.

51. E. K. Chambers, *The Elizabethan Stage*, 4 vols. (Oxford: Clarendon Press, 1923; repr., 1961), 2:9–11.

The children described in the ballad, however, may have had nothing at all to do with St. Paul's Cathedral. Professor Peter McCullough of Lincoln College, Oxford, and Canon of St. Paul's Cathedral, informs us that the St. Paul's school was never referred to as a hospital. The "children of the hospital" designated instead the orphaned children of Christ's Hospital, who resided in the former Greyfriars Monastery on Newgate Street (a site renamed Christchurch after the Dissolution).[52] Edward VI was instrumental in founding this institution late in 1552, along with the hospitals of St. Thomas and Bridewell. The children of Christ's regularly took part in London civic pageantry. In *Fool upon foole* (1605), Robert Armin describes how "On Easter Munday the auncient custome is, that all the children of the Hospitall goe before my Lord Maior to the Spittle [Hospital], that the world may witnesse the workes of God and man, in maintenance of so many poore people."[53] Machyn's *Diary* records their presence at London funerals in 1553 and 1555; they numbered one hundred children on the former occasion. A sermon at St. Mary's on April 19, 1557, was attended by the Lord Mayor, twenty-three aldermen, "and alle the chylderyn of the hospetall in blue garmenttes."[54] It would thus have been quite normal for the children of Christ's Hospital to be present in the churchyard for the Armada thanksgiving sermon.

Whether Elizabeth suddenly encountered Paul's Boys or the children of the hospital at the close of the Paul's Cross sermon, the question is why they were brought before her at all. Contemporary references suggest that they may have been present to perform one of two songs she herself wrote for the occasion. In *The Countrie Mans Comfort* (1637), John Rhodes printed "Two most excellent songs or Ditties, made by Queene Elizabeth . . . in the yeare 1588."[55] As Rhodes's book was entered in the Stationers' Register in 1588, it seems likely that a first edition of the work had been published in that year, no copies of which have survived. Moreover, Rhodes certainly had access to a copy of the first song he attributed to the Queen well before 1637, for in 1605 he published a version of it entitled "An Antheme often Sung in the royall Chappel of our late Queene Elizabeth, . . . Made in Anno Dom.

52. Private communication, December 16, 2012.

53. Armin, *Foole upon foole, or, Six sortes of sottes* (1605), *STC* 772.5, sig. C4.

54. Machyn, *Diary*, 32, 99, 131.

55. *STC* 20961, sig. D6.

1588."[56] A text of the second poem in MS SNG/4 at the National Maritime Museum, Greenwich, ties it explicitly to the thanksgiving ceremony of 24 November. It is entitled "A songe made by her majestie and songe before her at her cominge from white hall to Powles throughe fleetestrete in Anno Dni 1588 / songe in December after the scatteringe of the Spanishe Navy."[57] The first poem is the Queen's first-person prayer to God to deliver England from the alien threat. The second thanks the Lord for delivering his people and specifically Elizabeth herself from conquest, albeit its title incorrectly states that the procession began at Whitehall rather than Somerset House and took place in December rather than November.[58]

Both poems were, in fact, set to music by well-known composers with close ties to the court. Music for the Queen's first poem occurs among the anthems composed by Dr. John Bull, who had been appointed gentlemen of the Chapel Royal in 1586. In 1593 the Queen granted him a lease in reversion and a few years later recommended that he become the first reader in music at Gresham College. Thus Bull's setting may have stemmed from a royal commission, for he was a crown servant known personally to the Queen.[59] It supports as well Rhodes's assertion that the poem became "An Antheme often Sung in the royall Chappel of our late Queene Elizabeth." The second poem survives in a setting by William Byrd in British Library, MS Additional 31992, f. 43v. This manuscript provides only the work's incipit with a score in lute tablature. In 1575 Elizabeth granted Byrd, a gentleman of the Chapel Royal since 1572, a music publishing patent shared with his colleague in the chapel, Thomas Tallis. The Queen thereafter intervened to protect Byrd, a committed Catholic, from the harsh legal penalties levied against recusants.[60] Byrd's madrigal songbooks include

56. *A briefe some of the Treason intended against the King and State* (London, 1605), *STC* 20960, sigs. C3v–4.

57. EV 14009, in May and Ringler, *Elizabethan Poetry*.

58. These are poems 8 and 9 in *Queen Elizabeth I: Selected Works*, ed. Steven W. May (New York: Washington Square Press, 2004).

59. Alan Brown, "Bull, John," *ODNB*, http://www.oxforddnb.com/view/article/3905?docPos=1. A text of the poem in Bodleian Library, MS Rawl. poet. 23, p. 141, is closer to Rhodes's 1605 version than that of 1637. The manuscript is a mid-seventeenth-century anthology of religious verse copied from songbooks; while it omits the music, it does identify the composers.

60. Craig Monson, "Byrd, William," *ODNB*, http://www.oxforddnb.com/view/article/4267?docPos=2.

settings of several poems by courtier poets that circulated only in manuscript; thus he, too, was well placed to receive a text of the Queen's hymn of thanksgiving for deliverance from the Armada.[61]

If Elizabeth arranged for her thanksgiving poem to be "songe before her at her cominge from white hall to Powles throughe fleetestrete," as the title to the National Maritime Museum text affirms, where and when did the performance take place? If "at her cominge" means during the procession, the most likely occasion occurred at Temple Bar. There, according to Stow, the London waits were stationed over the gate to greet the Queen (*Annales*, sig. 4P1v). The waits, however, were an instrumental ensemble, and no source mentions a song or songs as part of the welcome. Afterward, the second ballad records of the livery companies that

> They songe and played wythe musyke sweete
> In sundrye places in the streete
> On Dyverse Instrumentes they thought meete.
>
> (2.121–23)

But it seems unlikely that Elizabeth commissioned these tradesmen to sing her poems, nor could she have heard them sung unless the performance were continuous among the sixty companies that this same ballad assures us lined the way (2.95). We take "at her cominge" to mean instead, on the occasion of her procession to and worship at the cathedral that November day. Could the clergy who sang the litany in the cathedral have appended the Queen's songs to their canonical devotions? Perhaps, although that would have been a lot to ask of men who were not professional musicians but sang parts of the service as merely one aspect of their clerical duties. By far the most likely occasion for the singing of Elizabeth's songs occurred when she was suddenly confronted with the children who appeared "before hyr face." This is in keeping with Rhodes's title to the Queen's poem of thanksgiving, which states that it was "performed at

61. Byrd's *Psalmes, Sonets, & songs* (London, 1588), *STC* 4253, for example, included texts of song 10 from Sidney's *Astrophil and Stella*, "My mind to me a kingdom is," of disputed authorship between the Earl of Oxford and Sir Edward Dyer; Oxford's "If women could be fair"; and Sir Walter Ralegh's "Farewell false love, the oracle of lies."

Saint Pauls crosse in London."[62] Testimony from the second ballad confirms that there was, indeed, singing after the sermon:

And when he hade the Sermon done
And psalmes Ryght solemply were songe
Hyr heighnes shewd hyr selff amonge
Hyr people th[e]re of London

(2.166–69)

The Queen's poems might reasonably be described as "psalmes"; as we shall see, they adapted much of their phrasing from the Psalter. The second poem seems to have been explicitly designed for the St. Paul's thanksgiving service, for in it Elizabeth describes herself

amongst thy priests offering to thee,
Zeal for incense reaching the skies,
Myself and scepter, sacrifice.[63]

This literally describes the scene in the churchyard that afternoon. Elizabeth was certainly in the presence of a great many priests on this occasion, while the mayor would have been prominently in sight holding her scepter. Accordingly, in this scenario, the Queen commissioned the children's choir to sing her poetry as set to music by Bull and Byrd. But which one? We find the choice difficult to arbitrate. There was no reason for the balladeer to single out the appearance before the Queen of the "Chyldren of the hospytall"—that is, Christ's Hospital—unless they were to play some part in the ceremony. Even if assembled in their hundreds for the occasion, they would have formed only part of the crowd in the churchyard that afternoon among many other subjects of the Queen. Although these children never performed plays at court or in public, as did Paul's Boys, they received a similar education. John Stow records that after attending Bartholomew Fair in 1555, the Lord Mayor and aldermen "came to Christs Hospital within *Newgate*, where they heard a disputation betweene the Schollers of *Paules* Schoole, *Saint Anthonies* Schoole, and the Schollers of

62. *Countrie Mans Comfort*, sig. D6v.

63. May, *Queen Elizabeth I*, poem 9, ll. 2–4.

the said Hospitall."[64] Upon her entrance into London as Queen on January 14, 1559, Elizabeth had encountered the children of the hospital at St. Dunstan's Church, where one of them greeted her with a Latin oration: "The child after he had ended his oration, kissed the paper wherein the same was written and reached it to the Queen's Majesty," who took it and declared "her gracious mind toward their relief." As good as her word, on 4 March following Elizabeth sent to Christ's Hospital ten pounds for the children's use.[65] Perhaps she nurtured a sentimental attachment to the hospital because her half-brother, Edward VI, had founded it. If so, she might have commissioned an ad hoc choir of these children to sing her hymn, whether or not singing formed a part of their schooling.

On the other hand, it is possible that the balladeer extended the customary phrase by referring to the children of Paul's as the "Chyldren of the hospytall." This solved the problem of working Paul's boys into his poem in an iambic tetrameter line (such as "The Chyldren of the hospytall"). The children of Paul's do not readily lend themselves to this meter: "The Children of St. Paul's School" is a syllable short, as is "The boys of St. Paul's School," while "The St. Paul's schoolboys" (or children) destroys the line's rhythm. "The boys of the cathedral school" will do it, but they were always termed the boys or children of Paul's, not of the cathedral. Its choir boys, moreover, were still part of an eleemosynary foundation, the master of the song school being the cathedral almoner. In his will of 1582, for instance, Sebastian Westcott, master of the song school who became schoolmaster of Paul's by 1557, described himself as "almoner of St. Paul's dwelling in the almonry."[66] The boys of Christ's Hospital and those of St. Paul's were thus very similar beneficiaries and residents of religious institutions. The poet could solve his metrical problem and still adequately describe Paul's boys by referring to them as "of the hospital" in that word's sense as a "charitable institution for the housing and maintenance of the needy."[67]

64. Stow, *Chronicles*, sig. 3Z2v.

65. Germaine Warkentin, ed., *The Queens Majesty's Passage and Related Documents* (Toronto: Centre for Reformation and Renaissance Studies, 2004), 93, 124.

66. Chambers, *Elizabethan Stage*, 2:12, 15n.

67. *OED*, "hospital," n. 2a. For further analysis of the Queen's role in the service with regard to her sense of privacy about her writings and in the context of the churchyard as physical space, see Steven W. May, "Queen Elizabeth's Performance at Paul's Cross in 1588," in *Paul's Cross and the Culture of Persuasion in England, 1520–1640*, ed. Torrance Kirby and P. G. Stanwood (Leiden: Brill, 2014), 300–313.

In their manner of composition, both of Elizabeth's songs resemble the prose psalm that opens the *Psalme and Collect of thankesgiving* that the Crown had published to guide her subjects' religious observances. This *Psalme* is a pastiche of verses adapted primarily from the Psalter, with scriptural citations in the margins. Worshippers who recited, for example, the verses "We will therefore give thankes whome the Lord hath redeemed, and delivered from the hand of the enemie. We wil confesse before the Lord, and prayse him for his goodnes: and declare the woonders that he doth for the children of men"[68] could then follow the marginal reference to Psalm 107, verses 2 and 21: "Let them give thanks whome the Lorde hath redeemed: and delivered from the hand of the enimie. . . . O that men would therfore praise the Lord for his goodnesse: and declare the wonders that he doth for the children of men."[69] Similarly, the Queen's poems echo the wording of both the prose and metrical Psalters. The opening of her first Armada poem, for instance—"Deliver me, O Lord my God, from all my foes that be"—resembles that of Psalm 59 in the Great Bible translation, "Deliver mee from mine enimies, O God" (sig. F2). Her second poem begins, "Look and bow down thine ear, O Lord," similar to verse 1 of Psalm 86 in the metrical Psalter, "Lord, bow thine ear to my request."[70] Other phrasing from Sternhold and Hopkins crops up in this song of thanksgiving, including "behold and see" (Psalms 66, l. 3 and 92, l. 33) and—for the Queen's "Thou hast done wonders"—"Thou workest wonders" (Psalm 86, l. 39), and "The wonders great which thou, O Lord, hast done" (Psalm 106, ll. 21–22). A few lines later Elizabeth writes, "My soul ascend his holy place, ascribe him strength and sing him praise," wording echoed by Psalm 56—"and keep my soul upright, / That I before thee may ascend" (ll. 50–51)—and Psalm 29, "ascribe unto the Lord worship and strength."[71] Key nouns throughout her poem—"handmaid" for "handmaids" (Psalms 86, l. 64 and 123, l. 5, "handiwork" (Psalm 28, l. 3), "thy priests" (Psalm 132, l. 25), "Israel's God" (Psalm 72, l. 74), "incense" (Psalm

68. Liturgies, sig. A3.

69. *The Psalter or Psalmes of David, after the translation of the Great Bible* (London, 1580), *STC* 2397.3, sigs. L2v, L3.

70. May, *Queen Elizabeth I*, poem 8, l. 1; *The Psalter or Psalmes of Dauid*, sig. I1v; *The whole booke of Psalmes . . . by Thomas Sternhold, John Hopkins and others* (London, 1567), sig. K5v (this edition cited hereafter by psalm and line numbers).

71. *The Psalter or Psalmes of David*, sigs. I2, C1, C3; May, *Queen Elizabeth I*, poem 9, ll. 1–2, 5.

141, l. 5), "his holy place" (Psalm 134, l. 6)—reveal how closely Elizabeth modeled her work on the poetic diction of the metrical Psalter. As sung by a boys' choir, it would have been indistinguishable to the crowd assembled in Paul's churchyard that afternoon from the psalms that were sung after sermons there from the beginning of Elizabeth's reign.

Despite these verbal parallels between the Queen's hymns and the Psalters in prose and verse, her message differed from the officially published *Collect* by assigning to God very different motives for his role in the national triumph. Although they fully agree in attributing the victory entirely to divine intervention, the *Collect* stresses that God initially sent the Armada "to the punishment of our sinnes." God then vanquished the Spanish attackers after realizing that they "came not of justice to punish us for our sinnes" but "utterly to root out the memorie of our nation from off the earth for ever." The Deity mercifully overlooked the "innumerable, and most greevous offences continually committed against thy divine majestie" by the English people.[72] From Elizabeth's standpoint, however, the Almighty's motives were entirely different. In Poem 8 she adapted phrasing from Psalm 59 to protest, "Mine enemies, O Lord, be strong, and thou the same doest know, / And that without offence in me, they seek mine overthrow."[73] Her own innocence is a frequent theme in Elizabeth's writings that here sets her completely apart from her sin-ridden people. God saves them despite their transgressions while the Queen describes metaphorically and in scriptural terms her relationship with the Lord, who "hath preserved in tender love / The spirit of his turtle dove."[74]

The manuscript ballads thus contribute many details toward a full reconstruction of the thanksgiving ceremonies, especially Elizabeth's personal role in their planning and execution. We know from the State Papers that she was directly involved in securing the French ambassador's attendance. Only the ballads, however, supply the fascinating detail that Châteauneuf expressed his and his government's attitude toward the actual occasion of the celebration by causing his gentlemen to be dressed in

72. Liturgies, sig. A4.

73. May, *Queen Elizabeth I*, poem 8, ll. 5–6. Cf. Psalm 59:3: "the mightie men are gathered togither against me without anie offence or fault of me." *The Psalter or Psalmes of David*, sig. F2v.

74. May, *Queen Elizabeth I*, poem 9, ll. 11–12.

black.[75] Meanwhile, Elizabeth had composed two verse prayers setting forth in her own voice her response to the Armada's approach and subsequent defeat. Her inspiration is easily understood. England's unlikely triumph seemed to confirm all that her loyal subjects had said throughout her reign about her leadership of God's true church and his chosen people, pitted against the powers of the Antichrist. But her use of at least one of these poems speaks to the Queen's skills in political theater as well as her piety, for she had her poetry set to music by royal musicians and sung before her at the conclusion of a patriotic, public religious service. Of the sources we have consulted, only the first ballad in Hanson's anthology testifies to the sudden revelation of the children immediately after Dr. Piers's sermon, and only the second ballad notes that psalms were sung after the sermon as well. The Queen intended the performance as something of a grand finale to the thanksgiving service. Afterward, according to the ballad, Elizabeth rose to face her subjects, perhaps as acknowledgment of herself as the first-person voice in one or both of the songs.[76] The Queen had everything to do with all the elements of that day of thanksgiving, and the two ballads following round out the historical record of the event.

Ballad 1

Note: We add line numbers to the verse as presented on the manuscript page at five-line intervals. This means that the line numbering fails to synchronize with the poems' technical form in both ballads. In ballad 1, the heptameter couplets are divided into four-line stanzas, while in ballad 2

75. No protocol governed this choice of color. The members of the French ambassador's retinue marching in Queen Anne Boleyn's coronation procession in 1533, for example, were "clothed in coates of blewe velvet with sleves of yelowe and blewe velvet." Edward Halle, *The Union of the two noble and illustre famelies* (1550), a Scolar Press facsimile of *STC* 12723 (Menston, UK: Scolar Press, 1970), sig. N4.

76. In his description of the thanksgiving service published in 1657, Samuel Clarke affirmed that after the sermon, "her Majesty herself, with most princely and Christian speeches exhorted all the people to a due performance of those religious services of thankfulness which the Lord expected and required of them." Clarke's testimony, however, is too late and unreliable to be accepted without reservations. He dates the Queen's visit to St. Paul's, for example, on 24 September and states that she departed for the ceremony from Whitehall rather than Somerset House. *Englands Remembrancer, containing A true and full Narrative of those two never to be forgotten deliverances: The one from the Spanish Invasion in Eighty eight: The other from the Hellish Powder Plot: November 5. 1605* (London, 1657), sigs. E7v–8.

the scribe discontinues copying repeated forms of refrains after stanza 2 (in so doing, he was probably following his copy, for printers also ordinarily stopped repeating broadside ballad refrains after the first few stanzas). Where the scribe creates unintentional ligatures between words, we separate them for legibility. The textual notes include variant readings from Mrs. Stirling's transcription of ballad 1.

f. 19] *A Joyfull newe ballad of the Royall entrance of Quene E[lizabeth]*[77]
in the Cetye of London the 24 of November in the 3i yere of hyr majesties
Reigne to gyve god prayse for the overthrowe of the spanyardes

Amonge the woonderous workes of god
for savegard of owre Quene
Agenst the heape of traiterous foes
Whiche have confounded bene
The great and Myghty over throwe
of Spanyerdes prowde in mynde
have gyven us all Just cause to saye
The Lord ys good and Kynde

And that we myght not thankeles be
unto owre gracyous god
That hathe in mercye cast awaye
hys greevous scurgynge Rod
and for the blessynges manyfold
Bestowed upon thys Land
The state wherof makes all the worled
Amazed for to stand

Owre noble Queene and peerelesse prynce
dyd make a straight Decre
That throughe hyr land a sollemne Daye
Unto the Lord shoulde be
To yeld all lawde and honor hye
Unto his gloryous name
Whose hand upholdes owre happynes
and hyr tryumphant Reigne/

The twentye foure of November
This Joyfull Daye was seene

77. Page torn.

whiche was made holye to the Lord
by owre most gr[a]cyous Queene
upon whose heade the Lord had plast
The Royall Englyshe crowne/
f. 19v] Thies thirtye yeires to weare the same
wythe glorye and Renowne

Therfore to lovelye London fayre
owre noble queene woulde goe
And at paules crosse before hyr god
hyr thankefull hert to showe
Wheare prynces and people Dyd consent
wythe Joyfull myndes to meete
To gloryfye the god of heaven
wyth psalmes and voyces sweete

Whearas a proper place was made
for hyr good[78] grace to stand
The comfort of good cittizens
and Joye[79] of All the Land.
The Cyttyzens no soner harde
hyr majestis intent
but for hyr welcome they prepared
all pompt the[y] cowlde[80] invent

And from Temple barre unto paules Churche
Alonge one syde the waye
The Cittizens in theyr lyveries
eache one in Ryche araye
wythe streameres fayre and Lyttyll [f]lages[81]
in order Due Dyd stand
wherin theyr armes weare Rychelye Drawne
To make each trade Decernd

The gentlemen of the Innes of Cowrte
from sergents Inne also
f. 20] from temple barre on thother side
Dyd make a seemely shoe° °*show*

78. Stirling: "great."
79. Stirling: "pride."
80. Stirling: "coule."
81. Stirling: "flags." Hanson wrote "slages."

and from that place unto paules Churche
on everye syde in Deede
The Cittizens of London stood
as yt was well Decreed

And everye companye by theym selves
as in theyr Railes they stood
had yongmen store in Velvet coates
And chaynes of gold all good
and each of theym ~~to theyr~~ to cleare the waye
As they Dyd wayttying stand
Dyd styll avoyde[82] the multytyde
wythe walkynge staves in hand

The streetes were hange[83] wythe tapystrey
of couleres freshe and bryght
and everye thynge provyded [f]ytt
for suche a gloryous syght
The Lord maior and hys brethrene
in Scarlet Rich arayd
upon theyr Steedes at temple barre
for theyr Dread soveraigne stayd

Then came hyr Royall majestye
most vyrgyn lyke in syght
and gloryouslye attyred was
in clothe of sylver whyte
and Eke the charyot wheare she sate
of sylver clothe Dyd shyne
and mylke whyte Steed[s][84] Dyd beare the same
all trapped Ryche and [f]yne

f. 20v] And When she cam to temple Bar
Whearas the maior Dyd stand
hys Sword on bended knees he gave
Into hyr heighnes hand
who gr[a]cyouslye Dyd take the same
before hyr nobles there

82. *OED*, v. 5a, expel, drive away.

83. Error for "hanged"? The *OED* records "hang" as the past participle from the thirteenth through the fifteenth centuries.

84. Stirling: "steeds."

and gave the maior a Scepter Rych
whiche he Dyd barehead beare

And[85] hundreth knyghtes and gentlymen
Dyd fyrst before hyr Ryde
on gallant, fayre and stately steedes
theyr servantes by theyr sydes
The aldermen in Skarlet gownes
dyd after take theyr place
Then Rode hyr heighnesse Trumpetters
soundynge before hyr grace

And all the Sergantes at the Lawes
in Scarrlet there were seene
The Lord cheeff baron and Judges grave
Rode all before owre Queene
in Scarlet Robes most Ryche in syght
and comelye to behold
wythe collers fayre abowt theyr neckes
of pure and per[f]ecte gold

The noble Lord heighe Chauncellor
moste[86] gravelye Rode in place
The archebyshoppe of Canterburyie
before hyr Royall grace
The Lord ambassador of france
and all hys gentylmen
f. 21] in velvet blacke amonge the Lordes
Dyd take hys place as then

The Lord marques of wynchester
bare headed there was seene
who bare the sword in comely sorte
before owre ~~lo~~ noble queene
the noble earle of oxford then
heighe chamberlayn of England
Rode Ryght before hyr majestye
hys bonnet in hys hand

85. Read "An."
86. Stirling: "Nighe."

Then all hyr graces pentioneres
on foote dyd take theyr place
wythe theyr weapones in theyr hands
to guarde hyr Royall grace
The Earle of Essex after hyr
Dyd Ryde the next in Deede
Whyche by a costlye sylken Rayne
Dyd leade hyr graces Steede

Then followed the Ladies fayre
of honor afterward
an[d] on each one of theym Dyd wayte
a yeoman of the Gwarde
Attyred in theyr coates most Ryche
all wrought wythe glystrying gold
whiche was a most delightfull syght
and joyfull to behold

And so to paules she Rode alonge
a mylde and soft[l]ye[87] pace
the people Crying Joyfully
Lord Jes[u]s save yowre grace
the grownd before the gates of paules
wythe tapystrye was spred
f. 21v] of purpose for hyr Royall grace
whan she Dyd lyght to tread

Whearas a table was prepared
in pryncely sorte that Daye
Whearat hyr noble grace Dyd Kneele
in humble sort to praye
before she entred in the Churche
even att the Temple gate
as soone as she was taken from
hyr chariot of Estate

And after by two noble mene
alonge the churche was Led
wythe a golden cannapye
carryed ore hyr head
The cleargye wythe processyon brought

87. Stirling: "softlye." *OED*, a.3, Of pace: Easy, slow, gentle. *Obs*.

hyr grace into the quyer
whereas hyr majestye was sette
the servyce for to heare

and afterward unto paules crosse
She Dyd Dyrectelye passe
wheare by the byshope of Salysburye
a Sermon preached was
The Ear[l]le of oxford openyng then
the wyndowes for hyr grace
The Chyldren of the hospytall
she sawe before hyr [f]ace

And everye tyme hyr grace Dyd come
To shewe hyr selfe in syght
The peoples hartes[88] were Ravyshed
wythe Joye and swete Delyght
f. 22] Whyche beyng Done wythe thankes to god
she Dyd to Dyner goo
To the byshope of Londons place
hyr noble peers also

And Dynner beying ended then
in order as she came
She Dyd Returne unto the Cowrte
wyth all hyr noble trayne
Delyveryng the sword agayn
into the Lord maior hand
a thowsand torches burnyng bryght
alonge the waye Dyd stande

Thus went owre noble Quene awaye
unto hyr heighnesse Cowrte
wheare multytudes[89] of people Dyd
contynuallye Resorte
Dysyryng god for evermore
hyr grace to keepe and save
That Longe unto hyr subjectes Joye
hyr presence we maye have
finis

88. Stirling: "hart."
89. Stirling: "multytude."

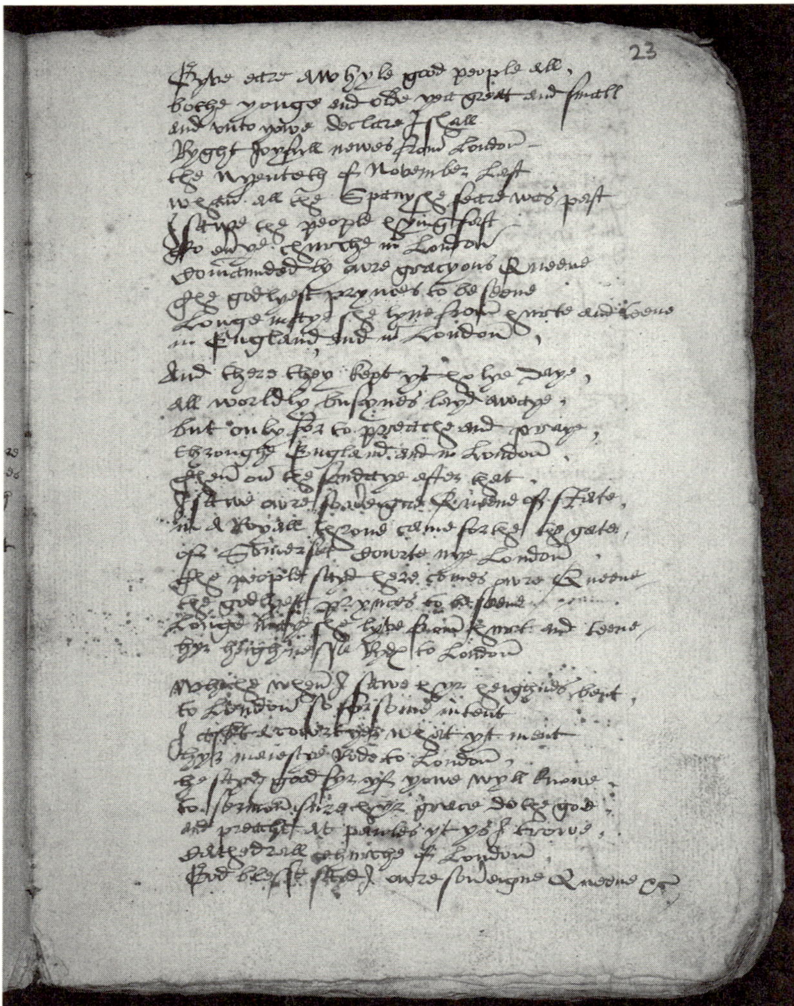

Figure 7. BL Add. MS 82370, f. 23. Beginning of second Armada thanksgiving ballad. Reproduced by permission of The British Library Board.

Ballad 2

f. 23] Gyve eare awhyle good people all,
bothe yonge and olde yea great and small
and unto yowe Declare I shall
Ryght Joyfull newes from London—
the Nyente[n]th of November Last
when al the Spanyshe feare was past
I sawe the people hying fast
To everye churche in London
Commaunded by owre gracyous Queene
The godlyest prynces to be seene
Longe maye she lyve from hurte and teene
in England, and in London,

And there they kept yt holye Daye,
all worldly busynes layd awaye,
but only for to preache and praye,
throughe England and in London.
Then on the sondaye after that,
I sawe owre sovereigne Queene of state,
in a Royall throne came forthe the gate,
of Somerset Cowrte nye London,
The people sayd here comes owre Queene/
the godlyest prynces to be seene
Longe maye she lyve from hurt and teene/
hyr heighnesse Rydes to London

Whiche when I sawe hyr heighnes bent,
to London so for some intent
I askt a cowrtyer what yt ment
hyr majestye Rode to London,
he sayd good syr yf yowe wyll knowe,
to sermon sure hyr grace dothe goe,
and preacht at pawles yt ys I trowe,
Cathedrall Churche of London,
God blesse sayd I owre sovereigne Queene &c/

f. 23v] yt was no neede to byd me hye
To London warde then by and by
That I the order myght espye
of hyr graces goyng to London

hyr pryncelye trayne abowte hyr there
of manye a Lord and noble peere
and gentylmene suche a number weare
dyd guard hyr Grace to London
and she the godlyest mayden quene
that ever eye on earthe hathe seene
hyr heighnes sat on a throne betwene
two palfrayes whyte throughe London

The heraultes that all armes Dysplaye
Amonge the nobles keepe the Ray,[90]
And Twentye trumpettores sound and saye
Queene Elizabeth comes to London
Whyche sound made all the Cetye glade
Yea, many thowsands had beene sad,
suche Longyng for theyr Queene they hade
to se hyr come to London/
~~Commaunded by owre gracious queene~~
~~The godlyest prynces to be seene~~
which ys the godlyest sovereig[n] Queene, &c.

me thought yt was a heavenlye syght
to se hyr lyke an angell bryght
yt made my heavye hart so Lyght
To see hyr Ryde to London
amydest hyr Lordes and ladyes fayre
a statlye trayne and troupe they were.
I never sawe non suche I sweare
before that Daye in London
god blesse I praye, owre sovereigne Quene &c/

f. 24] at temple barre hyr grace to meete
the worthy maior kneeld at hyr feete
gave up hys sword hyr grace to greete
most welcome Queene to London
hyr heighnes thankt hym for the same
and a pryncely Scepter gave hym again

90. *OED*, aphetic form of "array," order or position; here, precedence among the nobility as in the procession itself.

which he Receyved glad and fayne
to beare yt afore hyr in London
he thanked god & his good quene
that theare hys Dutye myght be seene
yt pleased hyr heighnes to esteme
of hym hyr maior in London

The aldermen in skarlet Red
in gravest sorte that maye be sayd
most Readye were wythe handes bespred
to welcome hyr grace to London
So weare the Judges and mene of Lawe
and studentes of the same I sawe
in order stood wythe Reverent awe
To welcome theyr quene to London
sayng all god save owre Royall Quene &c,

The worthye companyes one by one
Stood in theyr lyveryes everychone
in order as she past alonge
throughe fleetstrete fayer in London
the Draperes fyrst this present yeere
the merceres to theym verey neare
and groceres next theym Dyd appeare
as order ys in London
they crave of god to save theyr Queene,/ &c

f. 24v] To Longe to shewe yowe all the Rest
threescore in nommber be exprest
whyche god most bountyfullye hathe blest
all memberes good of London
all thies Dyd stand in order grave
in fayre Ryche furres and sylkes so brave
And stages for the nonce they have
to Receyve the prynce in London
and humbly they salute the Quene &c/

These companyes all, fayre banneres have
wherin theyr armes are sett out brave
set over theyr heades in wynde to wave
a sumptuous shewe in London

wythe Wyslers[91] in velvets fayre
and chaynes of gold whiche they do weare
in Rychelye sorte theyr orderes are
to Receyve the queene in London
and humbly they salute the Quene &c

Throughe [f]leetstrete as the queene past by
on bulkes belowe and wyndowes hye
Alonge the streetes Dyd thowsandes crye
Welcom sweet Queene to london
She gave theym pryncely thankes apace
to everye companye in suche place
I thanke yowe all styll sayd hyr grace
my subjectes good in London
So gracyous was owre sovereigne quene &c

f. 25] they songe and played wythe musyke sweete
in sundrye places in the streete
on Dyverse Instrumentes they thought meete
To Delyght the Quene in London
and all the penthowses covered weare
wyth carpettes Ryche and coverynges fayre
of Dyveres workes of cunnyng Rare
greate pleyntye were in London
and all to welcome owre good Queene.

Foorth on to Ludgate, she Dyd passe
wheare that hyr famous pycture was
So lyvelye made, as in a glasse
for hyr to see in London
kynge Lud wythe hys two sones also[92]
were there set up in syght to showe
The gate newe made awhyle agoe
at the Cytyzens charge of London
and all for the sake of theyr good queene &c/

91. The *OED* defines "wisseler" as a money changer or retailer (last citation, 1573).

92. Ludgate had been rebuilt in 1586; its architecture included statues of the legendary King Lud with his two sons and of the Queen. Ben Weinreb and Christopher Hibbert, eds., *The London Encyclopedia* (London: Macmillan, 1993), 501.

from ludgate, foorth she past a longe
to pawles church yeard wheare people thronge
and there alighted theym amonge
by west of paules in London
where the byshope and the Deane Dyd staye
and fi[f]tye clergye menne they saye
hyr heighnes kneelled there to praye
in paules churchyeard in London
Thys Dyd owre sacred sovereigne queene &c

These ~~chergye~~ clergye mene that Joyfull daye
dyd synge the letynye all the waye
up to the quyere, and there Dyd staye
in sancte paules churche in london
f. 25v] Then followed hyr heighnes to the Quyere
the solempe servyce for to heare
a heavenlye armonye to the eare
was songe in paules in London
To welcomme there theyr sovereigne queene/

Then Drue she neare the preachyng place
to a newe made wyndowe for hyr grace
dyrectlye agenst the precheres face
at paules crosse then in London
doctor pearce hys name was so
a grave Devyne he was I knowe
and byshoppe of Salesburye too I trowe
they sayd so there in london
he precht before owre sovereigne quene &c

And when he hade the Sermon Done
and psalmes Ryght solemply were songe
hyr heighnes shewd hyr selff amonge
hyr people th[e]re of London
and lovyngly to theym she spake
hyr hand att theym she oft dyd shake
Longe lyve she Queene for chrystes his sake
of England and of London
Oh god do graunt to owre good queene[93]

93. The scribe has left enough space for five or six more lines at bottom of this page.

f. 26] hyr grace went throwe the Churche agayne
awayghted on wythe noble menne
To the byshops palace went she then
To Dyne that Daye in London
My lord was glade I do well knowe
hyr heighnes Deynd to honor hym so
a sumptuous feast he dyd bestowe
to welcom hyr to London
and merye was owre sovereigne queene &c

And when the evenyng tyme was come
and hyr heighnes Readye to Ryde home
The companyes wayted all and some
in [f]lettestrete fayer in London
wythe a thowsand torchys burnyng bryght
To temple barre a Joyfull syght
wheare hyr majestye bade theym good nyght
hyr people all of London
manye good nyghtes have she good queene &c/

The lord maior awaighted styll
So dyd the aldermen wythe good wyll
They sought theyr Dutye to fulfyll
lyke subjectes good of London
at Cowrte gate humblye leve they take
besechyng god for chrystes sake
a longe lyved queene hyr grace to make
in England and in London
then thanked muche owre sovereigne queene
theyr lovyng kyndnes showne and seene
besechyng god to keep frome teene
hyr Realme and Cetye of London

f. 26v] Thus have I made a symple songe
to synge the contrye folke amonge
of all I sawe, as I paste alonge
throughe fleetestreete into London
and yf in ought I do offend
In thys whyche Rudlye I have pend
I gladlye would the same amend
for the Cytyes sake of London

and I wyll praye for my good queene
the godlyest pryncesse to be seene
god blesse hyr and the Realme from teene
To the comfort greate of London
finis Richard pygote

3

Verse and Prose from Other Printed Sources

Like many other collectors in the period, John Hanson drew readily upon printed sources for many entries in his household book. He attached no premium to materials that circulated only in manuscript. In addition to the broadside ballads celebrating victory over the Armada, he copied from at least five other printed sources, including another broadside and four books, only one of which he apparently owned. More than a quarter of the contents, nearly fifteen of the manuscript's fifty folios, can be traced to identifiable prints. These works occur in the following order, with the years indicating the earliest to latest dates of publication from which Hanson's transcription could derive:

f. 22v	*The Apologie or Defence*, 1584
ff. 27–29v	*Preceptes of Cato*, 1553–60
ff. 32–32v	"A Kalendar," c. 1520–57
ff. 47v–49	"An epitaph . . . Earle of Penbroke," 1570
f. 49	John Foxe, *Acts and Monuments*, 1570, 1576
f. 49v	Richard Tottel, *Songs and Sonnets*, 1557+

Clearly, Hanson was not dealing with these works in the order of their publication. The sequence of his transcriptions may indicate nothing more than when he happened upon them in the chronological formation of his household book. For example, Hanson copied verse epitaphs for Sir Henry and Henry Savile on folios 42v–45v. The only other epitaphs in the miscellany are Thomas Churchyard's broadside memorial for the first Earl of Pembroke (ff. 47v–49) and a Latin remembrance of the Emperor Frederick (f. 49). In between, Hanson copied from manuscript sources two poems attributed to Queen Elizabeth and, on folios 46v–47v, the Nativity poem beginning "When Jesus was born in Bethlehem." If he had previous access to the Pembroke poem, he clearly had no interest in grouping it with the Savile epitaphs. Similarly, the three full folios of moral adages taken from the *Preceptes of Cato* follow the second Armada thanksgiving ballad and precede the "byerley bouke" concerning regulations on the Manor of Clifton (ff. 30–31v). These contents appear in random order, apparently as the sources came to hand.

In three instances, however, Hanson may have intentionally positioned the material he copied from printed sources. On the bottom of folio 49 he squeezed in a title and the Latin epigram on the Emperor Frederick (d. 1250), excerpted from John Foxe's *Acts and Monuments*. This eulogistic epitaph appears next to and beneath the subscription to the Pembroke epitaph. Hanson was perhaps merely taking advantage of available space, or he may have associated Frederick's virtues with Pembroke's and decided to place their tributes together. Second, Hanson copied on folio 22v the King of Spain's style—that is, the formal listing of his royal titles. He may have placed it there on purpose, for it falls in between his copies of the two Armada thanksgiving ballads. Hanson generally began copying discrete works on rectos: the Eland feud narratives in verse and prose, the adages from the *Preceptes of Cato*, the "byerley bouke," and the mnemonic saint's day calendar verses all fit this pattern. His most notable exception to this rule occurred on folio 42, where he began his transcription of the verse Decalogue in the space left after the last stanzas of the feud ballad. He apparently ended the first Armada ballad on the recto of folio 22, left folio 22v blank, and continued with the second ballad on the recto of folio 23. To judge from the handwriting, Hanson filled in the intervening empty page with the King of Spain's style at a later date. It is noticeably less regular and more unevenly spaced than that of the adjacent ballads. He perhaps did so in order to savor the contrast between King Philip's hegemony over so many lands and his catastrophic failure to conquer England. Finally, Hanson's copy of "I lothe that I did love" on folio 49v is his next-to-last entry in the manuscript. The rough notes on various properties and their tenants on folio 50 could have been entered much earlier. Lord Vaux's poem may have appealed to the aging Hanson, who was in his early seventies at least when he transcribed the Armada ballads. He copied his text of Vaux's poem from the second or a later edition of Tottel's *Songs and Sonnets*, this being the only poem he took from that collection. It makes a fitting conclusion to the anthology he had compiled from so many sources.[1]

Hanson apparently relied on printed sources for a substantial portion of his household book for several reasons. His overall motive, however, in common with that of so many other collectors who copied from prints, was the creation of a text to his personal taste, needs, and specifications. He clearly valued the broadside ballads but would have had little incentive to transcribe them into his manuscript if he owned them; he probably borrowed them just long enough to copy them. The same is true for the *Preceptes of Cato*, although the abrupt beginning and ending of his transcription suggests that he may have been salvaging a fragmentary or damaged copy of the book. He perhaps owned the book of hours from which he took the mnemonic calendar verses on folio 32r–v, copying them out to have their record of saint's days readily to hand, along with the "byerley bouke" (ff. 30–31v), for reference in drawing up legal documents. He certainly owned the first volume of Foxe's *Acts and Monuments* from which he copied the epigram on Emperor Frederick (f. 49), apparently to complement the praise of another great man, the Earl of Pembroke, in the preceding poem. Again, the emphasis is on the text, the contours of the collection, and the preservation of all kinds of material that the compiler found interesting, valuable, or useful.

Titles of King Philip II of Spain

This text of the King of Spain's style was copied from the second English edition of *The Apologie or Defence, of the Most Noble Prince William, by the*

1. This poem is also found in the miscellany of another Yorkshire compiler, Richard Shanne (BL Add. MS 38599, f. 134v) in a section of the manuscript headed "Certaine pretie songes hereafter followinge drawn together by Richard Shanne 1611" (f. 133).

grace of God, Prince of Orange (London, 1584).[2] Hanson omitted a line after "marques," easily attributable to eye skip in any of the three printed copies of the work. However, in the 1584 imprint, the ascender of the *t* in "Zutphen" is almost entirely missing above the crossbar, making it look like an *r*. This explains Hanson's error, "Zurphen," thus identifying his copy text. The Spanish king's style was a fairly popular text for anthologists. Versions of it are found, for example, in Bodleian, MS Eng. Misc. e.859, f. 53v, and Huntington Library, MS EL 6162, f. 31a verso. Both are early seventeenth-century transcripts.

Beyond his unintentional errors of transcription, Hanson seems to have altered the text in a way that reveals his religious orientation. He faithfully copied the edict's title to the point where it describes William of Orange as "the cheif captayn." Thereafter, the printed text in all three imprints reads "and disturber," which is left out of the manuscript. Hanson continued with "of the state of chrystendome & specyally of these low contryes" but then omitted the proclamation's offer (set forth in the collations) of a reward for anyone who will assassinate the prince as a public enemy (sig. P3). Hanson's refusal to indict the Prince of Orange is further evidence of his commitment to the cause of Protestantism. He did not bother, however, to copy from the tract William of Orange's competing style (sig. B2), which overlaps with Philip's in claiming sovereignty over Holland, Zeeland, and Utrecht.

f. 22v] A proclamatcion & an edyct in forme of a
proscripcyon made by the majestie of the kynge owre
Lorde agenst william of Nassau prynce of
Orange, as the cheif captayn of the state of
Chrystendome & specyally of these low contryes
bygynyng thus

Philip by the grace of god king of Castyle
leon of Arragon of navare of naples of
Cicilie of maleorcha of Sardina of the
Isles of the ~~land~~ Indes and the fyrme land
of the occyon sea, archeduke of austr[i]che
Duke of burgndye of lothyer of brabant of

2. This was the second edition of the work (*STC* 15209), an English translation by Hubert Languet of the original Dutch tract. Its title page imprint, Delft, 1581, disguised its English origins. The first edition and its reissue with canceled title page were printed in 1581 (*STC* 15207.5, 15208).

lemburge of luxenbourg, of Gylderland & of
mylan County of hasburghe of Flaunders
of arthoys of Burgndye palatyne both of
haynolt of holland of zeland of namure
and of zurphen prince of Suave marques
of the Cetye Townes and cuntrey of utrych
of veryssell Gronninge and governore
in asia and affryke to all those that
shall see thies presentes gretynge &c.

Textual Analysis

Hanson's variants from the three printed versions of the text are listed below:

4 captayn] captain and disturber; 5 contryes] countries, by which every one is authorised, to hurt him and to kill him, as a publique plague, with a rewarde to him that shall doe it, and shall bee assisting and ayding thereunto; 6] *om.*; 8 leon] of Leon; 14 mylan . . . hasburghe] Millan . . . Habsbourg; 17 zurphen] Zutphen; Suave marques] Swave, Marques of the holy Empire, Lorde of Friseland, of Salines, of Malines; 19 Gronninge] and Groninge; 21 presentes] present writinges.

Preceptes of Cato

On folios 27–29v Hanson copied moral adages in eighty-six couplets taken from the *Preceptes of Cato, with annotacions of D. Erasmus*, a work that saw at least five editions between 1545 and 1560.[3] From the variant readings between the editions of 1553 and 1560 we conclude that Hanson was most likely to have copied from the latter of the two.[4] In addition to Cato, the

3. These are *STC* 4853.5 (1545), 4853.7 (1550), 4854 (1553), 4857 (1560). We have not seen the edition of 1545 but assume it closely resembles the next edition of 1550, the readings of which vary widely from Hanson's. Variant readings in the editions of 1553 and 1560 are markedly closer to Hanson's versions.

4. In number 19, line 1, where 1553 reads "his harte," Hanson and 1560 read "hys arte." While 1553 reads "slacking" and 1560 reads "flacking," Hanson transcribes the word as "flocckyng" in number 20, line 2. In number 70, line 2 the manuscript and 1560 have "at an other mans," while 1563 has "to anothers mannes." Finally, Hanson's "expectable" in number 71, line 2 probably derives from 1560's "exceptable" rather than 1553's "acceptable."

work includes precepts translated from "the seven wysemen of Grece," followed by "Wyse sayinges and pretye tauntes of Publius" (S1v–2).[5] The translator was Robert Burrant, who had previously brought out an edition of Sir David Lindsay's *Tragical death of David Beaton* (c. 1548), rendered from Scots into English.[6] Hanson began copying on signature S4v more than halfway into the *Preceptes*, in the last section of the book, the "Sayings of Publius" (Publilius Syrus). With a few exceptions, Hanson transcribed the majority of the verses over the next thirty-eight pages, skipping over some of the items either by mistake or because they didn't interest him.[7] The topics covered include covetousness (nos. 4, 8, 10, 12, 13, 79, 80), death (nos. 23, 24, 49, 57, 71), love (nos. 6, 9, 15, 26), old age (nos. 11, 15, 16, 85), friendship (nos. 18, 29, 67), women (nos. 2, 7, 26, 66), giving and generosity (nos. 14, 21, 25, 30, 44), poverty and social abjection (nos. 3, 36), and good name and reputation (nos. 31, 37). These are all treated from the point of view of the educated mature man and obviously appealed to the aging compiler. Hanson apparently tired of the task and wrote "finis" after reaching signature Y8v, more than fifty pages short of the end.[8] These entries are typical of the widespread Renaissance interest in "wisdom literature" and more particularly of the appetite for moral adages made memorable by being set forth in verse. Thousands of these tags occur in both print and manuscript. William Baldwin's *Treatise of Moral Philosophy* was one of the most popular of such collections, a mixture of the supposed sayings in prose and verse of pagan philosophers that saw more than twenty-two editions between 1547 and 1651. Hundreds of its verse aphorisms were selectively copied into contemporary manuscript miscellanies.[9]

5. The poetic maxims and sententiae of Publilius Syrus, a first-century freed Roman slave, were well known from ancient times up through the sixteenth century.

6. J. K. McGinley, "Burrant, Robert," *ODNB*, http://www.oxforddnb.com/view/article/4097.

7. He omitted four verses on signatures S5v–S6 and T7v–T8, perhaps because he turned two pages together as he proceeded through the printed book.

8. The selections begin out of order with couplets taken, respectively, from signatures S5 and S4v, then follow the order of the 1560 edition after this. Each of the verses in the printed book is embedded in a prose discussion that Hanson omits.

9. On this and other related practices, see Mary Thomas Crane, *Framing Authority: Sayings, Self, and Society in Sixteenth-Century England* (Princeton, NJ: Princeton University Press, 1993). Conventional wisdom is also to be found in the thousands of proverbs from the period: see Morris Palmer Tilley, *A Dictionary of the Proverbs in England in the Sixteenth and Seventeenth Centuries* (Ann Arbor: University of Michigan Press, 1950).

For clarity of presentation, especially since there are five instances in which Hanson transcribes couplets as a single line, we number and separate the eighty-six items he recorded.

f. 27] [1] Love thy father beynge gentyll and kynd
yf he be not so, obey wythe harte and mynde

[2] Extreme ys the love or thatrad° of a woman °*the hatred*
A thyrd thynge to be a meane to fynd no man cane

[3] They that be in povertye and myserye
be always suspectyd of Inyquytye

[4] The Covetous person that ys alwayes nedye
To hym self ^ys^ cause of hys own myserye

[5] yf anye thynge chaunce otherwyse then well
everye manne ys Redye the same for to tell

[6] Love cannot be sodenlye put awaye
But by lytyle and lytyll yt maye decaye

[7] Onelye a good woman thowe mayest knowe
when she openlye pleyethe the shrewe

[8] Thowe mayest sone perceyve a person averycious
yf thowe thy selff be not coveytous

[9] To be wyse and also to love/
ys scant gyven to ^the^ god above/[10]

[10] A covetous person Dothe no thyng well
untyll he passe eyther to heaven or hell

[11] Age beyng hyd neverso priviye/
yet at lenght yt dothe yt self Dyscrye

[12] A covetous manne yf he lose anye thyng
Dothe more styrre then one that hathe understandyng

[13] To the coveytous manne What ~~Doest~~ ^ woldest^ thou dyssyer
but onelye that he myght be a long lyver[11]

10. Hanson mistakenly placed "the" in this line before "to." For this proverb, see Tilley, *Dictionary of the Proverbs in England*, no. L558 ("It is impossible to Love and be wise").

11. Another pen has added at the bottom of the page a wavy vertical line ending in a squiggle.

f. 27v] [14] We Delyte beste wythe that that ys otheres
and that pleasyth theym, the whiche are owres

[15] for a yonge mane to Love ys pleasure & pastyme
And for an olde mane yt ys afoule faute & cryme

[16] An olde woman when she Dothe leape & dance
Unto Deathe she makythe myrthe & Dalyance

[17] he dothe soonne hym self Repente
which gyvethe quycke and lyght Judgement,

[18] prosperytye dothe get unto the° afrende °*thee*
and adversytye tryeth who ys unkynde

[19] The dysser° in hys arte howe muche he ys the conninger °*dicer*
In hys Demeaner so muche he ys the lewder

[20] abowe ys Dystroyed wythe overmuche bendyng
and ^so^ a manes Mynd wythe over muche flocckyng[12]

[21] That thyng ys twys welcomme in Dede
whiche ys voluntaryelye proferred in tyme of nede

[22] There commeth to no mane so good an howre
but yt ys to one or other cause of Doloure,

[23] That kynd of Deathe ys Doubled
whyche by an other ys adjudged/[13]

[24] That deathe ys good & to be wyshed
By the whiche all evyll ys extynguyshed

[25] he doth Recyve a good turne by gyvyng
Whiche Dothe bestowe yt upon Dyservyng

[26] The love of a woman ys sweete and pleasant
wone wythe fayere meanes & not by constraynt

f. 28] [27] A good dysposed mynde dothe never hym self gyve
To theyr servyce that in synne dothe lyve

12. The *OED* defines "flock" (v.) as "treat with contempt, set at naught; [less plausibly] to congregate, troop in great numbers."

13. In the left margin opposite lines 44–46 another hand has written "my i."

[28] To have done a good turṅe he that hym self Reporteth
The same to be done agayne he shamfullye asketh

[29] There ys the nearest and grettest kynred
wheare two faythfull myndes are cowpled[14]

[30] oftentymes to gyve abenefyte < >
ys to teache howe the same to Requyte

[31] A good name to amane ys more sure
Then anye worldlye Ryches or treasure[15]

[32] goodnes although yt be for the tyme suppressed
yet yt ys not for ever extynguysshed,

[33] he hathe a Double vyctorye
Who overcommeth hym selff & his enmye

[34] he ys twyse slayne and murthered
whiche wythe hys own weapen ys kylled

[35] he slepeth quyetlye and at Reste
who feleth not how yll ys hys neste

[36] It ys to good menne a greate dyshonestye
To se an honest manne lyve in myserye

[37] a good name although yt be unknown & in darkenes
yet yt kepeth styll [h]ys owne clere light & brightnes

[38] good thoughtes yf they fall owt of memorye
yet they peryshe [not] nor utterlye Dye

[39] he well and wyslye leasyth his money
when he gyveyt° to the Judge beyng gyltye °*give it*

[40] Good menne he dothe bothe hurte & greve
who so ever doth yll mene pardon and forgyve

[41] next to the vertue of Justice and equytye
[Is cruel dealing and severitie][16]

14. This is a version of the definition of friendship as "one soul in bodies twain."

15. Cf. Tilley, *Dictionary of the Proverbs in England*, no. N22.

16. Hanson mistakenly skips over the second line of this couplet.

[42] a good mans anger and furye a man maye sonne aleye &
pacyfye[17]

f. 28v] [43] That ys an honest and good shame
That sheweth us to avoyd blame

[44] for a manne to have mercye and petye
ys to hym self a good helpe & Remedye

[45] Suche thynges as menne have by theym daylye
be lytle estemyd & lytle set by

[46] yt ys cownted for verey crueltye
to chyde a manne in adversytye

[47] To whom thou hast ever gyven & doest hym nowe denye
Thowe commandest hym to take from the° vyolentlye °*thee*

[48] The pacyentes yll dyet & intemperancye
make the physicyon to handle hym more ungentlye

[49] his lyfe to hys frendes ys odyous, who of his death ys dessyrous

[50] The mane commeth the soner <to>into an hassard
When of the same he hathe no Regard

[51] of hyr husband a chast wyfe & contynent
dothe opteyn hyr purpose beyng obedyent

[52] a prowde mans pompe and glorye
ys sone turned into shame and Ignomye

[53] Thow shalt more wyne by good councellyng
then thowe shalt by brablyng & chydyng

[54] Sufferance and pacyence, ys to everye greyf a defence

[55] a merye companyon that can talke and clatter,
upon the heigh waye ys in steed of a horslytter

[56] The welfare of a wyckyd person, sone commeth to confusyon

17. Hanson transcribes this couplet as a single line, perhaps because he has reached the bottom of his folio page. He also does this for items 49, 54, 56, and 67.

[57] he to lyfe leyeth sawte° and blame °*assault*
whiche by death wold be Ryd of the same

[58] he that above the lawe hathe myght
wyll borowe a lytle more then Ryght

f. 29] [59] The daye that commeth next after,
ys to the day before a scholer

[60] To chyde a man when he ys in adversytye
ys to hurt hym when he had nede of Remedye

[61] Battell ys to be prepared lesurly
that thou mayest the soner overcom thine enymmye

[62] To call a man a churle who so dothe enterpryse° °*undertake*
dothe call hym all the evyll wordes that he can Devyse

[63] Do not speke evyll of thyn enimye/
howe so ever thowe thynkest of hym pryvelye

[64] upon thynges profytable take good advysement
leasure and Respecte are the best assurement

[65] Greyfe and sorowe dothe then cease
when thowe doest no thyng theym to encrease

[66] I had as leave thow toldest me a verey leasyng°[18] °*lie*
as to saye that a woman shall forgeyt her wepyng

[67] By debate & stryvyng frendshipp ys made more Lovynge

[68] upon that thyng take thou Respyte and laysure
whiche yf thow once promyse must ever endure

[69] The strenght and manhood of the soldier
ys the good councell of hys captain & governer

[70] a man ought to be hard of hearyng
onelye at an other mans compleynyng

[71] when owre mynde ys most Delectable° °*pleasant, delightful*
Then the state of Death ys most expectable

18. There is a manicule in the left margin next to this line.

[72] Feare least what to the° ys gyven thys Daye °*thee*
an other Daye wyll com and take yt awaye

[73] That whiche wythowt knowledge ys Demynyshed
ys for no losse to be suspectyd

f. 29v] [74] A verey Innocent beyng in torment and payne
ys constrayned to Lye and fayne

[75] In verey syne and naughtynes
yt ys mete to performe faythfulnes

[76] In that mane ys wysdome & happynes
whyche [h]ys owne fawt by an otheres can Redresse

[77] mene in myserye are of wytt verey scante
and of the same they are also abundant

[78] What a manne knoweth and hathe in memorye
The same to forgett ys somtyme necessarye

[79] Dyssyer of Lucre & verey° covetousnes °*true, absolute*
made fortun an heavenlye [G]oddesse[19]

[80] he that dothe covetousnes avoyde and flee
conquerethe a whole contrye

[81] he that hathe no howse wherin to put his head
ys as one wythowt a [grave][20] when he ys Deade

[82] Even they that do wronge and Injurye
do hate the same in an other extremelye

[83] A mane hys own contrye for to denye
ys asmuche as to suffer bannyshement wyllyngly

[84] Even one verey Smale hare,
hys shadowe with hym dothe beare

[85] Alas yt ys a verey wretchyd <syn> thyng
To Wax elder by feare and tremblyng

19. Hanson wrote "Doddesse."

20. Hanson left out the word "grave" (found in the printed text).

[86] A mysfortun dothe hurt theym verey lyghtlye
Whiche be promoted to heighe dygnytye/ finis

Calendar Verses from the *Primer*

These crude verses, adapted from a French original, appeared in at least thirty-three editions of the *Primer* of Salisbury Use (Use of Sarum) published between about 1520 and 1557.[21] The mnemonic purpose of these lines was to identify the saint's days ("holy dayes") in each month (but not "the days in every monthe" as Hanson states in his title). The printed texts divide the lines into syllables separated by periods. By counting these units to the point where the saint or feast is named, the reader could determine on what day of that month a saint's feast was celebrated.[22] As Curt Bühler notes, however, even the printed English texts failed to mark these conjunctions precisely. In January, for instance, "Paule" is the twenty-fourth syllable in the stanza, although the Feast of the Conversion of St. Paul falls on 25 January. Hanson either didn't understand or chose not to record this system. He retained most of the periods between words and syllables through the first two stanzas but thereafter ignored most of the punctuation in his copy. As all the editions that include this poem were set by compositors in France, it is not surprising that the text degenerated rapidly, yet we have not located overlapping errors with Hanson's version that would confirm any one of them as his certain source.[23] At line 3, for example, Hanson's implausible "grave. any good. wyne" is corrected in all the printed versions we have checked with "graffe [graft].ony.good.vyne." Elsewhere, the prints commit errors not found in Hanson's version. At line 44, editions of 1527, 1528, 1531, and c. 1533 read "and.sat.an" (sat. An in c. 1533), corrected by Hanson to "sant.anne." At line 23, editions of c. 1533, 1537, 1555, and 1556 read "tought.it" for Hanson's "thought yt."

21. TP 310 in William A. Ringler, Jr., ed., *Bibliography and Index of English Verse Printed 1476–1558* (London: Mansell Publishing, 1988).

22. Curt F. Bühler, "At Thy Golg First eut of the hous vlysse the saynge thus," *Studies in the Renaissance* 6 (1959): 230.

23. We have collated the manuscript version against the versions found in eight editions of the *Primer*: *STC* 15955 (1527), 15958 (1528), 15974 (1531), 15983 (1533?), 15995 (1537), 16055 (1551), 16068 (1555), and 16076 (1556).

Where Hanson wrote "Gregory" in line 10, editions of 1551, 1555, and 1556 read merely "go.ry." It could be argued that these and many other errors in the prints are obvious enough for Hanson to have corrected independently, but it is also possible that he copied from a lost edition or one we have not checked.

The inclusion of this poem in Hanson's anthology probably reflects less his religious devotion than his involvement with legal records. These regularly designate dates with reference to saint's days and feasts. Indeed, the four terms of the central courts at Westminster were named for just such festivals: Hilary, the winter term, after the feast of St. Hilary on 13 January, for instance, and Michaelmas, the fall term, after the feast of St. Michael, Archangel, on 29 September. Official accounts usually recorded entries between one feast day and another, while legal agreements of all kinds dated specific events with reference to saint's days and feasts. Several obligations in the "byerley bouke" are scheduled for the feasts of St. Michael Archangel and the Annunciation of the Virgin Mary (ff. 30, 30v). In 1562 Hanson witnessed an indenture between two of his neighbors that specified annual payments "of tenne shillynges in the Feastes of penticost and Sanct Martyn in wynter by evyn porc[i]ons."[24] This "Kalendar" poem and the "byerley bouke" that immediately precedes it in the manuscript were therefore useful aids in Hanson's work as law clerk and scrivener.

f. 32] *A Kalendar wherbye a manne may ķnowe the days in every monthe aswell holy dayes as otheres*

Januarye
Circumstantly thre. kynges.cam. by.nyght[25]
by.an hie.hill.or day light.
and thowe.wyll.grave.any.good.Wyne.
paule.call.for.thomas.alquyne.

February
Bride.mary.gil bert.har.de ly.
all.thy.frendes.standynge.the.by.
and pray wyth the to dyne.
peter ma.thi.and au.styne

24. WYAS, Calderdale, KM 256.

25. The periods between words in Hanson's text reflect a feature of the text printed in France.

Marche
david.of.wales.loveth.well.leekes
that will.make Gregory.leane cheekes
yf Edward.Do eate some wyth them
mary.sende hym to bedlem° °*Bethlehem*

Aprill
In aprill ambrose ys fayne
To se us washed wyth Rayne
oswold.furth.wyth sent victore
with George & marke to do so no more

May
James toke crosewasteres John to kyll
Nicholas.sayd do hym none yll
But wyth that came fayre helayne
and.Frances to depart theym twayne

June
In June Erasmus Dyd thynke
for to gyve barnaby drynke.
But then Botulph thought yt meter° °*more fitting, appropriate*
that John should Drynke.before peter

f. 32v] July
When mary visited Thomas
The freers° let theyr dogs owt passe °*friars*
then came forth mary magdalayn
James and marth and other twayne

August
Peter called for Jesu
and bad laurence to say true
Mary seeynge all theyr Debate
made Barthilmewe to breake Johns pate

September
Giles was cut to hys losse
mary sayd nay by thys crosse
for Edyth saw how that mathewe
dyd beate fir myn° cosine Mygh.ewe° °*Ferminius . . . Michael*

October
Full Lyght was Frances fayth at Rome
Denys could not Edwar over come

Tyll luke with a leven thow sand
made Crispyn & Symon to stande

November
Saintes soules in heaven bene sicker° °*secure, safe*
as sayeth martyn Bric.er° °*Bricius*
Record hugh & besse that tell can
Clement kathryn and sant.anne/

December
Loy was barbar to Nicol
mary pray thow for lucyes soule
and for grace pray good Thomas Inde
To chryst Stevyn John tho be kynde

Epitaph for the Earl of Pembroke

William Herbert, first Earl of Pembroke, who died in 1570, was a major power player from the late Henrician through the early Elizabethan periods. John Aubrey's colorful (but not especially accurate) biography of him calls him "a mad fighting . . . fellow" who killed one of the sheriffs of Bristol, fled to France, distinguished himself as a soldier and "was favoured by [Francis I] the king, who afterwards recommended him to Henry the VIII, who much valued him, and heaped favours and honours upon him." After the dissolution of the abbeys, Henry gave him the abbey of Wilton, which became the family's treasured Wiltshire estate. He married Anne Parr, Queen Katharine Parr's sister, and "was made Privy Councellor and conservator of King Henry the Eight's will."[26]

The history of Pembroke's involvement in national and international affairs is a complex one, highlighting his political and military skills and daring. Having served as executor of Henry VIII's will, he subsequently served as a member of Edward VI's council of regency, supporting Edward Seymour, Duke of Somerset, and taking responsibility for suppressing rebellions against the regime in Wiltshire and elsewhere. When Somerset was suffering greatly in popularity and under attack by political rivals, however, he withheld his military support and facilitated the

26. Aubrey, *"Brief Lives," chiefly of Contemporaries, set down by John Aubrey, between the Years 1669 & 1696*, ed. Andrew Clark, 2 vols. (Oxford: Clarendon Press, 1898), 1:314–15.

Protector's overthrow, aligning himself with the man who replaced Somerset, John Dudley, Earl of Warwick. Steadily amassing wealth, lands, and political authority and power in Wales, Wiltshire, and elsewhere, he was made Earl of Pembroke in 1551. Though he had supported plans to make Lady Jane Grey, rather than Mary Tudor, the next monarch, he reversed himself when support for Mary grew, helping her become queen. His loyalty to Mary was demonstrated in his leading role in suppressing Wyatt's Rebellion, and the queen restored him to his position as president of the Council of the Marches in Wales, from which he had been removed. He politically and militarily supported the queen's spouse, Philip II, favoring his involvement in English governance and assisting his army in northern France. When Mary died, however, he was part of the first Privy Council of Elizabeth's reign and bore the sword before the Queen in her entry into London in 1558. He supported William Cecil in the secretary's efforts to intervene militarily in Scotland and to oppose the Queen's marrying Robert Dudley, later Earl of Leicester, whose political faction he nonetheless later joined. Having become lord steward of the royal household in 1568, he supported the proposed marriage of Mary, Queen of Scots to Thomas Howard, Duke of Norfolk and suffered the Queen's displeasure and a period of temporary exile from court. He then dissociated himself from the leaders of the Northern Rebellion, the earls of Northumberland and Westmoreland, who had claimed his support, heading a military force to defend the Queen at Windsor. He died at Hampton Court in 1570.[27]

Pembroke's second marriage involved connections with south Yorkshire. Beginning in 1552, Pembroke had created a bond with the family of the most influential noblemen of that district, the Earls of Shrewsbury, by taking for his second wife Anne Talbot, daughter of George, fourth Earl of Shrewsbury. Thereafter, Pembroke's daughter and his son and heir also married into this family. Pembroke's presence in John Hanson's neighborhood through these marriages with the Talbots perhaps made this epitaph sufficiently interesting for copying into the miscellany. Hanson, of course, would have been aware of Pembroke's long and nationally visible public career, which the printed epitaph celebrates.

The poem, by Thomas Churchyard, had been entered in the Stationers' Register on 27 March 1570, ten days after Pembroke's death, and was issued

27. For these summary details of Pembroke's life, we draw upon Narasignha P. Sil's biography in the *ODNB*, www.oxford.dnb.com/view/13055.

as a black-letter broadside (*STC* 5227). With the Armada thanksgiving ballads, this text illustrates how readily London print culture infiltrated the hinterlands. The elegy concludes with a couplet entitled "A verse of farwell" in Roman type, the whole being subscribed "Quoth Churchyard." Why Hanson attributed this couplet to the Queen is a mystery, for there is no reason to suppose she had anything to do with its composition. Perhaps he felt it important to emphasize how great a loss to the Queen had been the death of this loyal royal servant. The poem not only makes the expected gestures of general praise of the departed nobleman as a loyal, courteous, and generous person and reminds the reader of the impermanence of worldly achievements and status but also particularly calls attention to the earl's place on the Queen's "councell" (l. 37), the military reputation of "manlye pembroke" (l. 73) as an English "hector" (l. 48), and his fondness for rich display ("clenely fynenesse trymly framed," l. 77). Though Aubrey's assertion that Pembroke could neither read nor write might be inaccurate, the poem concedes that "he no scole poynt knew" (l. 58). Of course, the poem is silent about his fierce temper, his political side-switching, and his unrestrained pursuit of wealth, property, and power. Whatever his virtues and vices, Pembroke was a major power player under four monarchs, involved in the processes of royal succession, instrumental in suppressing rebellions and insurrections, involved in foreign military adventures, and at the center of a governing political elite for decades. Even in the late 1580s, when John Hanson probably transcribed Churchyard's epitaph for him, placing it on folio 47v after the Armada ballads and Hanson's copy of the King of Spain's style, the earl still loomed large both in national and in west Yorkshire historical memory.

Hanson's relatives, the Saviles, had also allied themselves with the Talbots. No later than 1581, George Savile, son and heir of Henry Savile (d. 1569, eulogized in the verse epitaph on ff. 44–45v), had married Lady Mary Talbot, daughter of George, sixth Earl of Shrewsbury.[28] The match is mentioned in a curious verse elegy for Henry Savile in the younger John Hanson's heraldic manuscript (unfoliated; c. ff. 130v–31). The poet,

28. Although the marriage has been dated to 1583, before the birth of the Saviles' son and heir—P. W. Hasler, *The House of Commons 1558–1603*, 3 vols. (London: History of Parliament Trust, 1981), 3:348—an acrostic poem addressed to "Ladi Mari Savile" in Thomas Howell's *Devises* (sig. K1v) shows that the marriage had taken place by the time of its publication in 1581. Howell was a retainer of Henry, second Earl of Pembroke and his countess, Mary, née Sidney.

Gabriel Savile, writes that Henry's "sonne & heire / he linckt with noble Lyne, & doughter grave / of the triumphant Talbot virgin faire." As this marriage occurred more than a decade after Henry's death in 1569, the elegy is clearly retrospective and, in its poetic high style, quite similar to Churchyard's elegy for Pembroke. In his poetic preface, Gabriel even invokes Churchyard: "Helpe Chaucer Gower Lidgate yowe bring Churchyeards statlie stil[e] / that drew the dreadefull dragons death to waile with us a while." This refers to the Pembroke crest, a wyvern vert (green dragon), and thus alludes to the same broadside elegy copied by Hanson.[29]

f. 47v] *An epitaph of the honorable Earle of penbroke*
baron of cardyf and knyght of the most noble order
of the garter who Dyed Lord Stuard of the quenes
majestie's howshold and the privy councell and so dyed

Synce playntes wantes wantes [*sic*] powere to pearce the skyes
or Rayse the Deade from grave
no teares nor syghes may well suffice
To wayle the Losse we have

Then Lordynges wype yowre blobered eien° °*eyes*
and sighe no more alas
for Deathe and Destanye dothe assigne
the lyfe lyke shade shall passe

No seate nor septer certan ys
the hye and Lowe allyke
In spyte of pompe and wordly° blysse °*worldly*
fall bothe amyd the Dyke° °*ditch*

f. 48] But whan a proppe that stayed the state
Drope down as yowe maye see
the lokeres on in masze do stand
at crake° of suche a tre °*breaking, fracturing*

Which leaves the world in mournyng woo
byhynd to wayle the Losse
whyle frute ys flede from brannce & bowe
as golde forsakes the Drosse

29. WYAS, Calderdale, SPC 118. Terming the dragon (and therefore the poem's honoree) "dreadful" alliterates the line rather ineptly but in agreement with the poem's many other infelicities.

O penbroke wylt thou parte so sone
what hast hath hadde the° hence *°haste . . . thee*
had I bene warned I hade perfumed
Thy Tombe wythe frankensence

but called so swyftlye to my penne
The swete Incence I wante
Yet sweare I by the sacred godes
Thoughe skylle and sence be skant

Tho[u] shallt not have in cottes of clay
thy Ryche Rare gyftes of kynde
nor scraplynge° wormes, shall make theyr pray *°scraping*
upon thy noble mynde

The Cowrte that knewe thy constant harte
bydes the° Retorne agayn *°bids thee*
that arte for trouth & frendshipe fast
a perfecte patern playn

A father wheare the councell sate
of tonge and ta[l]ke Devyne
As he at byrth hade stollen the grace
of all the muses nyene

his lookes Dyd speake when sylent lyppes
lokt up great thynges in head
yea everye word past penbrokes mouth
peazed° well a pound of lead *°weighed*

f. 48v] [No l]ightnes Lodged in his brayne
but suer a manne in dede
that well myght Ryse from trojanes Rase
and honor hector his sede

of Nature noble voyd of blotte
in Cowrte and contrye throwe
as curteys as the lytyll lambe
or falcon gentyll nowe

In bounty Dyd his harte abound
Wheare cause made place before
not wone by feare but held by love
what myght be wyshed more

To suche as favored learnynges Lore
Thoughe he no scole poynt knewe
his purse and hande as closlye crept
as hawke weare clapt in mue° *°cooped up in a cage*

To those that semed somwhat to be
whose hertes he sawe aspire
he gave good hope in sygne of happe
To further theyr Dyssyer,

To prynce and contrye true as stele
no blaste cowld beare hym Downe
he kept his promesse faythe & othe
in Cowrt in feild and towne

Devout to god his lyfe well shewes
his Death Dothe that declare
one° chryste alone the cornerstone *°on*
he onely layeth his care

O manlye penbroke yet me thynkes
I se the marche upryght
Thy Jesture & thy jolly porte
stand styll before my syght

f. 49] Thy clenelye fynenesse trymly framed
Sprange owt of noble breste
And all thow dydest wythin thy Dayes
A noble mynde exprest

But nothyng here so trym or gaye
can kepe thy lyfe alive
bothe welthe and Lordshyppe~~s~~ leapes away
Whan Deathe owre dat dothe Dryve° *°date [of death] doth impel, force*

yet Deathe whan he had done hys worst
Dare not molest the spiryte
whiche god doth claym and angeles thynke
for abrahames bosome mete/

A Verse of farwell
I Lost a losse, yowe Lost no lesse
Who least lost, lost to muche

Who lokes to lyght, upon the like
In cowrt shall fynd fewe suche./
finis quod Elizabetha/

Textual Analysis

The printed text of the epitaph comprises some 658 words. Hanson's departures from it show him committing some thirty substantive errors for a factor of error of 4.5 percent, or about one mistake in every three lines. This is quite a high rate of error, yet Hanson copied nearly twice that many words from the *Preceptes of Cato* with only thirty-seven substantive variants (counting an omitted line as six errors) from the edition of 1560. His factor of error, less than 3 percent, is a bit over half that for Churchyard's elegy. His three errors in the 330 words of Lord Vaux's poem copied from Tottel's *Songes and Sonnets* on folio 49v yield only a .9 percent factor of error. It seems possible at least that Hanson copied the Pembroke elegy from another manuscript rather than directly from the print, and if so this might also explain the interpolated attribution of the last stanza to Queen Elizabeth.

Collation with *STC* 5227: *Title* An] The; and the privy] and of her privie; and so dyed] *om.*; 1 wantes wantes] want; 6 sighe] sob; 8 the] all; 14 Drope . . . maye] dropps . . . do; 15 masse] muse; 17 woo] weeds; 18 wayle] weepe; 19 whyle] Whyles; 22 hadde] hyed; 29 have] hyde; 31 scraplynge . . . theyr] skrawling . . . no; 42 loke] lockt; 45 brayne] browes; 46 but] and; 48 hector his] Hectors; 72 layeth] layd; 76 stand] stands; 81 trym] cleane; 82 thy] the; 85 had] hath; 86 spiryte] spreete; 87 whiche] That; 89 losse] friend; 93 finis qd Elizabetha] Quoth Churchyard

Elegy for the Emperor Frederick II

Hanson copied this epitaph for the Holy Roman Emperor, Frederick II (1194–1250), from the second or a later edition of John Foxe's *Acts and Monuments*, popularly termed the "Book of Martyrs."[30] The title is presumably

30. The verses are found in the editions of 1570 (bk. 4, p. 417), 1576 (bk. 4, p. 320), 1583 (bk. 4, p. 339), and 1596 (bk. 4, p. 287). Our search for this text was greatly facilitated by access to "John Foxe's The Acts and Monuments Online," http://www.johnfoxe.org.

Hanson's own, however, for the printed verses are untitled. Foxe celebrated the emperor as a victim of papal secular ambition and meddling: Frederick was indeed twice excommunicated by Pope Gregory IX and deposed by Pope Innocent IV. In his will of 1599, Hanson left to his grandson Robert Hanson "my first booke or parte of the actes and monumentes of the Church." This was no doubt his source for the epitaph, as Foxe's work was published in two volumes, with book 4 in volume 1. Hanson probably owned either the 1570 or the 1576 edition of the *Acts and Monuments*, in both of which the spelling in line 2 is "virtutum," as it is in the manuscript, changed to "virtutem" in the editions of 1583 and 1596. In addition, given the poem's diminutive italic font in the editions of 1570 and 1576, Hanson might easily have mistaken the *t* in "gratia" for a *c*.

f. 49] fredericus imperator in hoc
epigramma affixit
Si probitas sensus, virtutum gracia census
nobilitas orti possent Resistere morti
non foret extinctus, fredericus qui jacet intus

Lord Vaux's "I lothe that I Dyd love"

"I lothe that I did love," written by Thomas, second Lord Vaux of Harrowden (1509–56),[31] is presented without ascription in the section of poems by "Uncertain auctours" in Tottel's *Songs and Sonnets*, though texts of the lyric are to be found attributed to "lord vaws" in Bodleian Library, Ashmole MS 48 (ff. 23v–24v) and British Library, Harleian MS 1703 (f. 100r–v). Thus Tottel's popular *Miscellany* joins the Armada ballads, the *Preceptes of Cato*, a book of hours, and Foxe's *Acts and Monuments* among the printed works Hanson both had access to and found worthy of copying, in whole or part, into his manuscript.

Vaux's lyric is far more a memento mori than a renunciation of love: its speaker dwells upon the infirmities of old age as "The herbenger of

31. Lord Vaux is credited with a dozen poems in *The Paradise of Dainty Devices*, an anthology that saw nine Elizabethan editions (1576–1600), making it the age's most popular printed anthology of secular verse. While the *Paradise* did not include a text of "I lothe that I did love," the poem was well enough known for Shakespeare to adapt lines 9–12 and 29–32 to be sung by the Gravedigger in *Hamlet* (5.1.71–74, 94–97, 120–21).

Deathe" and concludes by reminding his reader, "so shall ye wast to dust" (ll. 25, 56). As this is the last verse entry in his collection, it seems likely that Hanson transcribed it after 1588 and perhaps not long before his own death in 1599. That would explain, at least, why he singled out this one poem from hundreds more in Tottel's volume for inclusion at the end of his personal household book. He did not select for transcription in his manuscript any of the dozens of love poems from this landmark anthology, perhaps because he was a mature man, who because of his age and the hostility of his generation to amorous lyrics as the "toys" of youth,[32] was uninterested in them, preferring the traditional moral wisdom embodied in Vaux's lyric.

f. 49v] *The aged lover Renounceth Love*[33]

I lothe that I Dyd love/ in youthe that° I thought swete °*that which*
as tyme Requyres for my behove/ me thynkes they are note mete
My lustes° they Do me leave/ my fansyes all be flede °*desires*
and tracte of tyme begynes to weave/ gray heares upon my head
For age wythe stelynge steps,/ hathe clawed me wythe his crouche° °*staff, crutch*
and lustye lyfe awaye she leapes, as there hade bene non suche,
My Muse dothe not delyght/ me as she dyd before
My hande and pen are not in plyght,° as they have bene of yore °*good condition*
For Reason me Denyes, This youthelye Idyle Ryme/
And Daye by Daye to me she cryes, leave of thies toyes in tyme
The wrynkyles in my browe/ the furrows in my face
say lympyng age wyll hedge hym nowe/ wheare youthe must gyv[e] hym place
The herbenger of Deathe/ to me I se hym Ryde
The coughe the colde and gaspynge breath, Doth byde me to provyde
A pike ax and a spade/ and eke a shrowdynge shete
a howse of claye for to be made for suche a gest most mete
me thynkes I heare the clerke that knowlles the carfull knell

32. On this attitude toward erotic poems as a characteristic of an early Elizabethan generation, see Richard Helgerson, *The Elizabethan Prodigals* (Berkeley: University of California Press, 1976).

33. In the left margin opposite the title, Hand D has written "John."

And byds me leave my wofull warke/ eare nature me compell
me° keperes knyt the knot, That youth dyd laugh to s[c]orne °*my*
of me that cleane shalbe forgotte as I hade not bene borne
Thus must I yowthe ~~up~~ gyve up/ whose badge I longe dyd weare
To thym I yelde the wa[n]ton cup/ That better maye yt beare
Lo heare the bared ~~sk~~ scull/ by whose balde signe I knowe
That stoupynge age away shall pull/ whyche youthfull yeirs dyd sowe
For bewtye wythe hyr band/ thes croked cares hath wrought
And shippyd me into the land/ from whence I fyrst was brought
And ye that byde byhynd/ have ye non other trust
as ye of claye weare cast by kynde° so shall ye wast to dust. °*nature*

Textual Analysis

In all, another seven transcribed texts besides that found in the Hanson miscellany are known, counting the incipit for a musical setting in British Library, MS Add. 4900, f. 62v.[34] Hyder E. Rollins collated the Ashmole, Harleian, and MS Add. 38559 versions in his edition of Tottel;[35] a wide range of variant readings emerges between these texts and the print. Hanson's text, however, departs from the printed version in only three substantive readings, and it includes the title found in *Songs and Sonnets*. Hanson no doubt copied from the second (1557) or a later edition of the work, which reads "crouche" at line 10 for the first edition's "cowche."

Collation with Tottel's *Song and Sonnets*, eleven editions, 1557–87: 10 crouche] cowche 1st ed., 1557; crowch 2nd ed., 1557 and all later eds.; 28 and gaspynge] the gasping; 38 me] My; 42 wa[n]ton] wanton

34. British Library, Add. MS 4797, f. 4; Add. MS 38559, ff. 134v–35 (c. 1611); and Add. MS 26737, f. 107v; Gonville and Caius College, Cambridge, MS 218/233, pp. 89–91.

35. Hyder E. Rollins, ed., *Tottel's Miscellany (1557–1587)*, rev. ed., 2 vols. (Cambridge, MA: Harvard University Press, 1965), 2:284.

4

Other Texts from Manuscript Sources

In addition to the Eland-Beaumont feud ballad, several other literary items in the Hanson manuscript appear to have been copied from manuscript sources. These range from two epitaphs for members of the Savile family to two poems attributed to Queen Elizabeth, a verse Decalogue, a Nativity poem, a fragment of a seventeenth-century poem transcribed in available space at the bottom of folio 26v in a hand other than Hanson's, and two short poetic fragments. The last of these are the opening words of two common verse tags, both probably written as pen trials. On folio 26v, the hand we have tentatively identified as that of John Stanhope III has written, "In my beginning god be my speede." Lacking is the concluding line forming the couplet, "In grace and virtue to proceed." This brief prayer probably dates from the late fifteenth century: an early variant of the formula reads, "At my begynnyng Crist me spede / In vertu and lernyng for to spede." In the first half of the sixteenth century we find "At owre beginynnyng God be my spede / Wyth grace and vertue to procede." One Ambrose Corbet of Shropshire changed "grace and virtue" to "grace and fortune" and used the couplet to personalize his entry in the national lottery of 1567–68.[1] The verse circulated widely in manuscript throughout England, and many other variations could be cited. On the manuscript's inside back cover, hand F has written "The Text" followed by "The man is blessed that." The latter passage constitutes the opening words of at least a dozen Tudor poems, including translations of Psalms 1, 32, 41, and 112. Without more of the text it is impossible to say which (if any) of these known poems the scribe had in mind.

The Savile Epitaphs

Two unique verse epitaphs for members of the Savile family on folios 42v–45 contribute to this miscellany's regional tenor but are also directly connected with the Eland-Beaumont feud. A postscript to the ballad notes of Sir John Eland that

> his full syster hys heire she was
> and savile wedd the same
> thus Lord of Eland savile was
> and styll enjoyes the same
>
> (f. 42r, st.124)

Among these Savile descendants was Sir Henry of Thornhill, who served as sheriff of Yorkshire in 1537–38, 1541–42, and on the Council of the North, 1542–49. He died in 1558 and is highly praised in the first epitaph (ff. 42v–43v). Sir Henry's male heir, Edward, was "of weak intellect."[2] By 1567 his relative from a junior branch of the family, Henry Savile of Lupset, was legally possessed of most of Sir Henry's estate.[3] His death in

---

1. Rossell Hope Robbins and John L. Cutler, eds., *Supplement to the Index of Middle English Verse* (Lexington: University of Kentucky Press, 1965), no. 430.5; William A. Ringler, Jr., *Bibliography and Index of English Verse in Manuscript 1501–1558*, ed. Michael Rudick and Susan J. Ringler (London: Mansell, 1992), TM 220, 221; Steven W. May and William A. Ringler, Jr., *Elizabethan Poetry: A Bibliography and First-Line Index of English Verse, 1559–1603*, 3 vols. (London: Continuum, 2004), EV 12077.5, 12078.

2. J. W. Clay, "The Savile Family," *Yorkshire Archaeological Journal* 25 (1920): 14. See also Joan Kirby, "Savile family (*per*. c. 1480–1644), gentry," *ODNB*, http://www.oxforddnb.com/view/article/71873/74822?back=,71873.

3. P. W. Hasler, *The History of Parliament, the House of Commons: 1558–1603*, 3 vols. (London: HMSO, 1981), 3:349.

1569 is mourned in the second unique epitaph (ff. 44r–45v), where he is identified as Lord of Baropye (Baraby, Lincolnshire), which he owned by right of his second wife, Joan Vernon. The poem also mentions his offices as surveyor of the lordship of Wakefield and (by 1558) as member of the Council of the North.[4] Hanson's interest in these epitaphs is easily explained by the fact that the seat of this locally powerful family at Thornhill was less than ten miles southeast of Rastrick. (For Hanson's kindred and ongoing ties with a cadet branch of this family, see the introduction).

The first "Epitaph for Sir Henry Savile," which begins with some conventional wisdom about the folly of worldly desire (ll. 1–16), is a patronage poem for the Savile family that has a specific social and political agenda. First, it serves the usual purpose of funerary poetry in praising the deceased as a morally exemplary member of his class. Savile is portrayed as a just, honest man in an unjust world: he served as "sheryfe twyse" (21) by appointment of the king's council and as "head stuard . . . of pomfrait" (25–26) "wythotten brybe or fine" (29), discharging his duties in impeccable fashion, even though bribery and graft were common practices. He practiced noblesse oblige as "A kyndelye knyght truly, to menne of all estates" (30) and he fearlessly prosecuted criminals in his jurisdiction, holding to the standard of "truthe and true Justice" (40). Second, as someone who could himself claim to be "of Royall bloode" (64), he was a stout defender of the king's cause against "Rebeles Rowt" (65), presumably at the time of northern revolt of 1536–37 called the Pilgrimage of Grace, siding with his Talbot relative, "The Earl of shrewsburye" (68). Both features of his behavior relate to the Eland-Beaumont ballad, which, in Sir John Eland, has an example of a bad sheriff, and whose social antagonisms relate to the Tempest-Savile feud. As noted in chapter 1, Sir Richard Tempest had unwisely sided with the rebels and paid the social and political price for this error. From the vantage point of 1558, the date of Savile's death, Sir Henry's victory over Sir Richard Tempest in his local power struggle could be commemorated along with his other achievements. Presumably the poem was designed to be inscribed on a Savile funeral monument, to which it calls attention: "Lo henry Savile knight / entumbed here yowe see" (17–18). The wider community looking at the monument and reading the poem was an important secondary audience.

4. Kirby, "Savile family."

[Epitaph for Sir Henry Savile]

f. 42v] No wyght can well Dyscryve° °*write down (obs. except Scots.)*
The woo and wretchednes
We have here in thys wretched lyfe
wythe greife and great Dystres

Yf one mane myght acheve
even all the worled at wyll
nought shoulde he gayne but grudge and greife
when Deathe shall worke hyr wyll

No castylls towne ne towere
Nor such lyke lyvynges ° heare °*property*
can tracte ° owre tyme no Daye nor howre °*lengthen out*
yf present Deathe appeare

Why mynde we than so muche
on suche to sett owre harte
sence we ne wotte° howe sone from suche °*don't know*
suere are we to departe/

Lo henry Savile knyght
entumbed here yowe see
who hade of late hys hertes delyght
in landes and dygnytye

The sheryfe twyse was he
of yorkeshyer as I fynde
of Councell by the kynge trulye
in hys countrye assynd

The head stuard was he
of pomfrait° in hys tyme °*Pontefract*
The honor[5] Rewled he Ryghtlye
wythotten brybe or fine/

f. 43] A kyndelye knyght trulye, to menne of all estates,
To craftye knaves a scourge was he, a staye to° all Debates °*preventer of*

Yf Roberye weare commytte
the Thef cowld never escappe

5. The Honor of Pontefract was a "seigniory of several manors" governed by a single lord.

Thys knyght was of such worthy wytt
Some wayes he wold hym trappe

Well, well, I saye no more
the contrye shall hym mysse
Whose helpe they had here longe before
in truthe and true Justice

For helpe that comes by lawe
ys costlye and ful badde
and wayes and meanes to overthrawe ° °*overthrow*
The truthe maye there be hadde

For please the cheife in place
wythe gaynes or gold in hand
one maye possesse hys owne purpasse
hys cause can non wythstand

But thys most noble knyght
suche k[na]vry wold Dysgrace
wythe suche Deceiptes so that no wyght
durst come before hys face

God gave hym suche a grace
Such craftes to spye and knowe
the same also wold he Deface
wherso ever he sate in Lawe

f. 43v] no gaynes nor gold trulye
hys conscyence cowlde perverte
who bedd° hym brybbes, wyth theym wold he °*offered*
Be wrothe and overthwart° °*unfriendly, opposed*

A faythfull hert bare he
To god and to the kynge
he shewed hym self most certanlye
of Royall bloode to spryng

Agenst the Rebeles Rowt[6]
in armore bryght Rode he

6. This appears to refer to the Pilgrimage of Grace. For a discussion of the sociopolitical context of this revolt in West Yorkshire, see R. B. Smith, *Land and Politics in the England of Henry VIII: The West Riding of Yorkshire: 1530–46* (Oxford: Clarendon Press, 1970), 165–212.

unto the talbot true and stowt
The Earl of shrewsburye

The savilles Dyd Resort
To Sir henrye theyr head
The crowned kynge for to support
and shewe theyr frendly ayde

Eland and Thornhill eke
Wythall the contrye crye
Wheare they were wont theyr helpe to seke
heare Deade nowe dothe he lye,[7]

The second (also apparently unique) commemorative poem, "an Epitaphe of Master henry Savile of thornehille," commemorates the life and acts of a member of the Savile family who was from its junior, but still quite distinguished, branch. The poem is designed for the tombstone of a corpse "closed cold in claye" (5), not for someone enshrined in a family monument. This "esquyer" (6) achieved "wurshippe . . . and welth" (14), moving from being "lord of Baropye" (26) to inheriting Sir Henry Savile's estate of "Lupset" (25). He had important positions of service as "sur[ve]yer and Stuard" (30) of Wakefield, "head stuard and guyde" (31) of hatefeild," and "sherife of the shyer of yorke" (35). The poem calls attention to his service on the Council of the North from 1558 until his death in 1569. But though it celebrates him as a clever man who achieved wealth and the respect of his community, it concentrates on his charity and social benevolence. In praising Savile for this, the poet relies on the pre-Reformation religious belief in the spiritual merit of one's good acts (53–60). The poem highlights the dangers of worldly wealth both to oneself and to one's descendants (73–76), insisting on charity as the only path to heaven. Although in this poem moral status is made to trump social status, by the time of his death, Henry had succeeded to the lands of the senior branch of the family and had risen in the social hierarchy (though he was never knighted).

f. 44] *an Epitaphe of Master henry Savile of thornehille*

O earth earth take unto ° heare — ° *unto thee?*
the corpes that taken was owt of the° — °*thee*

7. The name "John" appears below this line in Hand D, whom we tentatively identify as John Stanhope III (1629–93).

That earth to earth as everye wheare
maye here also converted be

heare hast thowe closed cold in claye
the corpes of henry savile esquyer
The speret to heavens now toke the waye
as was hys hope and cheif Dyssyer

O cruell nimphes why Dyd yowe spyn
The threde so short of saviles lyfe
whiche sought hys wyttes howe he myght wyn
In everye coste° to staye all stryfe °*territory, part of the country*

he hade a heade cowlde wel devyse[8]
wurshippe° to wyn and welth all °*honor*
The same to spend in wyttye wyse
a harte he hade as lyberall

unto his frendes a frend was he
unto his foes foo was he non
his frendlye favor so shewed he
his fooes to hurtte but fewe or non

That head that cowlde so wele contryve
The contrye to kepe in quyetnes
ys nowe berefte bothe breath and lyfe
To all owre greif and great Dystres

of Lupset Lo heare lyeth the heire
that late was lord of Baropye
In Right of vernones Doghter & heire
somtyme hys wyfe most certanlye/

f. 44v] Of Wakefeld Lordship large and wyde
also sur[ve]yer and Stuard he was
of hatefeild chase head stuard and guyde
Wythe mo promocyones° in manye a place °*preferments, appointments*

In the costes° of the north contrye °*districts, lands*
of the quenes councell he was also
sherife of the shyer of yorke trulye
wyth heighe promotyones many mo

8. There is a faint manicule in the left margin next to this line.

But marke me heare the myserye
of thys vayn lyfe that we be nowe in
whan all thys welthe and Dygnytye
was newlye nowe bestowed on hym

Came Deathe alacke the more petye
and qwyte bereft hym on ° theym all °of
that we myght marke the vanytye
in thys vayne lyfe we toyle for all

Nought ys thys wretched worled we see
But greifes well mo than can be told
nought ys the wordlye Dignytye
nought ys in store of sylver and gold

Yf he hade lefte byhynd hym heare
heapes lyke hylles of sylver and gold
The porest wyght thys Daye he weare
Throughowt the worled of yonge and old

hys cheifest Riches nowe ys thys
That he bestowed upon the poore
layd up in heaven for sothe yt ys
hym to promote for evermore

f. 45] He kept howse for poore and Ryche
To everye wyght both franke and free° °generous
he sought hym self for to enryche
before the Devyne majestie

The author herof hathe knowne and sene
the poore have felt his Charytye
In place oft tymes wheare he hathe bene
petyfull on the povertye

O yowe that passe herby yet stay
consyder upon thys gentylman
thoughe he lye heare what he can saye
To yowe and everye mortall manne

When yowe shalbe as I ame nowe
no store of gold nor suche lyke pelfe
here left byhynd can profett yowe
Se to the poore and helpe yowre selfe

The good° wythe wronge that yowe shall wynne °*goods, wealth*
To prosper yowre posterytye
maye theym confound and all theyr kynde
and slea yowre soule eternallye

Wythe craftes & wyles to catche and cleike[9]
ys not the wayes the heavens to wyn
that Joyfull place yf yowe wyll seke
truthe ys the waye to enter in

of this vayne worled make yowe no store
seke not to muche for Ryches therin
yowe se they last not evermore
lyfe everlasting seke to wynne

f. 45v] After this Lyfe Do I beleve
Chrystes promyse can never Deceyve
in suche a place as can be no greife
lyfe everlastyng for to Receyve

Thys waye that I have walked heare
Thoughe yowe shall walke wythowten fayle
once shall we mete and quycke° appeare °*alive*
wheare we shall never wepe nor wayle.

That this maye be god graunt amen
Lyve welle, and fare yowe well tyll then

The Poems Attributed to Queen Elizabeth

Hanson's choice of two poems attributed to Queen Elizabeth is a revealing one. In the serial transcription of his manuscript, he seems to have copied them out in a period following the Armada, therefore after the 1587 execution of Mary, Queen of Scots. Mary was the "daughter of debate" or "foreign wight" in the first of these poems, "The dowt of future foos." She was threatened in the original context of the poem's composition after the Northern Rising of 1569–70. A Yorkshireman's inclusion of this piece in his compilation was an

9. *The English Dialect Dictionary*, ed. Joseph Wright, 6 vols. (Oxford: Oxford University Press, 1898), defines this Yorkshire dialect word as "cleek . . . 2. To snatch hold of, to seize hastily, roughly, eagerly." The *OED* has "2. To seize with the clutch or hand; to lay hold of, clutch, grasp, or seize, firmly, suddenly, or eagerly" (northern dialect).

act professing his allegiance to the Queen in the context of his home county's troubled history of rebellion (the 1536–37 Pilgrimage of Grace as well as the 1569 Northern Rising) and the religious resistance of the numerous Catholics in that part of England who continued to trouble the central government, forcing it to make special efforts to enforce conformity to the state religion. Whereas the poem would have been read close to the time of its composition as the Queen's show of strength after the defeat of the northern rebels and her pointed warning both to Mary and her supporters in the aftermath of Mary's execution and the victory over the Spanish, it would also have been read as a reaffirmation of that threat (to potentially rebellious English Catholics) and as testimony to Elizabeth's strong rule. Putting it into his collection, Hanson in effect signaled his religio-political loyalty to the Crown.

The other poem attributed to Elizabeth but probably not written by her (see the textual discussion below), "Nowe leave and let me Rest," was consistent with the Queen's projection of her public image as not only a strong and resolute leader but also an emotionally sensitive woman—one whose affection for her people was rooted in her feminine sensitivity to their needs. Jennifer Summit has deftly defined the Queen's strategy of publicizing her allegedly "private" writing as part of the projection of her dual image as steadfast ruler and emotionally responsive human being.[10] The Queen affectionately reached out to her subjects, portraying herself, in the period after it was clear she would not marry and have children, as wedded to them. In fact, the wish to attribute a poem such as "Nowe leave and let me Rest" to the Queen testifies to her success at portraying her two royal "bodies" to her subjects. Even as she asserted at Tilbury Camp during the Armada crisis that she had "the heart and stomach of a king, and of a king of England too," she also admitted to having "the body but of a weak and feeble woman,"[11] and it was to this vulnerable, human side of her nature that some readers of the second lyric responded. Transcribing a piece associated with Elizabeth's softer side was like reciprocating the affection she directed at her people, and that, we believe, is what Hanson was doing. Although apparently the Queen did not compose "Nowe leave and let me Rest," the important thing

10. Summit, "'The Arte of a Ladies Penne': Elizabeth I and the Poetics of Queenship," *English Literary Renaissance* 26 (1996): 395–422, reprinted in *Reading Monarch's Writing: The Poetry of Henry VIII, Mary Stuart, Elizabeth I, and James VI/I*, ed. Peter C. Herman (Tempe: Arizona Center for Medieval and Renaissance Studies, 2002), 79–108.

11. Steven W. May, ed., *Selected Works of Queen Elizabeth I* (New York: Washington Square Press, 2004), 77.

is the connection in the minds of readers of this piece, and some other writings associated with her name, with a female monarch they respected and loved. As Summit and others have shown, the Queen had a politically canny method of self-presentation, and certainly this lyric was consistent with it.[12]

Together with the two Armada thanksgiving ballads, these two poems attributed to Queen Elizabeth signal Hanson's interest in the larger national environment in which he lived. Although the Queen did not go on progress into the North and although so many of the items in the Hanson manuscript focus on provincial history, local personages such as the Saviles, local real estate matters, and the immediate world of work and leisure in which the scribe participated, his interest in the Queen, her court, and the distant but relevant metropolitan environment is signaled by a number of the entries he made in his book. These entries also reveal that despite his remote, provincial location, Hanson had access to both printed and transcribed texts that came to him from the nation's cultural center. The Armada thanksgiving broadsides were, of course, printed in London, and evidently spread to the provinces through ballad sellers and their distribution network. Similarly, scribal networks transmitted the two lyrics attributed to the Queen quite as readily into the hands of yeoman scribes living in distant, rural areas.

["The dowt of future foos"]

f. 45v] *certan verses made by the quenes majestie Eliz &c anno Regni xij°*

The dowt° of future foos, exiles my present Joye °*fear*
and wytt me warnes to shunt suche snares
as threatyns myn anoye
For falshod nowe dothe flowe, and subjectes faythe doth ebbe
whiche should not be, yf Reason Rewld or wisdom weave the webbe
But clowdes of Joyes untryd/ do cloke aspyryng myndes
Whiche turnes to Rue of late Repent, by chaunged course of kyndes[13]
The toppe° of hope supposed, the Roote of Rwe shalbe °*flowering head*

12. For a discussion of Elizabeth's techniques of making allegedly "private" communications "public," see Giovanni Iamartino and Angela Andreani, "In the Queen's Name: The Writings of Elizabeth I between Public and Private Communication," in *The Language of Public and Private Communication in a Historical Perspective*, ed. Nicholas Brownlees, Gabriella Del Lungo, and John Denton (Newcastle Upon Tyne: Cambridge Scholars' Press, 2010), 116–34.

13. Hanson's corrupt wording here seems to mean that the rebels regret their recent repentance by virtue of a change in their nature ("kynde"). The critical text of the poem below preserves the Queen's metaphors involving vegetable growth and weather.

and frutles all theyr grafted guyle/ as shortlye yow shall see
Theyr Dasled eies wythe pryde° whom false ambytion
blyndes °*eyes dazzled with pride*
shalbe unfyled[14] by worthy wyttes/ whose forsight falshood fyndes
The doughter of Debate, that Dyscorde aye° doth sowe °*always*
shall Reape no gayn, wheare former Rewle
oulde peace hathe taught to knowe
No forren banyshed wyght, shall enter in this porte
owre Realme brouke° no sedicions, let theym elleswheare
Resort °*brooks, permits*
my Rustye sworde throughe Reste
shall fyrst his edge imploye
To pole° theyr toppes that seke suche chaunge °*poll, lop off*
or gapes for future Joye.
finis quod Elizabetha

Textual Analysis

In order to simplify the list of variant readings, we have collated the text in the Hanson MS against the superior text in Folger, MS V.b.317, f. 20v.[15]

Verses made by the Queen's Majestie

The doubt of future foes exiles my present joye,
And wit me warnes to shun such snares as threatins myne anoy,
For falshod nowe dooth flowe and subjectes' faith dooth ebb,
Which should not be if reason rulde or wisdom weavde the web.
But cloudes of joies untride doe clook aspiring myndes,
Which turns to rage of late repent by chaunged course of windes.
The top of hope supposde, the root of rue shalbe,
And fruitles all theire grafted guile as shortli you shall see.
Their dazlde eies with pride, which great ambition blindes,
Shalbe unsealed by worthi wightes whose forsight falshod findes.
The daughter of debate that discord ay dooth sowe,
Shal reap no gayne wher former rule stil peace hath taught to knowe.
No forein, banisht wighte shall ancre in this porte;

14. Error by Hanson or his source for "unsealed," referring to the dazzled eyes of the rebels.

15. The poem in this manuscript is transcribed in four-line stanzas, breaking the long-line couplets into two lines of trimeter, one tetrameter, and a closing trimeter line. This probably represents the format in which Elizabeth squeezed these lines onto her diminutive tablet and how Lady Willoughby copied them from it. We print the poem according to its actual poetic form, expand contractions, normalize i/j, u/v, and add clarifying capitalization and punctuation.

Our realm brookes no sedicius sects, let them els where resorte.
My rusti sworde through rest shal first his edge employ
to pul their tops who seke such chaunge or gape for future joy.
Vivat Regina

Queen Elizabeth wrote "The doubt of future foes" (f. 45v) during the winter of 1569–70 as a defiant rebuke to Mary Queen of Scots and to those who had participated in the Northern Rebellion on her behalf. Hanson's version of the poem is marred by at least a dozen faulty readings, most of them unique among the eleven transcribed and two printed texts that offer substantive witnesses to the Queen's poem.[16] Sir John Harington, Elizabeth's godson, explained that the poem entered general circulation after Lady Willoughby copied it "covertly" from Elizabeth's tablet, for which theft the Queen gave her a good tongue-lashing. Carlo A. Bajetta proposes that Harington's source for this anecdote was probably Anne Neville, who became Lady Willoughby in 1553 when she married Fulke Greville, Lord Willoughby de Broke.[17] Her son, the courtier poet Fulke Greville, was Harington's close friend. The Northern Rising was of immediate family concern to Lady Willoughby, whose nephew Charles, sixth Earl of Westmorland, was one of its most prominent leaders. Understandably, she would have had a heightened personal interest in the Queen's response to the uprising. Perhaps Anne was motivated to circulate the poem as royal propaganda out of her loyalty to the regime on which her immediate family's prosperity depended.

Whichever Lady Willoughby copied Elizabeth's poem, her version is presumably *W* in the stemma below, the source for Sir John's own version of the poem in the Arundel Harington MS, as well as in the 1776 print in *Nugae*

16. For the variant readings of twelve of these texts and a tentative stemma of their relationships see Steven W. May, "Queen Elizabeth's 'Future Foes': Editing Manuscripts with the First-Line Index of Elizabethan Verse (a Future Friend)," in *New Ways of Looking at Old Texts*, no. 3, ed. W. Speed Hill, Renaissance English Text Society Special Publication (Tempe: Arizona Center for Medieval and Renaissance Studies, 2004), 8–9. In addition to the Hanson anthology, a twelfth transcribed text, Reading University Library MS 233, has come to light since the results in May's chapter were published.

17. Bajetta, "'Most peereles Poëtresse': The Manuscript Circulation of Elizabeth's Poems," in *Representations of Elizabeth I in Early Modern Culture*, ed. Alessandra Petrina and Laura Tosi (New York: Palgrave/Macmillan, 2011), 105–21 (113). Steven W. May, *The Elizabethan Courtier Poets* (Columbia: University of Missouri Press, 1991), 47n11, suggests the thief was Margaret Willoughby, who had served in Princess Elizabeth's household with Harington's parents. However, she married Sir Matthew Arundel in 1560 and was henceforth Lady Arundel, not Lady Willoughby. The anecdote with a copy of the Harington family's text of the poem was published under the auspices of Henry Harington in *Nugae Antiquae* (London, 1769), 1:58.

Antiquae, also taken from Harington family papers. But if Elizabeth genuinely resented Lady Willoughby's theft, that should have ended matters and all the other texts of the poem should descend from *W*. Instead, our textual analysis shows that the poem reached most of its copyists along two independent lines of descent represented by the hypothetical sources *Δ* and *Σ*. This can only mean that versions of the poem were released into scribal circulation not once but twice, and both times independently of the Willoughby version. It is difficult to believe that anyone but Elizabeth herself could have authorized this breach of royal privacy. "The doubt of future foes" is, in fact, a spirited expression of the Queen's determination to resist any effort to overthrow her government, and specifically, any rebellion attempted on behalf of "The doughter of Debate" (l. 11), the captive Queen of Scots. Our textual analysis of this poem strongly suggests that Elizabeth was, in this instance, a "scribal publisher" who purposely released her poem into the broad currents of manuscript circulation. She apparently favored at least two persons with copies, or at least access to copies of her lyric.

But the textual evidence may tell us even more about how, when, and why the Queen published her poem and her motive for doing so. Its eleven contemporary texts are preserved in documents that fall into two chronological groupings. Two descendants of Lady Willoughby's original copy of the poem, *F* and *R* (see the list of sigla below), are miscellanies of the 1560s and '70s. *RD*, a single, undated leaf, could very well also date from c. 1570 to judge from its handwriting, while nothing about *AH* or *NA* suggests that their reconstructed ancestor, *β*, was transcribed later than the 1570s. By contrast, none of the six manuscripts that descend from *Δ* and *Σ* can be dated before the 1580s. Puttenham's text appeared in 1589, in his *Arte of English Poesie*. Peter Beal describes the Ottley manuscript's watermark as "almost identical with" that of paper in use in 1580–86,[18] while Robert Commander compiled the Egerton manuscript between about 1585 and, at latest, his death in 1609. The Harleian manuscript was transcribed about 1581–87, while the contents and handwriting of both the Inner Temple and Digby manuscripts suggest transcription during the same general era rather than pre-1580.[19] Thus all the descendants of *D* and *S* certainly or

18. Peter Beal, "Poems by Sir Philip Sidney: The Ottley Manuscript," *The Library* 33 (1978): 284.

19. Bajetta, "'Most peereles Poëtresse,'" 110, notes that the watermark on folio 3 of the Petyt manuscript, on which "The doubt" was transcribed, also occurs in documents dated 1587–96.

probably date from the 1580s or later. The existence of this chronologically later and textually distinct group of copies may be most easily explained by considering the historical context in which they occur.

Discovery in August 1586 of the Babington plot to murder Elizabeth ratcheted up the pressure on the Crown to condemn the Queen of Scots to death as accomplice in the plot. Elizabeth avoided taking decisive action as long as she could: beyond her natural aversion to bloodshed,[20] she understandably did not wish to set a precedent for executing monarchs in England. She finally signed Mary's death warrant in January but claimed that she withheld permission to enact it. Members of the Privy Council, however, took matters into their own hands, and the Queen of Scots was beheaded on 7 February 1587; in the language of the poem, her top was polled (l. 16). The Catholic community at home and abroad condemned the regicide. Elizabeth thus had good reason to reissue her defiant lyric during this crisis as a means of defending her action before her own subjects. Her verses had explicitly warned her competitor that she would stir up further trouble in her realm at peril of her life. The texts descended from *Δ* and *Σ* apparently bear witness to her very politic recycling of the poem for release into the scribal medium. This was altogether a more subtle dissemination of her poetic apologia than setting it forth officially, and rather brazenly, in print (albeit Puttenham managed that for her a few years later by presenting her work, in however corrupt a state, in *The Arte*). In her insightful analysis of "The doubt of future foes," Jennifer Summit argues for the "feminine and aristocratic associations" of scribal culture that also conveyed a mystique of privacy even as the text circulated with unrestrained freedom throughout the kingdom.[21] Elizabeth knew that her name attached to the poem would give it momentum and appeal among copyists. Indeed, no copy is anonymous: each is ascribed to Elizabeth. The fact, moreover, that so many copies survive from her reign testifies to her poem's considerable popularity, for these extant witnesses are the survivors among many hundreds if not thousands of contemporary copies. The Queen thus conveyed to her subjects her defense of Mary's execution as a confidential message discreetly circulated by means of private scribal transmission.

---

20. For the Queen's reluctance to sign or implement death warrants see Peter Beal, "Elizabeth's Execution Warrants," in *Elizabeth I and the Culture of Writing*, ed. Peter Beal and Grace Ioppolo (London: British Library, 2007), 173–200.

21. Summit, "'The Arte of a Ladies Penne,'" 409–11.

Given the propaganda advantage of this sort of publication of the poem, we must wonder if Elizabeth was entirely aloof from its release into the scribal network in 1570. She apparently did not ask Lady Willoughby to surrender her copy of the work or forbid her to share it with others. Helen Hackett notes that while the poem's circulation appears to have been "a calculated exercise in apparently unwilling publication," Elizabeth benefited from it: "Not merely was a private artefact brought to public light, but its very privacy was strategically publicised in the process," thus enhancing its value to readers.[22] Now, Lady Willoughby was justly rebuked if she opened the Queen's diptych-shaped writing tablet to steal the poem, but what if it had been left open and unattended instead? Was Elizabeth so calculating as to invite one of her attendants to initiate scribal publication for her by leaving her finished poem in full view and unattended? Just years before, in another incident involving her rivalry with Mary, she had staged an invidious display of her musical talent for the Scottish ambassador, James Melville. One afternoon during Melville's embassy to England in the fall of 1564, Elizabeth grilled him at length on how she compared with Mary, Queen of Scots. The embarrassed Scot was asked to compare their height, hair, learning, and various accomplishments. After dinner that evening the Queen's kinsman Lord Hunsdon escorted Melville "up till [to] a quyet gallerie that I mycht heir some musik, bot he said he durst not advow it, wher I mycht heir the Quen play upon the virginelis." Melville eavesdropped on the concert, then confronted Elizabeth, who at once stopped playing and assured him "that sche used not to play before men, bot when sche was solitary hir allaine [alone], till [to] eschew melancholy; and askit how I cam ther."[23] For Elizabeth to leave her poem in plain sight to be copied, then pretend outrage at the theft, is of a piece with the innocently transparent duplicity she used to show off on the virginals before the Scottish ambassador.

Elizabeth's publication of "The doubt" resembles her passive publication of the two poems she inscribed on a wall at Woodstock Palace during her imprisonment there by Mary I in 1554–55. Her self-assured protestation of innocence, "Much suspected by me, / Nothing proved can be. / Quod Elisabeth the prisoner" circulated in manuscript (and even more widely in

22. Hackett, "Courtly Writing by Women," in *Women and Literature in Britain, 1500–1700*, ed. Helen Wilcox (Cambridge: Cambridge University Press, 1996), 174–75.

23. Sir James Melville, *Memoirs of His Own Life, by Sir James Melville of Halhill M.D.XLIX.–M.D.XCIII.* (Edinburgh: Roxburgh Club, 1827), 166.

print) during her reign.[24] The second poem is a ten-line reflection on God's apparent injustice in allowing "the guilty to be loosed / From bands where innocents were enclosed" (herself being just such an innocent, of course). The poem concludes, "So God send to my foes as they have thought."[25] These verses share a defiant tone with "The doubt of future foes," which is itself an assertive, even militant piece in which the sword-wielding speaker threatens to behead her opponents. Elizabeth may well have encouraged her self-representation as a strong, even militant ruler. She did nothing to deter access to her verses at Woodstock, and she was surely responsible for the release of "The doubt" into manuscript circulation on one occasion, if not two.

Hanson's version of "The doubt of future foes" is so corrupt that it is not entirely clear whether he worked from a copy of its first or second "publication." Its placement on folio 45v immediately after the Savile epitaphs may indicate that he entered it not long after the death of Henry Savile of Lupset in 1569. Or he may have been working from a collection of papers dating from the 1550s and '60s. The poem occurs in his anthology many folios after the two ballads on the Armada thanksgiving celebration (ff. 19–22, and 23–26v), texts that were necessarily transcribed in late 1588 at the earliest. Hanson's copy of the Queen's poem could therefore derive from its "second edition" of 1586–87, and indeed its variant readings lean somewhat in that direction. His text agrees in error with the *Nugae Antiquae* version (but not the related Arundel Harington text) at line 6, "kyndes."[26] But Hanson avoided diagnostic errors that connect the Harington and *Nugae Antiquae* versions at lines 6 ("report"), 7 ("topps, suppose"), and 9 ("the"). He also avoids the key error, "rage" in line 6 found in all versions derived from Lady Willoughby's theft of the poem c. 1570, yet he replaces it with a different error ("rue"), anticipating the occurrence of that word in the next line. Hanson's text does, however, share one doubtful reading

---

24. May, *Selected Works of Queen Elizabeth I*, poem 1. Bajetta analyzes the printed contexts in which the couplet appears in "'Most peereles Poëtresse,'" 108. Janel Mueller, "Elizabeth I: Poet of Danger," in *Approaches to Teaching Shorter Elizabethan Poetry*, ed. Patrick Cheney and Anne Lake Prescott (New York: Modern Language Association of America, 2000), 204, points out that this epigram is also a claim that her accusers cannot *prove* possible charges against her, which is a different thing than saying she is innocent. We are grateful to the anonymous Cornell University Press reader for pointing us to this essay.

25. May, *Selected Works of Queen Elizabeth I*, poem 2. Elizabeth's poems at Woodstock were a highlight of the palace as a tourist attraction.

26. Harington, *Nugae Antiquae*, ll. 58–59.

with documents descended from Δ and Σ: with *D, H, I*, and *O* at line 10 ("wyttes"). The relationship of Hanson's copy with the other texts may have been obscured by independent variation, or it may represent a fourth independent line of descent from the archetype in the stemma below. Given the contradictory evidence of these and other readings, we conclude that Hanson's text cannot be confidently placed in the stemma. Similarly, the variant readings of *D2* at lines 6 and 7 are corrective interpolations to the original version of the poem in the Digby MS; they offer too little evidence to align their unknown source text with any of the other witnesses.

The wide circulation of these texts along all three lines of descent confirms that the efficacy that Harold Love attributed to seventeenth-century scribal publication was very much in play by Elizabeth's reign.[27] The descendants of Σ, the Harleian and Inner Temple anthologies, were probably compiled in London, where a related text no doubt reached Puttenham as well.[28] Both descendants of Δ, however, were transcribed not far from the Welsh border. The Ottley family was seated at Pitchford Hall, Shropshire, southeast of Shrewsbury. Commander, the Egerton anthologist, was Sir Henry Sidney's chaplain and stationed with him at Ludlow Castle in his capacity as Lord President of the Marches of Wales. These manuscripts along with Hanson's show how effectively Elizabeth's apologia for Mary's execution could be widely disseminated among her subjects through the national scribal network. Within a few years, a decade at most, it had reached the northern border of Wales and deep into rural Yorkshire, where Hanson found it worthy of preservation. Of course, Hanson's location in heavily Catholic Yorkshire made Elizabeth's rebuke of the northern rebels particularly relevant to local politics. The threatening rhetoric from the royal center of power in the South warned against any similar uprising in the wake of Mary's execution. This must have been just the effect that Elizabeth had hoped for on the national level when she allowed those two additional copies of her lyric to circulate through the scribal medium.

In the list of transcribed sources below, only *Ha*, copied from Puttenham's *Arte* (*P*) in the eighteenth century, is not of Elizabethan vintage. *Ha* is thus the only text directly transcribed from an extant copy of the poem.

27. Love, *Scribal Publication in Seventeenth-Century England* (Oxford: Clarendon Press, 1993).

28. For most of the time from 1577 until his death in 1590 or 1591, Puttenham was a fugitive from the law hiding out from the authorities in the liberty of the White Friars, London. See Steven W. May, "George Puttenham's Lewd and Illicit Career," *Texas Studies in Literature and Language* 50 (2008): 155–59.

Sigla

Lemma *F*	Folger MS V.b.317, f. 20v
A8	Additional MS 82370, f. 45v
R	Bodleian Library, Rawlinson Poet. MS 108, f. 44v
E	British Library, Egerton MS 2642, f. 237v
D	Bodleian Library, Digby MS 138, f. 159 (original readings)
D2	Bodleian Library, Digby MS 138, f. 159 (as emended)
H	British Library, Harleian MS 7392(2), f. 27v
AH	Arundel Harington Manuscript, f. 164v, ed. Hughey (1960)
I	Inner Temple, Petyt MS 538.10, f. 3v
P	George Puttenham, *The Arte of English Poesie*, 1589, sig. 2E2v
Ha	British Library, Harleian MS 6933, f. 8
NA	*Nugae Antiquae . . . By Sir John Harington* (London, 1769), 1:58–59.
O	National Library of Wales, Ottley MS, f. 5v
RD	Reading University Library, MS 233

Title] verses made by the Quenes Matie *R*, Certen verses made by the Queenes moste excellent Matie against the Rebells in the North partes of England and in Norfolke & other places of the Realme A[nn]o D[omi]ni 1569 & 1570. *E*, E Reg *D*, Reginam *left margin, I*. The following Ditty . . . was composed by Q Elizabeth and was printed not long after, if not before, the beheading of the said Scots Queen *Ha*, certan verses made by the quenes ma[jes]ti Eliz. &c A° R xij° *A8*. Certaine verses made by the queenes majestie and wryghten with hir one hand *RD*; *Om*. *AH P NA O*; 1 doubt] dread *AH NA*; future] futures *E*; foes] force *D*; exiles] exyle *AH*; 2 shun] shunt *A8*; threatins] threaten *R E D H AH NA I P Ha O*; myne] my *Ha*; 3 subjectes] subject *P Ha*; 4 should] woud *Ha*; weavde] wove *AH NA*; weave *A8*; 5 joies untride] joyes vntyed *R*, Joye untried *E O*, toyes untryed *H Ha D*, toie untride *I P*; doe] doth *AH I NA*; aspiring] aspired *E*; 6 turns to rage] storme to reigne *E*, turne to ende *D2*, turne to Rayne *D H I P Ha*; turne to rage *AH NA*; turnes the raigne *O*; turnes to Rue *A8*; repent] report *AH NA*; by] bee *E*; chaunged course of] course of changed *P Ha NA*; windes] minds *AH*; kindes *NA A8*; 7 top] topps *AH NA*; hope] happe *O*, Joy *D2*; supposde] supprest *R*, suppose *AH NA*; root of rue] roote upreard *R*, Roote of ruyne *E O*, roote of Rule *D*, Roote of Ruthe *H I P Ha*; shalbe] will be *Ha*; 8 all] of *AH NA RD*; theire grafted guile] the grafted guiles *H Ha*, their graffed guile *AH*, their guiles *I*, their graffed guiles *P*; you] ye *P Ha*; 9 Their] the *R AH NA*, Then *P Ha*; with] which *H*; which] with *AH*, And *NA*, that *O* whom *A8*; great] false *A8*; blindes] blynde *AH NA*; 10 unsealed] unsold *I*, unfyled *A8*; by worthi wightes] by woorthye wyttes *D A8*, of worthy wittes *H*, of worthie wi*tes* *I*, through worthy wittes *O*, by worthey weyght *RD*; forsight] presight *E*, foresightes *I*; 11 that] which *RD*; discord ay] discord eake *H I*, eke discord *P Ha*; dooth] dyd *R*; sowe] showe *I*; 12 gayne] reigne *O*; stil] till *E*, oulde *A8*; stil . . . knowe] hath taught stil peace to growe *P*, hath taught Peace still to grow *Ha*, Still Peace hathe taughte to flowe *NA*; 13 wight] wyeghtes *D*; ancre] enter *A8*; 14 realm] Calmes *O*, Callme *D*; brookes] brouke *A8*; no] not *R E D RD*; sedicius] sedicions *A8*; sectes] sect *I, om. A8*; brookes . . . sectes] it brookes no strangers force *P Ha*, brooke no seditious sectes *O*; 15 My] Owr *D H I P Ha*; sworde] swords *D I*; through] with *P Ha*; rest] ruste *I*; his] theire *I*; 16 pul] povle *R E H AH I P Ha NA O A8 RD*; their] the *AH I NA*; who seke] that sekes *R E D AH RD*, that seeke *H Ha NA O A8*, w*hi*ch seke *P*; gape] gapes *E D AH A8*, hopes *RD*; for future joy] for further Joy *AH*, and gape for joy *P*, and gape for lawless Joy

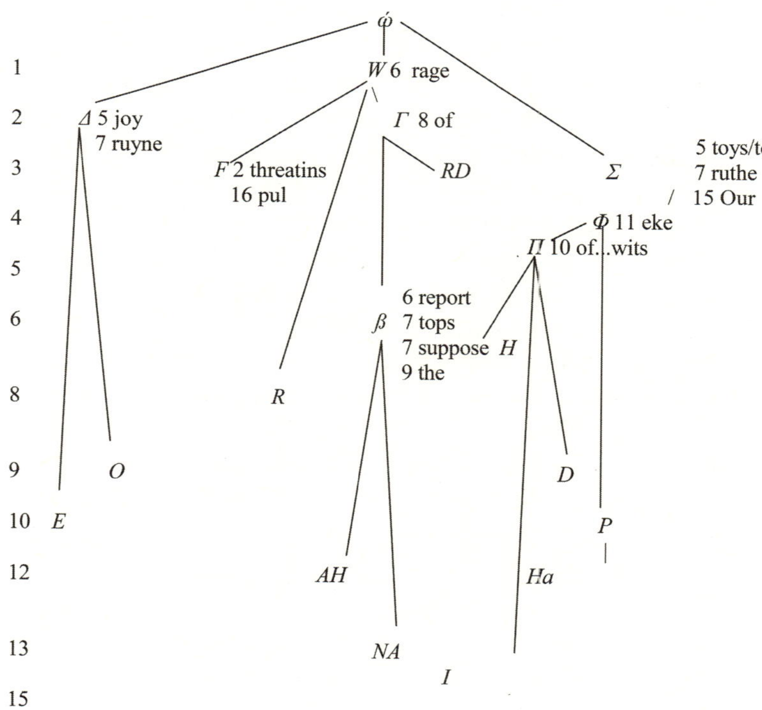

Ha, for such like joye *NA*; Sub. FINIS E. Reg *D*, EL *H*, ffinis Elizabetha Regina *AH*, Elizabetha Regina *O*, Finis w m *RD*.

["Nowe leave and let me Rest"]

f. 46] *Certan other verses made by owre sayd sovereign [Lady]*[29]

Nowe leave and let me Rest, Dame pleasure be content
Go chuse amongst the beste, my dotyng Dayes be spent,
By sundrye signes I se, thy profferes are but vayne
And wysdom warneth me, that pleasure asketh payn
And nourtur that dothe knowe, howe tyme hir steppes doth trye
Gyve place to paynfull woo, and byd me learne to dye
Synce all fayre earthlye thyng, sone Rype wyll sonne be Rotten
And all the pleasant sprynges sone wythered sone forgotten
And youthe that yeldes newe Joyes, that wanton lust desyeres
in Age Repentes the toyes, that wretchelesse youthe Requyeres
All whiche Delyghtes I leave, to suche as folye traynes
by pleasur to Decyve, tyll they Do fele the paynes
and from vayne pleasures paste, I flyte and fayne wold knowe
the happy lyfe at Last wheareas I hope to go
For wrothe, or wyse Reportes, nor yet examples gone
Can brydill youthfull sportes, tyll age cum steallyng on
The pleasant Courtlye games, that I Dyd pleasure in
My elder yeires nowe shones, suche folies to begyn
And all the same ys strange, that fonde delyght brought forth
I do intend to chaunge, and cownt theym no thyng worth
for I by prosses worne, ame tought to knowe the skyll
What myght have bene forborne,
in my yonge wretchildesse ° wyll ° *reckless*
By whiche good wordes I flete
From wyll to wytt agayn
In hope to sett my fette
In suertye to Remayne/ finis quod Elizabetha Regina

Finis Elizabethe Carminum Compositur
Carmina compositur[a] jnprimis Discendest[30]

29. The top of this page is torn, resulting in some loss of text. Hanson transcribes the poem by combining two lines into one; our lineation follows the poem's technical form in iambic trimeter lines rhyming *abab*.

30. These lines are added to the text by another hand using different ink.

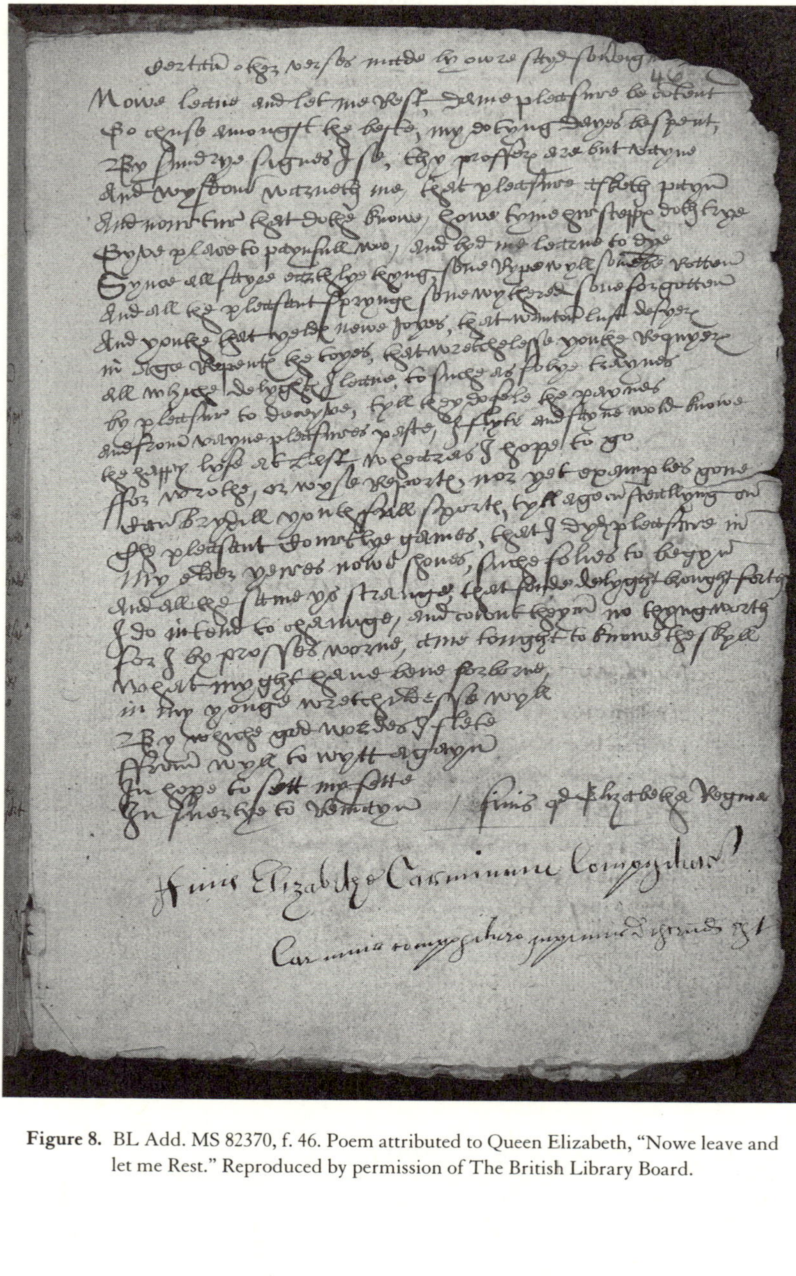

Figure 8. BL Add. MS 82370, f. 46. Poem attributed to Queen Elizabeth, "Nowe leave and let me Rest." Reproduced by permission of The British Library Board.

Textual Analysis

To date, our understanding of "Now leave and let me rest," including its authorship, has been based on the evidence of three manuscript witnesses, *AH, C*, and *Hy* in the list of sigla below. Only *Hy*, an anthology compiled between about 1585 to 1590, offers a (somewhat tentative) attribution to Elizabeth by erasing its original subscription, "H. C.,"[31] and replacing it with "Regina." The two unattributed texts, *AH* and *C*, were plausibly derived from sources at court, for the former was compiled by the courtiers John Harington and his son Sir John, while *C* is the anthology of Henry Stanford, chaplain and tutor in the household of George Carey, second Lord Hundson, lord chamberlain of the royal household. Had the Queen written this lament, it seems odd that neither of these collectors would have known or recorded the fact. In light of this evidence, in his edition of Queen Elizabeth's poetry, Leicester Bradner classified the lyric as "of Doubtful Authorship," adding in his notes, "I do not believe that Elizabeth wrote this poem."[32] The editors of the Queen's *Collected Works* argued, however, that Bradner's "reasoning is unpersuasive" and accepted the poem as fully canonical.[33] Steven W. May labeled the poem "possibly" by the Queen.[34]

We supposed at first that Hanson's second and unambiguous attribution of the poem to Elizabeth would clinch her authorship despite the fact that its content seems inappropriate to a queen, especially Elizabeth. The confession that "My doting days be spent" alludes to a frivolous and self-indulgent past life that few would accuse her of leading. Would Elizabeth have openly renounced in her writing the "vain pleasures" and "toys / That reckless youth requires," even if she felt herself to have been subject to them? The hedonistic, idle lifestyle rejected in this poem is difficult to align with the Queen's generally prudent, cautious behavior.

31. We are grateful to Jessica Edmondes for reconstructing the initials beneath the cross-out in this manuscript.

32. Bradner, ed., *Poems of Queen Elizabeth I* (Providence, RI: Brown University Press 1964), 77.

33. Leah S. Marcus, Janel Mueller, and Mary Beth Rose, eds., *Elizabeth I Collected Works* (Chicago: University of Chicago Press, 2000), 305.

34. May, *Selected Works*, 28–29.

She took little pleasure, moreover, in dwelling on the fact that "all fair earthly things / Soon ripe, will soon be rot, / And all that pleasant springs, / Soon withered, soon forgot." These repentant lines were perhaps a fictional, poetic exercise for Elizabeth quite in the vein of Lord Vaux's "I lothe that I Dyd love" (f. 49v), but for her they lack autobiographical resonance.

A yeoman farmer living in rural Yorkshire certainly could provide reliable testimony about his sovereign's authorship of a poem or any other writing in scribal circulation provided the information reached him on a reliable line of scribal transmission from the court to his farmhouse. This, however, does not seem to have been the case for this poem. In addition to Hanson's version, evidence from two more heretofore unstudied copies in contemporary manuscripts invalidate the ascriptions to Elizabeth.

Our work on this poem has greatly benefited from Hilton Kelliher's discovery of a fifth, fragmentary version of it in British Library Additional Manuscript 70516. This is a damaged, unattributed text that lacks nearly a third of the poem's forty-eight lines. Its margins are quite visible enough to establish, however, that this version was neither entitled nor subscribed with any indication of authorship by Elizabeth or anyone else. The sixth text is found in Derbyshire Record Office, D156M/A/2, a booklet of thirteen folios of accounts, notes on the Gospel of John, and a smattering of verse. "Now leave and let me rest" occurs on ff. 2r–v after copies of three unique love poems. The text is untitled, unattributed, and followed by two additional stanzas (supplied in the collations) that provide a godly conclusion to the poem. These unique verses may well be of the copyist's own composition.

We list below the variant readings among these six witnesses as collated against Hanson's text:

Lemma *A8*	BL Add. MS 82370, f. 46
AH	Arundel Harington MS, ed. Hughey, no. 242
C	Cambridge University Library, MS Dd.5.75, f. 44v
D	Derbyshire Record Office, D156/M/A2, ff. 2–2v
Hy	BL Harl. MS 7392 (2), ff. 49v–50
L	BL Add. MS 70516, f. 52 (damaged; ll. 8, 12–13, 17–46 fully legible)

Title: certan other verses made by owre sayd sovereign [Lady] *om. AH C D Hy L.*; 3 amongst] among *AH C Hy*; 4 be] ar *D Hy*; 9 nourtur] Nature *AH C Hy*; 10 howe] Her *AH*; 11 Gyve] gives *AH C D Hy L*; 12 bid] bids *AH C*, bides *Hy L*; 13 Synce] seinge *D*; earthlye] yerthly *D*, youthfull *Hy, corrected from* youthly; thyng] things *AH C D Hy L*; 14 wyll sonne be] & sowne are *D*, sound be within *L*; rotton] rot *C*; 15 the] that *AH C D L*; pleasant sprynges] pleasure bringes *D*; 16 forgotten] forgot *C*; 17 yeldes] yeldeth *D*; new] men *C*, all *Hy*; 18 lust desyres] lustes desires *D*, youth requiers *Hy*; 19 Repentes] repeat *D*; 20 wretchelesse] reckless C; Requyeres] desires *Hy*; 21 whiche Delyghtes] such delightes *D*, such desire *Hy*; 22 folye] follow *Hy*; 23 by] in *D*; pleasur] pleasures *AH C Hy L*; Decyve] receave *D*; 24 fele] file *D*; 25 from] so *D*, for *AH*; pleasures] pleasure *D Hy*; 26 flyte] feele *D*, fly *AH C*; 27 happy] happiest *D L*; lyfe] day *D*, place *Hy*; 28 wheareas] wherein *AH*, wherto *C Hy L*, wheir *D*; I hope] I doe hopes *D*; 29 wrothe] words *AH C D Hy L*; or] nor *D Hy L*; wyse] wast *L*; Reportes] report *D*; 30 nor] ne *C*, ore *D*; yet] all *Hy*; 31 can] gan *C*; youthfull] wilfull *Hy*; soirtes] sport *D*; 32 com] comes *AH*, cam *C*; steallyng] creping *Hy L*; 33 The] These *Hy*; 34 did pleasure] do pleasure *C*, had pleasure *D*, delighted *Hy L*; 35 My] myne *AH*; yeires] yeres, *corrected in margin*: age *Hy*; shones] shames *AH C Hy*; Shame *D*; 36 folies] folly *C D*; 37 the] these *D Hy*; same ys] Fancies *AH C D Hy L*; 38 that] which *D*; fond] found *D*, vaine *Hy*; brought] brough *D*; 39 intend] Intent *D*; to change] & count them all *L*; 40 cownt] compt *AH D*; *sub.* but vayne & nothinge worthe *L*; 41 prosses worne] *corrected from* prooffes am taught *C*; profes am warnd, *corrected in margin*: worne *Hy*; p ~~roe~~ es worne *L*;[35] 42 ame] And *Hy*; the] throw *D*; 43 might have been] ought to be *Hy*; 44 wretchildesse] retcheles *AH C D Hy L*; 45 by which] Which by *Hy*; wordes] will *AH*, proofe *C*, woorkes *L*; *sub.* wheirof good proves I Flitte *D*

After 48 in D:
for certenly I know
that god will served be
<in pleasure to receve>
<the> of him I stand in awe
& will doe till I dye

35. The original reading of this damaged text was, apparently, "process worne" (with "ro" in "process" abbreviated).

And accompt those pleasures great
& greatest gayne of all
to gayne that lyfe so sweete
which is celestiall

Subscribed: finis qd Elizabetha Regina (*and in a different hand and ink*) Finis Elizabethe Carminum Compositur Carmina compositura jnprimis Discendest] Finis *AH*, FINIS ~~HC~~ Regina *Hy*

Our analysis of these variants shows that Hanson's version of the poem, with eleven demonstrable errors,[36] is the second most corrupt of the six witnesses. With eighteen errors, *D* is the most corrupt but also the earliest datable version. The accounts on folios 9–13 of this booklet are dated between 1574 and 1583, suggesting that the scribe entered "Now leave and let me rest" by 1583 at latest. Corrupt readings in Hanson's text agree with those in *L* at lines 32 and 45, and with *Hy* at lines 15, 32, and 45, revealing that these three manuscripts descend from a common ancestor.[37] *AH, C*, and *D* are unrelated to these three texts or each other and offer independent witness to the Queen's text, with *AH* and *C* being by far the most reliable versions. The following diagram charts these relationships and calibrates the relative accuracy of these texts with the number of errors in each as enumerated in the left margin.

If the attribution of this poem to Elizabeth (found only in *Hy* and *A8*) was transmitted from the archetype (*O*) through the hypothetical intermediaries *X* and *Y*, the *L* scribe, oddly, did not record it. With eight and nine errors, respectively, *L* and *Hy* are almost as textually corrupt as *A8* (*L* actually more so, for its errors occur in only thirty-three of the poem's forty-eight lines). Accordingly, the Hanson and *Hy* attributions to the Queen stem from the same source and thus amount to a single witness to her authorship. Moreover, the testimony of *L* suggests that these attributions were missing at the text's point of origin, then interjected in

36. At lines: 9 nurtur; 11 Give; 12 bid; 15 the; 26 flit; 29 wrothe; 32 cum; 35 shows; 37 same as; 44 wretchildesse; 45 workes.

37. At line 32, the present tense verb "com" in *A8, L*, and *Hy* fails to pattern with "Can brydill," a past tense construction. In line 45, the experience ("skill") attained by the writer over time ("process") provides "proof" of the proper course of action, not "wordes" (*A8, Hy*) or "woorkes" (*L*). In line 15, "the pleasant springs" (*A8, Hy*) makes "springs" a noun, whereas in context it is a verb referring to all plant life "that pleasant springs" and that is soon "withered."

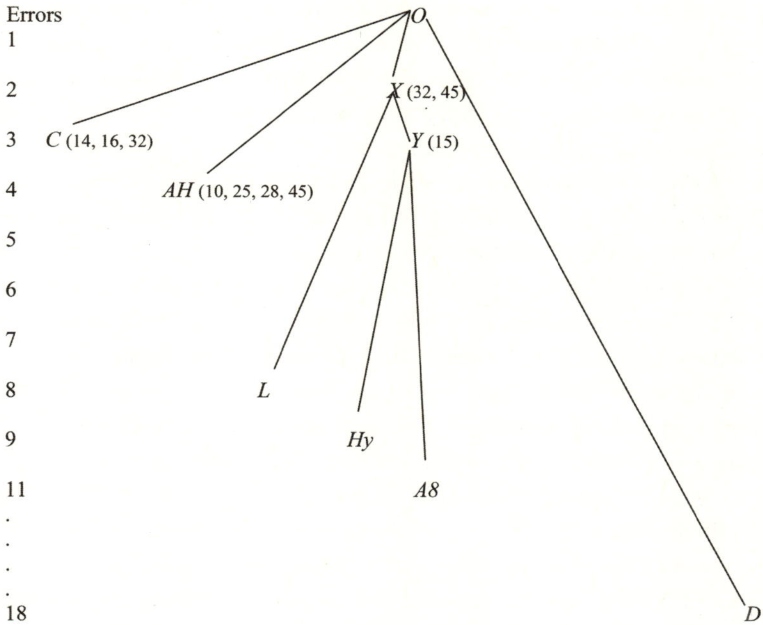

the course of transmission at some point after *X* and perhaps as late as *Y*. The independently derived texts, *AH, C*, and *D*, establish three further lines of descent from the archetype that lack any indication of the poem's authorship. *D*'s inclusion here suggests that the poem was not attributed to the Queen in the earliest years of its circulation. The *A8-Hy* subscriptions therefore amount to a single and almost certainly inaccurate assertion of Elizabeth's authorship that crops up only in two terminal texts on a highly unreliable line of the poem's transmission.

What case, then, can be made for Elizabeth's claim to the poem? The editors of the *Collected Works* argue that Harington and Stanford might not have known that Elizabeth wrote this lyric "given the private, even secret, nature of Elizabeth's poetic production at court." The aura of secrecy was such, they allege, that "manuscript attribution was not to be expected from her intimates."[38] But this aura was in fact quite permeable. As we have seen, it was ignored wholesale with regard to "The doubt of future foes," for every extant text is attributed to the Queen. Lady Willoughby

38. Marcus, Mueller, and Rose, *Collected Works*, 305n1.

obviously had no qualms about exposing her mistress's authorship, and that is duly recorded with the text found in the Arundel-Harington anthology. Similarly, what should have been Elizabeth's very private response to a poem addressed to her in 1587 by Sir Walter Ralegh (his "Fortune hath taken thee away, my love") entered scribal circulation almost immediately. Excerpts from both poems were attributed to their authors in Puttenham's *Arte of English Poesie* (1589). The full text of Elizabeth's answering poem was attributed "Per Reginam" in a contemporary manuscript anthology, while a redaction of both poems was even entered for ballad publication in the Stationers' Register on 13 June 1590.[39] Both Harington and Stanford attributed other entries in their anthologies to the Queen, but if they believed she wrote "Now leave and let me rest," they inexplicably declined to note it. If the source of the version in *D* was attributed to Elizabeth, this copyist too, found it not worth recording. Given her subjects' generally high regard for whatever she wrote as the nation's premier "celebrity" author, three such oversights are simply incredible. It is far more likely that a text would be wrongly attributed to Elizabeth through guesswork or wishful thinking than that an ascription would be overlooked by multiple scribes copying her authentic writings.

Further, the editors of the *Collected Works* attempt to substantiate the revised attribution to Elizabeth in the Harleian manuscript by asserting that its text preserves spellings that are "idiosyncratically characteristic" of her, citing "ar" for "are" and "oldar" for "older."[40] This argument relies on several questionable or demonstrably false assumptions. Even if these spellings were diagnostic of Elizabeth's writing, and the *Hy* scribe allowed his copy texts to influence his spelling (an unproven assumption), how could they have survived in a text that was otherwise filtered through a succession of flawed intervening copies? Not only does *Hy* descend from *X* through *Y*, but any number of additional copies may well have intervened between the presumed royal archetype *O* and the version finally copied by the *Hy* scribe. Is it likely that all these scribes preserved the royal orthography? These spellings are not found in *A8* and *L*, the texts related to *Hy*. It is not true, moreover, that "ar" was a particularly unusual spelling for "are"

39. These attributions and the textual circumstances are set forth in May, *Elizabethan Courtier Poets*, 317–21.

40. Marcus, Mueller, and Rose, *Collected Works*, 305n1.

among Elizabethans. The Harleian scribe, for instance, preferred "ar" to "are" by a ratio of more than five to one throughout his anthology and in texts neither by nor attributed to Elizabeth.[41] While it is true that the Queen sometimes spelled "er" suffixes "ar," this second word is even less persuasive as evidence of any connection between Elizabeth and the Harleian text, for "oldar" is a misreading. The initial letter is manifestly *e*, and the word is thus "elder." The final two letters might possibly be interpreted as "ar," and that would make it a very unusual spelling indeed, for the *OED* cites "eldar" as a fifteenth-century Scottish spelling. Yet the word is clearly spelled "elder" in the Harleian manuscript on folio 74v, line 5, and we contend that the actual spelling on folio 50 is the same, with the second *e* merely ill formed so that it resembles an *a*.[42] We conclude that nothing in the orthography of the Harleian text of "Now leave and let me rest" suggests that it derived from Elizabeth's holograph or a close copy of it.

In summary, to believe in Elizabeth's responsibility for this lyric requires the acceptance of a series of suppositions that in aggregate we find untenable. It is hard to believe that, despite their ties to the court, neither Stanford nor the Haringtons were aware that the Queen wrote this poem, or if they did, chose not to attribute it to her in their miscellanies, in both of which they attribute other texts to her.[43] It is equally difficult to believe that the scribes of MS Additional 70516 (*L*) and *D* were likewise so uninterested in their sovereign's work as to omit the attribution, and that only when the text at last came to Hanson and the *Hy* scribe did it reach copyists who valued the information transmitted on the *O-X-Y* line of descent and found it worth recording. Finally, we cannot reconcile the poem's expression of repentance for a frivolous and misspent youth with Elizabeth's biography. Her most public displays of "youthfull" folly might reasonably be assigned to her flirtatious courtship with the Duke of Anjou between

41. Examples of "ar" for "are" in this manuscript occur, for example, on folios 12v, 19, 23v, 24v, 27v, 28 (four instances), and 29.

42. In her edition of MS. Harley 7392 (2) as her doctoral dissertation (in progress) at the University of Sheffield, Jessica Edmondes transcribes the word "elder."

43. In addition to "The doubt of future foes," the Queen is credited with a translation of the first ninety lines of Petrarch's "Triumph of Eternity" in the Arundel Harington MS, in *The Arundel Harington Manuscript of Tudor Poetry*, ed. Ruth Hughey, 2 vols. (Columbus: Ohio State University Press), 1:276–77, 360–63, nos. 238, 320. Stanford entitled his copy of Elizabeth's speech to Parliament in March 1576, "oratio Elizabethae reginae" (f. 28).

1579 and early 1582. But, as we have seen, "Now leave and let me rest" was apparently in circulation by 1583 at the latest. In so short an interval, Elizabeth could not plausibly have made the transition from the "youthfull sportes" that "wretchelesse youthe Requyeres" (ll. 31, 20, to shunning those "vayne pleasures paste" in "My elder yeires (ll. 25, 35).

This second poem that Hanson attributed to the Queen provides a striking example of how textual analysis, here the macro reconstruction of the scribal network that transmitted these six versions of the poem, can help us answer larger questions about the work in question. Ironically, in the context of this analysis, the discovery of a second attribution of this poem to the Queen severely weakens her claim to it.

The Decalogue

Hanson transcribed a verse Decalogue in available space at the bottom of the page on folio 42 following the conclusion of the Eland-Beaumont ballad. There are numerous verse Decalogues from the period found in both manuscript and print. The most well known, perhaps, is the poem included in the editions of the Sternhold and Hopkins English metrical paraphrases of the Psalms from 1560 onward, probably written by William Whittingham. It was printed with the musical tune to be used to sing each stanza:

Attend my people and geve eare,
    of ferly° things I will thee tel: °*marvelous*
se that my wordes in mynde thou beare,
    and to my preceptes listen wel.

    1 I am the soveraine Lord and God,
Which have thee brought from careful thral.
And eke reclaimed from Pharaos rod,
Make thee no Gods on them to cal.

    2 Nor facioned forme of any thing,
In heaven or earth to worship it,
For I thy God by revenging,
With grevous plagues this sinne wil smite.

    3 Take not in vaine his holy name,
Abuse it not after thy will,

For so thou mightst soone purchase blame,
And in his wrath he would thee spil° °*destroy*

4 The Lord from worke the seventh day ceast
And brought al thinges to perfect ende,
So thou and thine that day take rest,
That to Gods hestes you may attend.

5 Unto thy parents honor geve,
As Gods commaundements do pretend°, °*assert*
That thou long dayes, and good maist live,
In earth where God a place doth lende.

6 Beware of murder and cruel hate,
7 Al filthy fornication feare:
8 See thou steale not in any rate,
9 False witnes against no man beare.

10 Thy neighbors house wish not to have,
His wyfe, or ought that he calth myne:
His field, his Oxe, his Asse, his slave,
Or any thing which is not thyne.[44]

Verse Decalogues different from this or the one found in the Hanson manuscript survive in a number of manuscripts. For example, a seventeenth-century manuscript found in the University of Leeds Brotherton collection has:

Hark Israell & Jacob hear my Law
Hear it to keep it (& thy selfe in awe)
I am Jehovah (I with mighty hand)
Brought thee from bondage out of Egypt land
Adore me onely for thy God & Lord
With all thy heart in every deed & word
Make thee none image (not of any sort)
To thy own works my Glory to transport

44. We cite this text from *The Whole Booke of psalmes collected in English meter by Thomas Sternhold, J. Hopkins and others* (1567), sig. Ri^{v}-Rii. For a list of other print and manuscript texts of this piece, see May and Ringler, *Elizabethan Poetry*, 1:378–79. For the attribution to Whittingham, see Beth Quitslund, *The Reformation in Rhyme: Sternhold, Hopkins and the English Metrical Psalter, 1547–1603* (Aldershot, UK: Ashgate, 2008), 126.

Use not my name without respect & fear
Never blaspheme neither thy selfe for swear
Six dayes worke for thy food but yow (as I)
Rest on the seaventh & to my temple hie
To thou that gave thee life, due reverence give
If thou desire long in the land to live
Imbrue° thou not thy hand in humane blood °*stain*
Staine not anothers bed, Steale noe mans good
Bear no false wittness, covet not to have
Thy neibours wife his oxe his Asse his slave
His horse his land his Cattell or his coyne
His place his grace or ought that is not thine

(Lt 91, f. 27)[45]

The verse Decalogue in the Hanson manuscript is in 4/3/4/3 ballad meter, but, probably to adjust to the available space on the page, lines 2 and 3 as well as 11 and 12 are combined to form one line each.

f. 42] *[Decalogue]*

No gods but one, shalt thowe adore
Nor Idols grave° to the, [/] avoyd vayne swearying evermore °*engrave, carve*
the Saboth sanctyfye
honor thy parentes Reverentlye
Murder and thefte forbeare,
from vile adultrye se thow flee
beare no false wytnes here
Thy neboures wyfe thou covet not
nor any thyng of his
kepe these preceptes & dout thou not, [/] of heven thou shalt not mys

45. A version of this appears in Yale Osborn MS b.137, p. 122. For other Decalogue poems from the period, see Bodleian MSS Rawlinson Poetry 148, f. 110v ("Believe one God 'gainst whom no oath commence") and 153, f. 40 ("No other Gods create but me") and the Arundel Harington MS. See Hughey, *The Arundel Harington Manuscript*, 1:367–68 ("Theise are the Hollie Commaund'ments tenne"). There is a fourteen-quatrain poem about the Ten Commandments drawn from *Speculum Christi* in Bodleian MS Ashmole 61, ff. 16v–17: see George Shuffleton, ed., *Codex Ashmole 61: A Compilation of Popular Middle English Verse*, TEAMS, Middle English Texts Series (Kalamazoo: Medieval Institute Publications, Western Michigan University, 2008), 59–60. Shuffleton, 437–40, discusses the background of this kind of didactic text, which was designed as a handy way for children and illiterate laypersons to remember the Ten Commandments.

Nativity Poem about the Magi

On folios 46v–47v there is an apparently unique eighteen-stanza poem about the visit of the Magi to Bethlehem by way of an interview with the deceitful and envious King Herod. Especially in its first stanza, it closely follows the account in the second chapter of Matthew's Gospel, which, in the Geneva Bible translation reads:

> When Jesus then was borne at Bethlehem in Judea, in the dayes of Herod the king, behold, there came Wise men from the East to Hierusalem,
>
> 2 Saying, Where is the King of the Jewes that is borne? for we have seene his starre in the East and are come to worship him
>
> 3 When king Herod heard this, he was troubled, and all Hierusalem with him.
>
> 4 And gathering together all the chiefe Priestes and Scribes of the people, he asked of them, where Christ should be borne.
>
> 5 And they sayd unto him, At Beth-leem in Judea: for so it is written by the Prophet,
>
> 6 And thou Beth-leem in the land of Juda, art not the least among the Princes of Juda: for out of thee shall come the governour that shall feede my people Israel.
>
> 7 Then Herod privilly called the Wise men, and diligently inquired of them the time of the starre that appeared,
>
> 8 And sent them to Beth-leem, saying, Goe, and search diligently for the babe: and when yee have found him, bring me word againe, that I may come also, and worship him.
>
> 9 so when they had heard the king, they departed: and loe, the starre which they had seene in the east, went before them, till it came and stood over the place where the babe was.
>
> 10 And when they saw the starre, they rejoiced with an exceeding joy,
>
> 11 And went into the house, and found the babe with Mary his mother, and fell downe, and worshipped him, and opened their treasures, and presented unto him gifts, even gold, and frankincense, and myrrhe.
>
> 12 And after they were warned of God in a dreame, that they should not go againe to Herod, they returned into their country another way.

If we compare this biblical passage with the poem, one of the interesting divergences is in the definition of the Messiah's rule: while the text in Matthew states that Christ will be "the governour that shall feede my people Israel," the poem speaks a language more relevant to a sixteenth-century reader:

A captayn come nowe unto me
shall Reignne And Rewle Right well
In truthe and in all equytye
my people of Israell

(ll. 29–32)

The term "equity" would have resonated in the contemporary political context in light of the increasing caseloads during Elizabeth's reign in the Court of Chancery as an equity court or "court of conscience," and in the Court of Requests, the principal court of "poor men's causes."[46]

This Magi poem is in the tradition of Nativity poems popular in medieval verse. Rosemary Woolf, for example, observes, "In the fifteenth century . . . the joy most commonly celebrated independently was the Nativity, and carols on this subject are particularly abundant. . . . Many of them deal with the adoration of the Magi and with the annunciation to the shepherds and their adoration of the Child."[47] Composed in 4/3/4/3 ballad stanzas, the poem copied by Hanson was probably intended for singing.

f. 46v] Whan Jesus was borne in bethleem
In tyme of herod kynge
Wyse menne came to Jerusalem
even from the este saying

46. J. H. Baker, *An Introduction to English Legal History*, 4th ed. (Oxford: Oxford University Press, 2007), 106–7, 120. In a proclamation of February 21, 1594, "Vagabonds," "Irishmen," and other undesirable persons were barred from entering royal palaces, although anyone who "shall have cause to prefer any complaint or request to her majesty or to her council being in the court, it shall be lawful for any such person to come to one of the masters of the requests, to whom a room is appointed near to the court to receive daily such requests." Paul L. Hughes and James F. Larkin, eds., *Tudor Royal Proclamations*, 3 vols. (New Haven: Yale University Press, 1969), 3:136, proclamation 762.

47. Rosemary Woolf, *The English Religious Lyric in the Middle Ages* (Oxford: Clarendon Press, 1968), 302, and Carleton Brown and Rossell Hope Robbins, eds., *The Index of Middle English Verse* (New York: Columbia University Press, 1943), list many Epiphany poems: numbers 20, 320, 1785, 2109, 2333, 2339, 2730, 2732, 3526, 3527, 3931, 3975. Richard Leighton Greene, ed., *The Early English Carols*, 2nd ed. (Oxford: Clarendon Press, 1977), 67–79, prints a number of these. There is a poem specifically about the journey of the three kings reproduced from the Trinity College, Cambridge MS 323 in Carleton Brown, ed., *English Lyrics of the XIIIth Century* (Oxford: Clarendon Press, 1932), 39–41.

Wheare ys this blessed babe nowe borne
That kynge of Jewes shalbe
Whose starre we sawe shyne us before
fare in the easte contrye

And we be come wythe gyftes nowe here
To honor hym Reverentlye
Whan herod kyng of thys land herd
A troubled head hade he

So was than all Jerusalem
troubled wythe hym certayn
And called the clergye unto theym
to searche the truthe owt playne

Where chryste messyas should be borne
who answered Directlye
In bedlem Juda as befornne
was wryten in prophesye

And nowe to make the matter playn
As truthe in Dede yt was
The[y] Rode before the kynge certayn
The prophet Micheas[48]

And thowe bedlam Ephrata[49]
art not the least of all
amongst the princes of Juda
for owt of the ° there shall °*thee*

f. 47] A captayn come nowe unto me
shall Reignne And Rewle Right well
In truthe and in all equytye
my people of Israell

Then herod called secretlye
To ~~th~~ hym the sayd wyse men
and searchyd owt what tyme trulye
The starre appered to theym

48. The prophet Micah.
49. Ephrata (or Ephrath) is another name for Bethlehem. See, for example, Genesis 35:19.

And sent theym unto bethelem
Saying searche owt trulye
Wheare thys chylde ys of truthe certayn
And shewe agayn to me

Lykewyse as yowe also that I
wythe harte and fayth unfyeld° *°undefiled, unfouled*
myght com my self Right Reverentlye
And wurshippe that same chylde

But nowe whan they had herd the kyng
Awaye they went with spede
And loo the starre all glytteryng
whiche they had sene in Dede

In the easte contrye whan they weare
The waye before theym yoyde° *°went*
unto the place wheare as the childe weare
and ther above yt stoyd[50]

This wonderous starre nowe whan they see
Ryght Joyfull wyghtes° they weare *°persons, men*
and then Rejoysyng Joyfullye
The howse they entred theare

This blessed babbe whearas they found
wyth hys mother Marye
and fell Down groveling on the grownd
Before hym Reverentlye/

f. 47v] And opened theyr treasures theare
offeryng wythe Reverence
unto this blessed babe nowe heare
gold myre and frankeincence

The angell of the Lord so bright
in sleppe nowe warned theym
by herod kyng that cruell wyght
not to Retorne agayne,

50. This may be a dialect pronunciation and spelling of "stood," rhyming with "yoyde" ("yode"), obsolete form of "to go/went."

Theym selves wyselye could theym convey
and that wythe spede trulye
To theyr contrye an other waye
from herodes crueltye/

A Seventeenth-Century Lyric Fragment

In available space on the bottom half of folio 26v following the second Armada ballad, a hand later than that of John Hanson's has transcribed two stanzas of a three-stanza seventeenth-century lyric found in its full form in Folger MS V.a.345:

As I walked forth in one summers morning
For to heare the smal birds sing
My fancy soone me thence recalled
To heare of such a thing
I hard a maiden sore complaining
Far from any towne
Singe al my joyes that were so jolly
Now are turn'd to foolish folly
Downe gentle belly downe
Downe gentle belly down

Once I was a wealthy mans daughter
And eke in Essex borne
But now my life is turn'd to laughter
& I am made a scorne
My freinds which once of me did take a pleasure
Now they doe fret and frowne
And my joyes that were so jolly
Now are turn'd to melancholy
Downe, &c.

Once I was proud of my proper beuty
So long as it remaind
But now I am weary of my wicked nature
& beuty I disdaine
Many country maids I have disdain'd
For their beuty browne

Sing al my joyes ~~nor turnd~~ that were so jolly
Now are turn'd to melancholy.
Downe gentle belly downe &c.

(pp. 224–25)

This poem about a gentlewoman who bemoans the loss of her home, her social status, her friends, and her reputation because she had sex and got pregnant is a song text. The copy of its first two stanzas in the Hanson manuscript is faint, stained, and faded, impossible to transcribe fully.

f. 26v] As I walked forth in to a somers morning
For to heare the sweet bird sing
my mind full quicklie me recalled
for to heare < > thing
I heard a maide sore complaineing
farre from anie towne
sing all my joyes that were so jolly
now art turned to ^foolish^ foollies
downe jentle bellie < >
downe jentle bellie, downe
Once I was a wealthie man[s] daught[er]
and eke in Essex borne
butt now my dayes are turned to laughter
and I am made a scorne
my frends which once < > me did take a pleasure
[ ] frett & [ ]
Sing all my joyes that were forgott[en]
now are turned into ~~follie~~ melanchollie
downe jentle bellie, downe gentle bellie,
downe

This is the least legible of the contents of the Hanson manuscript, and the scribe appears to have run out of space before he could record all three stanzas of this poem. The item would seem, however, to be the last one entered into the manuscript in space the later scribe found available in the middle of the book.

5

Recipes for Ink and Stink Bait plus Other Utilitarian Items

Manuscript miscellanies and household books containing both prose and verse typically include practical items such as medical recipes, accounts, and other forms of useful information.[1] For example, John Ramsey's miscellany (Bodleian MS Douce 280) has medical recipes, a translation of one book of Caesar's *Commentaries*, comments on theology and history, a mathematical explanation of the prime number, a list of the offices of England and of the kings since the Norman Conquest, and a list of lords, knights, captains, bishoprics, and counties. The *Book of Secrets*, a late fifteenth-/early sixteenth-century manuscript household book associated with Catherine Tollemache of Helmingham Hall, East Anglia, contains a variety of instructional texts, including the following: advice on how to plant and graft fruit trees; recipes for ink and for making colors for

1. For a discussion of late medieval and early modern manuscripts and printed works containing informational material, see Carrie Griffin, "Instruction and Information from Manuscript to Print: Some English Literature, 1400–1650," *Literature Compass* 10, no. 9 (2013): 667–76.

dyeing and for illuminating books; a treatise on fishing (excerpted from the fifteenth-century "Treatise of Fishing with an Angle"—see below); prognosticatons, charms, recipes, and puzzles; and a list of medicines for specific ailments.[2] The composite manuscript of Robert Reynes of Acle, who was a church reeve and, like Hanson, "a professional scribe, to whom villagers could turn for legal documents," contains both literary and utilitarian material.[3] The Hanson household book, in fact, appears to have been begun with such utilitarian purposes, devoting its first eleven folios to ninety-two separate items, including recipes for different-colored inks, instructions on moistening parchment and making glue, and recommendations on how to catch rabbits, birds, and many different kinds of fish. Hanson seems to have combined both professional and recreational interests in this section of his manuscript, including material related to his legal work with wills and real-estate transactions. These items could have served as a handy repository of information that Hanson himself might have used but also as instructions for his own son, who seems to have followed his father's profession as scrivener and carried forward his practices—for example, in producing legal documents and doing color illustrations of heraldic shields.

The language of this section of the Hanson manuscript is colloquial, with, for example, such Yorkshire dialect words as "kelynges" (f. 5),[4] "goytt" (f. 6),[5] and "suddled" (f. 7v).[6] What we have here are items of a personal and familiar character, information communicated in the local idiom. Some details of Hanson's transcription show that some material he recorded was derived from external sources, not his own experience. For example, in a recipe for making "whyte leade" on folio 7 and another "to take byrdes or anye other foole" on folio 11v he left blank spaces, indicating that he could not read all the words in his copy texts. In a fish-bait

2. See Jeremy Griffiths, ed., *The Tollemache Book of Secrets*, completed by A. S. G. Edwards (London: Roxburghe Club, 2001).

3. Cameron Louis, ed., *The Commonplace Book of Robert Reynes of Acle: An Edition of Tanner MS 407* (New York: Garland, 1980), 30.

4. The *OED* defines "keelings" as a Scottish and northern English dialect term for codfish.

5. The *OED* has "goit" or "gote" as chiefly a northern dialect word, defining it as a "watercourse; any channel for water; a stream."

6. The *OED* has the verb "suddle," meaning to stain or sully, as a Scottish and northern English dialect form.

recipe "for a pycke" (pike) on folio 9v, moreover, he repeated the phrasing "and put theym and put theym," a sure sign of copying. The entries may not be in the high rhetorical register of some of the manuscript's items from elite culture, but they reflect the social as well as the personal contexts of the yeoman compiler.

Recipes for Different-Colored Inks

Many manuscript miscellanies from the period contain recipes for ink, usually for the black ink for normal scribal use. Since, as Adrian Johns notes, ink was not really commercially manufactured until the mid-seventeenth century, ink making was normally done in the home with locally available ingredients.[7] There are four recipes for black ink in Hanson's manuscript. For example, the second of these offers the following instructions:

> *To make fyne blacke ynke*
> Take a quarteron of galles half a quarteron of gren[e]
> coperus or vitrial and half a quarteron of gume arabyke
> and put theym to a quart of well collored Red wyn or new
> worte° or good stayll olde alle styrryng theym ofte   °*unfermented beer*
> together
> and let theyme stand two or three dayes and than wryt with them. (f. 1)

As Peter Beal notes, traditional recipes for black ink since ancient times used "galls" (usually oak galls), iron sulphate (copperas), and gum arabic.[8] Such ingredients could have been purchased at a local apothecary shop—some of them, including both gum arabic and gum mastic (the latter mentioned in another recipe on folio 3), would have been imported commodities. The alternative possibilities for the main liquid ingredient in Hanson's recipe for black ink (red wine or new beer or stale ale), however, suggest the practical experimentation of home industry and personal experience of the writer.

7. Johns, "Ink," in *Materials and Expertise in Early Modern Europe: Between Market and Laboratory*, ed. Ursula Klein and E. C. Spary (Chicago: University of Chicago Press, 2010), 105.

8. Beal, *A Dictionary of English Manuscript Terminology 1450–2000* (Oxford: Oxford University Press, 2008), 202. Beal notes that the other standard recipe was carbon-based, using lampblack or soot.

Hanson offers another recipe for black ink that includes much more detailed practical information about the process of making the ink as well as of refreshing inks that have been produced:

> *Alio modo*
> Take jd° worth of galles & breke theym lyghtlye in a °*one penny*
> morter a half penye worthe of coperous & put theym into
> a halfepenye cupe so that the sayd stuff & water fyll you[r]
> cupe nye full but Remembre that you [use] water that yow
> make ynke wythe be eyther of suche water as hathe
> standed longe in or upon a hole of a tre or el[les] suche
> suddes or leavynges of suche water as they lett powreout
> or castawaye after lyttyng of blacke clothe or elles barke
> woys[9] and blend yowre coperus galles and water all together
> in a pott, and let theym stand and Remayn ij dayes
> [and p]ut a penyewoth of gume arabyke, and yf ye melt
> youre gume wythe yowre saydes water or ye put yt in
> yt ys not the worst, and wryte therwythe whan the same
> hathe stand awhyle often tymes ye must styr yt withe
> a styke for ofte styrryng makys yt thyke and good ynke
> than powreowt the cleryste ynke into hornes or other vessell[s]
> and take and fyllvp yowre sayd ynke cupe or vessell
> groundes or levynges wythe one of yowre forsayd wateres as
> ye dyd before, and make newe ynke thervpon wythe a lyll
> curtesye or Refreshyng of every of all the aforsayd thynges
> viz galles coperus and gume/ and makeyt verey thyn thatt
> whan yowre princypall ynke waxeth olde and thyke yowe
> maye put of yowre thynner Enke therto and temper yt
> to yowre pleasure for when mene puttethe water to
> Enke, they mar yt, and also yowre second Enke
> wyll serve Sir John° wythe one spore,° and bycause all °*a priest* °*spur*
> maner of stuffe are not equall in valor, therfore yf
> ye make yowre Enke thycke and perfecte at the fyrst
> tyme, yt ys the best waye for as of half a quarter of
> malte maye be made mykyll aylle° or lyttyll thon° good °*much ale . . . the one*
> for the hert and bellye, thother nought nether in bellye nor

9. The *OED* cites "bark-wose," apparently "bark ooze," in a single reference dated 1483 ("bark, n., Compounds, C1.a, attrib. or objective").

> schon[10] so in lyke case ye maye order yowre Enke The most
> pryncypall Decernyng of Enke good and well mad ys yf
> yt be not fast and sure, blakeshynyng and well collored
> put more gume therto for yt ys princyypall, and yf yt
> be oveare thyn and one semyth olde and more than [thin] put
> more of yowre coperus and galles therto for in yowre [en]
> yowre dyscressyon lyethe all makyng of good Enke,
> And kepe yt ever in somer in a lowe howse owte of the heate
> and from fresyng in wynter. (ff. 1–2)

Especially at the end of this set of instructions, it looks as if Hanson is offering the fruits of his personal experience in ink making to someone close, probably his own son. This is not simply a recipe for ink making transcribed for his own use; it is the communication of knowledge to whoever else might consult his book.

Some of what Hanson writes has more the character of practical advice than actual recipe. For example, the fifth item in the manuscript states, "Coperus maketh Inke blacke & thycke / Galles maketh yt blake and causeth yt to sattell welle" (f. 2). The eight lines that follow this are bracketed in the left margin to call attention to their importance:

> water thyn or thyke as yt ys mesured
> Gume settethe and maketh all Enke fayre, faste & sure,
> and Longe to endure,
> by mackyng of theys iiij properties make yowre Enke for
> enye tyme wythin the space of asenyght° ye maye putt °*a sevennight*
> to anye of thies iiij princypalles at yowre dyscressyon
> but not after, and specyally water, for newe freshe
> water marrythe Enke quod nota. (f. 2)

It is not unusual to discover recipes for black ink in personal commonplace book collections, but the Hanson manuscript also contains a variety of recipes for colored inks. Johns points out that traditionally "ink recipes were typically juxtaposed to instructions for producing pigments for painting or colors for illuminating manuscripts, with dyes for textiles, and with

10. Skin; the *OED* cites this as a pre-seventeenth-century Scottish spelling.

medicines."[11] This is certainly the case with the Tollemache manuscript, which has recipes for red, white, green, blue, russet, yellow, sable, gold, and silver inks.[12] Some printed books, such as *A very proper treatise . . . for the arte of Limming* (1573), offer recipes for producing colored inks and pigments as well as offering advice about the preservation and use of limning materials.[13] In this work there are several items on the same topics as those found in Hanson's manuscript, though the specific texts differ: "To temper Vermelion" (sig. Bi) (Hanson: "To temper vermelon to wrytt wythe" [f. 2]); "To temper redde Leade" (sig. Bi^{v}) (Hanson: "To make Reade leade" [f. 7]); "To Temper greene Byze" (sig. Bii) (Hanson: "To Temper bice" [f. 2v]); "To temper Vergrese, called Spanishe greene" (sig. B.ii^{v}) (Hanson: "To temper vertgrease[14] to wrytte or turne wyth" [f. 3]); "To make letters of the colour of gould without gould" (sig. Cii) (Hanson: "To made golde water to wryte wythe" [f. 6]). Many of the ingredients required to produce various colors, as explained on the next to last page of the printed work (sig. Civ), were available at apothecary shops. These include the following items mentioned in the recipes found in Hanson's manuscript: bize (or bice),[15] vermilion, red lead, black lead, green bize, vertgrese, gum arabic, galls, green coperas, turpentine, whites of eggs, white wine, and white vinegar.

The colored inks included in Hanson's manuscript would have been useful in drawing illustrations of coats of arms—as noted in the long title of a 1573 printed publication on "the arte of Limming," which refers to the "painting or tricking of armes in their right colors."[16] As noted earlier,

11. Johns, "Ink," 108.

12. See folios 8–11v of that manuscript (section 7 in Griffiths, *Tollemache Book of Secrets*). Robert Reynes's manuscript also contains recipes for red and blue ink, as well as for black ink. Louis, *Commonplace Book*, 171–72.

13. See also *A Booke of Secrets: Shewing divers waies to make and prepare all sorts of Inke, and Colours . . . Necessaire to be knowne of all Scriveners, Painters, and others that delight in such Arts*, translated out of the Dutch into English by W. P. (1596), sigs. A3-C3, and Henry Peacham, *The Art of Drawing with the Pen, and limming in Water Colours* (1606), esp. 49–63.

14. The *OED* defines verdigris as a "green or greenish blue substance obtained artificially by the action of dilute acetic acid on thin plates of copper (or a green rust naturally forming on copper and brass), and much used as a pigment, in dyeing, the arts, and medicine; basic acetate of copper."

15. Short for blue bice, a pigment made from smalt (finely ground deep-blue glass; a pigment called green bice was made by adding orpiment (a bright yellow arsenic trisulphide) to smalt.

16. The full title of this work is *A very proper treatise, wherein is briefly sett forthe the arte of Limming, which teacheth the order in drawing & tracing of letters, bnets, flowers, armes and Imagery, & the maner how to make sundry sises or grounds to laye silver or golde uppon, and how silver or golde shalbe layed or limned uppon the sise, & the waye to temper golde & silver and other mettales and diverse kyndes of colours to write or to limme withall uppon velym, parchement or paper, & howe to lay them*

there is a manuscript in the hand of John Hanson Jr. (WYAS, Calderdale, SPC: 118) containing color illustrations of a number of coats of arms, especially of families in the part of the country in which he lived. The fact that John Hanson Sr. recorded the colored-ink recipes suggests that he too was engaged in producing images of this sort. Since, for this purpose, parchment rather than paper would have been preferable (as it was for legal documents), it is not surprising that Hanson included in this section of the manuscript, instructions on how to moisten parchment before using it as a scribal medium (f. 4v).[17] He also gives instruction on how "To make an Instrument to portray wythe[18] upon a walle parchment paper or where ye lyke with the blake color" (f. 5).

Examples in Hanson's manuscript of recipes for colored inks include the following, the first of which is bracketed to call attention to its importance:

> *To temper vermelon[19] to wrytt wythe*
> Vermelon Take vermelon and grynd yt upon a marblestone with cleare
> water alonge whyle, for the more yt ys grone the fayrer yt
> wylbe, and the more easye to wrytte or to wyrke wythe/ and whan
> yt ys grone, gather yt up layng yt one a fayre playne chalke
> stone and sett yt in the sonne to° yt be drye, but yf ye have no °*until*
> chalkestone, drye yt upon a fayer clene papyre and whan yt
> ys hard dryed gather yt from the stone, puttyng yt in fayer paper
> and whan ye lyst occupye yt, take asmuche as ye lyke & temper yt
> agayn upon a marble stone wythe strong glair[20] viz of ij or iij
> dayes old/ and also wythe j or ij droppes of the yolke of the egge or

upon the worke which thou entendest to make, & howe to vernish yt when thou hast done, with diverse other thinges very mete & necessary to be knowne to all such Gentlemenne, and other persones as doe delite in limming, painting or in tricking of armes in their right colors, & therfor a worke very mete to be adjoined to the bookes of Armes, never put in printe before this time (1573). Nicholas Hilliard relied on this work in his somewhat more detailed descriptions of how to prepare and use colors in his treatise on the subject compiled c. 1600. His tract has been edited from University of Edinburgh Library MS Laing La.III.174 as *Nicholas Hilliard's Art of Limning*, ed. Arthur F. Kinney (Boston: Northeastern University Press, 1983), 6, 28–35.

17. The documents relating to property transactions that Hanson produced or witnessed, of course, were parchment.

18. White.

19. Vermilion.The *OED* 1.a has "Cinnabar or red crystalline mercuric sulphide."

20. Egg white. Item 19 in the manuscript (f. 4v) offers advice about how "To kepe gleire" (from spoiling).

asmuche as ye thynke nede wythe one droppe of gummewater
and whan ye lyst floryshe wythe vermelon temper yt in ahorne
wyth weke gume water or one droppe of glair. (f. 2)[21]

To temper synopyre[22] for wrytyng or towrnyng[23]
Take synopyre and grynd yt upon a marble stone or upon
a glasse wythe a molett of aflyntstone wythe gummed
water commenlye styff but not styff as for bye and yf
yt be commyn synopyre yt must have more gryndyng
whan yt ys groune put yt into ashell & temper yt with
yowre fynger/ whan ye have done therwythe yt wolde
have a waike[24] gummed water, nevertheles som mene temper
yt wythe clar,[25] but that ys in the workyng nether
easye nor fayre. (f.3v)

To make zalowe° coloures *°yellow*

Take a herbe called wodwys and cut yt small grynd yt [page torn]
astone, temper yt wythe glaire in ashell
Itm take mastycoyll[26] and temper yt wythe waykegummed water

21. Cf. the instructions in *[T]he arte of Limming*, sig. Bi, "To temper Vermelion": "Grynde Vermelion on a Painters stone, first drye, & then therto a litle glayre of egges, & grinde it againe, untill the brightnesse be fordonne, with a litle of the yolke, and let it stand a day or more, untill it be wel fyned. And when thou dost worke therewith, stirre it well together, and if it be thicke as lyme, doe a litle water thereto: and if it shall have an ill savour, then put into it three chyves of Saffron, and it will take awaye the evil sente." A late fifteeenth-century manual, *Crafte of Lymnynge of Bokys*, has the following: "To temper vermelone to wryte therewith. Grynde vermelone one a stone with newe glayre, and put a lyttylle of the holke of an ay hereto, and so wryte therewith: and if thou wylle temper it to floryche with bokys, take and grynde hit smalee, and temper tyt with gum water." Cited from J. O. Halliwell, ed., *Early English Miscellanies in Prose and Verse* (London: Wharton Club, 1855), in Griffin, "Instruction and Information," 669. Griffin, ibid., 674n13, refers to a manuscript of this work produced between 1460 and 1500, National Library of Wales Ms Brogyntyn II.i.

22. The *OED* defines "sinople" or "sinoper" as the color green, especially in heraldic uses.

23. The *OED* defines "turning" figuratively as "Shaping, moulding, fashioning (of literary work, etc.)." It is possible that this word has a different meaning in the local dialect.

24. The *OED* identifies "waik" as a Middle English and Scots form of "weak," related to an Old Norse word. It may be a case of language conservatism in Hanson's Yorkshire.

25. The *OED* defines this obsolete word, from the German "clär" (clear), by offering two citations that refer to finely ground and powdered burnt and calcined bone ashes. This may be the substance used in the manufacture of "bone china," dibasic dicalcium phospate dihydrate (CaHPO4 -H2O).

26. Mastic oil. The *OED* defines the mastic tree as "an evergreen shrub of the Mediterranean coastal region, *Pistacia lentiscus* (family Anacardiaceae), closely related to the pistachio, the bark of which yields mastic; = *lentisk n.* Also (usu. with distinguishing word): any of several trees of related genera which yield a similar gum." This substance is yellow in color.

in ashell and wyrke wythe yt whan ye wyll
Itm take iiij or v clyves of saffron or as muche as ye lyke
temper yt wythe alytyll glaire and no other lycour, color that wythe
what ye wyll, the thynner yt lightethe the feyrer yt ys. (f. 4)

To temper turnsall[27] to floryshe wythe

Turnsall Take a pece of turnsall and put in a shell wythe a lytyll
cleare water let yt stepe a nyght, than wryng yt into the
same shell put therto ij or iij droppes of glaire/ and take a lityll
earewax and temper yt together, than set yt in the sonne unto° it °*until*
thyken, yf ye have haste set yt agenst a wayke fyere and than
wryt therwythe,
but yf ye wyll have a sadder coloure then take whan ye have
wronge yt owt of the fyrst pece that ye steped as muche as ye
maye geytt, then put an other pece in the same collore and do therwith
as ye dyd wythe the fyrst and do so forthe as manye as ye lyst
unto ye have a substancyall colour as ye lyke/
and yf ye wyll have a sadder coloure than anye of thes
take a lytyll vertgress grynd yt and put therto, or yf ye have
haste shave yt wythe a knyffe as smale as ye cane, the more
vertgresse ye put therto the more sadder yt wyll be. (f. 4)

Whereas vermilion, or scarlet red ink, was used for scribal purposes, as the first of these recipes suggests, the other colors would have been used for artistic purposes, in, for example, the color illustrations of coats of arms.[28]

Hanson also collected recipes for black and white pigments:

To make whyte color to portray[29] on paper or parchement

Take glover spetches[30] steppe theym to they be thorowe weytt
than wrynge owt the chalke of theym, and yf ye have no spetches

27. *OED*: "A violet-blue or purple colouring matter, obtained from the plant *Crozophora tinctoria* . . . formerly much used for colouring jellies, confectionery, wines, etc., and later as a pigment." See the recipe "To temper Turnesoll" in *[T]he arte of Limming*, sig. B.i.

28. The official colors used in heraldry, in addition to silver and gold, are red, purple, orange, blue, green, and black.

29. The *OED* has two obsolete meanings for this word: "1. *trans.* To paint, adorn, or decorate (a surface or object) *with* an image or images" and "2.a *intr.* To make drawings, pictures, or statues."

30. See *OED*: "1. A patch or strip of undressed leather, a trimming of hide, used in making glue or size."

> take cuttynges of parchment together puttyng theym in a brasse pott or elles a panne wythe water lettyng theym sethe[31] over a fyer unto a quart be brought to apynte, than take that water and put yt into avesell and let yt stonnd to yt be colde and congylled together, this maner of lycoure ys collye[32] colle, and take marow bones of oxen bryn° theym to they be thorowe whyte then gryne [*sic*] them one astone of marbyll wythe the aforsayd gya[ ] Ryght as ye wold do vermylon/ (f. 4)
>
> °*burn*
>
> *To make blake color to portray wythe upon awall, or anye other place*
>
> Take sea cooles the bryghtest ye can geytt and grynd theym upon astone wythe cleire water as ye wold do vermylone and whan yt ys dryed into powder, yf ye wyll noytte yt or occupye yt temper yt agayn upon astone wythe the forsayd gyllye and portray then wythe upon awalle (f. 4v)

The uses envisioned for these pigments extend beyond paper and parchment to walls and other places that might be decorated.

Other Utilitarian Material

Some of the other recipes and advice in this section of the Hanson manuscript deal with writing materials and colors, with parchment use, and with glues. Hanson, for example, gives directions for making a reed paint applicator:

> *To make an Instrument to portray wythe upon a walle parchement paper/ or wheare ye lyke with the blake color*
>
> Take a good bygge Reede and cut of the knottes at bothe endes than cleve yt even in the mydwarde and fyll bothe the sydes wythe the same coloure but that whiche shalbe put in the Reede must be as thyke as yt maye be tempered whan bothe

31. The *OED* defines this as an obsolete or archaic term for boil.

32. The *OED* identifies this as an obscure or dialect word: "Dirtied with coal-dust or soot; grimy; coal-black."

sydes are [f]yllyd laye theym even together and bynd the[fold]
from the one ende unto the other wythe a threde and ley [yt][fold]
wheare yt may drye, whan ye wyll occupye yt cutt the [fold]
the ende therof as ye wold do a plummett and fest° yt alway *°fasten, bind*
Just, breath theron oft tymes to yt be able to wyrke wythe
Itm take a eller° styke cleve yt have owt the pythe and do *°alder*
thus wythe on the same wyse/ (ff. 4v–5)

There are five recipes for glue, the first of which is quite elaborate:

To make glewe for bookes

Take sowndes[33] of stockefyshe or of kelynges. or elles bothe together
put theym into a panne or pott wythe clere water/ yet ye must
nedes have an other vessell wythe warme water by yowe that
yf yt drye inn ye maye put more of the warme water therto,
when yt ys sodden a lyttyll whyle take yt up & klens yt
wythe a knyffe cleyn, than put yt in the vessell agayn
and let yt sethe to yt be tender, take yt up by lyttyll & lyttyll
braye[34] yt in a morter, whan yt ys smale, take yt owt of the
~~water~~ morter and leye yt in a vessell of pewder than take
the brothe that was sodden in and strayn yt thorowe a clothe
that doyne take bothe the brothe and the brayed sowndes and
put theym agayn into the forsayd vessell & let theym
have a whaline° in the vessell together, whan yt waxethe *°haling, dragging*
thyke take yt forthe of the vessell puttyng yt in a powder
dyshe and let yt gyllye together and so stand ij dayes at the
thyrd day turne yt up syde downe, and afterward cut yt
in Longe peces honging yt up to drye so that ther on
no sonne ne fyer therto; and yf ye wyll ye maye take small
flowere° suche as syngyng breade[35] ys mad of temper yt *°flour*
wythe ayle and so wyrke yt forthe, thys done take the
parchement that ye wold glue together & raysse bothe the
peces softlye wythe a knyffe and specyally by the egges° and *°edges*
than sett the glue theym Joynyng theym so together. (f. 5r–v)

33. Swimming bladders.

34. The *OED* defines the verb "bray" as "to beat small; to bruise, pound, crush to powder; usually in a mortar."

35. The wafer used to celebrate Mass.

This glue recipe is for joining sheets of parchment, an activity that would have related to Hanson's activities as a legal scribe as well as to his compiling separate parchment pages into book form.[36] There are other items dealing with bookmaking: "To clens a bouke that ys soddelled" (suddled, that is, soiled) (f. 5v); "To make sysse[37] to laye on bookes & gylt thereon" (f. 6); and "yf ye wyll make a sasse for pryntyng of bookes wythe gold" (f. 6v). In addition to recipes and general instructions, Hanson also includes advice that seems drawn from his practical experience. For example:

> *Yf ye wolde [keep] vermylon from stynkyng*
> Breake a gall and put yt into yowre glaire or° ye temper yowre vermelon, Itm put alytyll salt therto and yt shall not smell nether stynke. (f. 6v)
>
> °*ere, before*

Hanson offers technical advice also for working with gold: "yf ye wyll wryte & floryshe wythe gold," "yf ye wyll make asysse for golde," and "To make golde water to wryte wythe" (f. 6).

On the top half of folio 7v (see figure 9), Hanson transcribed two items ("To make Reade leade" and "To make glewe whiche fyer ne water shall not lyghtlye leysse [undo]"), but the three entries on the bottom half of the page were made by two other scribes. The first has instructions on how to catch rabbits:

> *Howe to take Conyes*
> Take Oates and vervine and cutt the vervine small & seeth them well in wine Dreggs or Ayle Dreggs & then drye it and cast it before the Conye holes and when they eate thereof they shalbe Drunken that yow maye take them with your hands. (f. 7v)

The second item, in the same hand (Hand B), is a simple (and probably ineffective) treatment for someone who has been bitten by a rabid animal:

> *For byting of a wood Dogge*
> Take rew honye & salt & stamp altogether & plaster it well therto. (f. 7v)

36. It is interesting that another legal scribe, Robert Reynes, also had a glue recipe in his commonplace book. Louis, *Commonplace Book*, 172.

37. The *OED*, 1.a defines "size" as a "glutinous or viscid wash applied to paper, parchment, etc., to provide a suitable ground for gilding, painting, or other work."

The final item is in another hand (Hand C):

> *To make red sealing wax*
> Take to one pound of wax 3 ounces of cleare turpentine in summer in winter 4; melt them together with a soft fire, then take itt

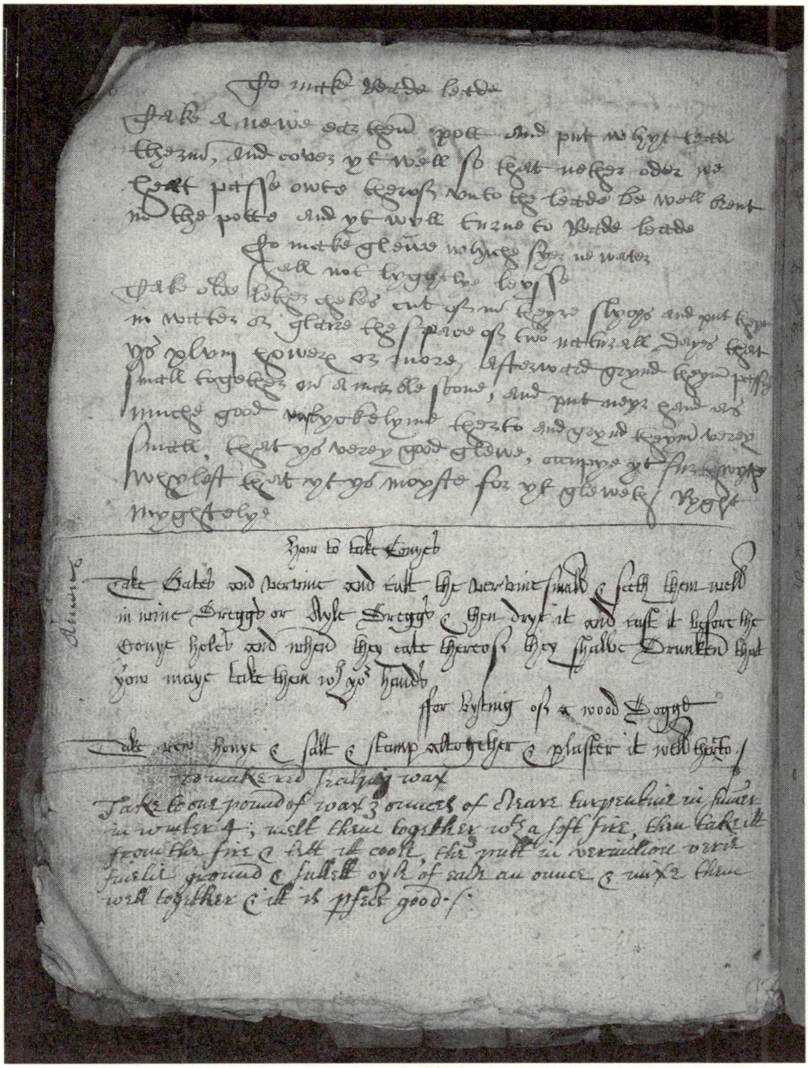

Figure 9. BL Add. MS 82370, f. 7v. Page of manuscript showing three different hands. Reproduced by permission of The British Library Board.

> from the fire & lett itt coole, then putt in vermilion verie finelie ground & sallett oyle of each an ounce & mixe them well together & itt is perfect good./ (f. 7v)

This page illustrates the way Hanson's utilitarian material was supplemented by new information added by later users of the manuscript.

Instructions for Fish Bait and Bird-Catching Concoctions

The best-known late medieval fishing manual, "A Tretyse of Fysshynge wyth an Angle," was, for a long time, attributed to the fifteenth-century prioress Dame Juliana Berners. It was added to *The Booke of Hawkyng, Hunting, and Blasing of Arms* (published originally 1486) in Wynkyn de Worde's 1496 edition and much reprinted thereafter.[38] In *The booke of haukyng huntyng and fysshyng with all the properties and medecynes that are necessary to be kept* (printed by William Copland, probably in 1566), the treatise on fishing follows the separate one on hunting, which ends with some miscellaneous material, including moral apothegms, a satirical poem on friendship, a long list of terms used to refer to groups of different beasts and birds, and a list of English shires and bishoprics (sigs. Hiii–Iii).

In this classic work on fishing we find advice about how to make a fishing rod, fashion different-colored fishing lines of varying strength, and craft hooks, weights, and floats. There is advice about how to fish in various bodies of water, how to avoid being seen by the fish, how to adjust to varying weather conditions, how to select the best times of day for angling, and what baits to select for different kinds of fish. With regard to the last, take, for example, the advice given to catch grayling:

> The Grayling by an another name called Umbre is a ryght delycyous fishe to mannes mouthe, and ye may take hym like as ye doo the Troute, and these ben his baytes, In Marche and in Aprill the red worme In May the

38. See *STC* 3308-15. For a short, skeptical biography of Juliana Berners (or Bernes or Barnes), see Julia Boffey's entry in the *ODNB*, http://www.oxforddnb.com/view/article/2255. For the relationship of the printed compilation of treatises in *The Boke of S. Albans* (which did not originally include the treatise on fishing) to Berners's authorship and to the manuscripts related to the separate treatises, see Rachel Hands, "Juliana Berners and *The Boke of St. Albans*," *Review of English Studies*, n.s., 72 (1967): 373–85. Sections of the fishing treatise are reproduced in Griffiths, *Tollemache Book of Secrets* (ff. 20–25).

greene worme, a lytle braysed worm,[39] the docke Canker and the hawthorne worme. In June the bayte that breedeth betwene the tree and the barke of an Oke. In Juill a bayte that breedeth on a ferne lefe and the great red worme, and nyp of the head and put it on your hooke and Codworme before in August the red worme and a Docke worme, and all the yere after a red worme. (sig. Mi^v^)

Some fishing manuals, such as Leonard Mascall's *A Booke of fishing with Hooke & Line* (1590), go beyond recommending using available natural baits and give instructions for concocting chum or for enhancing natural bait. For example, Mascall's book, in addition to recommending different kinds of worms and other natural bait, suggests the following way "To take Loches or small fish":

> Take the branne of wheate meale, two pound, of lenten pease, halfe a pound, mixe them together, and beate them with a sufficient quantitie of brine, and put thereto half a pound of sessame. Then shall ye part it in peeces, and throw them here and there: for as soone as ye have thrown it in the water, all the small fish will come unto it, and remaine in one place, although they be 300. paces off. (p. 38)

Mascall gives instructions about how to make bait pellets "To take Perch":

> The Perch is not so easily taken with hooke, nets, or bownet, but rather with proper baites made and used in a troubled water: therefore ye must make baites with the liver of a Goate, and the snaile, or take the yellow butter flie which flyeth: of Goates whay, called *fromage de chevereau* of each foure drams, *oppavicis* two drams, hogges bloud foure drams, galbony[40] four drams, beate all well together, and sprincle it all over with pure wine, and make thereof small pellets, or as ye make perfumes, and drie them in the shade. (p. 39)

Instead of just recommending such natural baits as "the guttes of a pegeon" (f. 9v), "yelowe frogge" (f. 9v), and "the blake sneyll" (f. 10) or suggesting the use of a simple chumming mixture, Hanson records some quite complicated recipes for concoctions to be used to anoint bait to make it more attractive and effective, some of them for what modern fishermen

39. An error for "brayled worme"; the *OED* cites this passage from the 1496 edition with the tentative definition of "brailed" as perhaps a ringed worm.

40. Galbanum, a plant-extract gum resin.

call "stink bait." For example, he offers the following recommendation for creating bait to catch pike: "Take oleum benedictum assafetida and oyle of exeter Juce of fenell and a quantytye of heory then put theym all on a sawcer one the fyer tyll they be hotte and anoynt the bayte what so ever yt be and specyallye a lampron" (f. 8). The "oleum benedictum," or "blessed oil," is created by infusing and cooking roots of carduus (a thistle), valerian (a garden plant), St. John's wort flowers, wheat, oil, cypress turpentine, frankincense, and white wine. The use of such an ingredient as blessed oil possibly points to a connection between practical knowledge and religious superstition.[41] Another substance, "asafoetida" is defined in the *OED* as a "concreted resinous gum, with a strong alliaceous odour, procured in central Asia from the *Narthex asafœtida* and allied umbelliferous plants; used in medicine as an antispasmodic, and as a flavouring in made dishes." *The greate Herball* (1561), chapter 5, has "Assa fetida, that is stinkinge, is hote & dry in the iiii degre. It is gomme of a tree that groweth beyond the sea, & is gadred in the Sommer. It may be kept long withoute corruption. It ought to be kept in a metelye drye place. The more it stynketh the better it is. It hath vertue to consume, to drye, dissolve and to sprede" (sig. Aiii^{r-v}).[42] Hanson has another bait recipe using asafoetida (one of several under the heading "To take all maner of fyshe"): "Take assafetyda & campher a quantytye of oyle oleve and braye theym together tyll yt come to a fyte oyntement than put yt into a boxe and anoynt yowre bayte whan ye wylle angle" (f. 8v). There are earlier examples of using asafoetida and other unusual ingredients found in late medieval manuscripts. For example, British Library MS

41. Richard C. Hoffman, *Fishers' Craft and Lettered Art: Tracts on Fishing from the End of the Middle Ages* (Toronto: University of Toronto Press, 1997), observes in his study of German and continental fishing manuals in manuscript and print, that "some fishers clung to the edges of popular religious magic. The first recipe in the Bodensee memorandum anoints a bait with 'blessed oil' (*oleum benedictum*), a lubricant handled by a pope or holy man and used to cleanse the dead and exorcise demons" (334). Hoffman's study is the most comprehensive discussion of late medieval and early modern fishing lore to date.

42. The seventeenth-century handbook *Natura Exenterata; or Nature Unbowelled* (1655) has a recipe for a fish-luring concoction using asafoetida: "Take *Assafedita*, Henbane seed, Quick-silver, and Vinegar, fry it together in a pot-sherd, put it in a linnen bag, tye it with a line to a Pole, Dip it in the water, the f[l]avour will make all the Fish to be above the water, that you may take them, as long as the bagg is in the water" (402). See also the recipe for using asafoetida in a mixture to anoint fish bait in *A New Book of Knowledge; Treating of Things, Whereof some are Profitable, some Precious, and some Pleasant and Delightful* (1697), 12: "To take FISH / Take *Assa Fatida*, Milk, Honey, Wheat-flower, and make an Ointment, and anoint the Bait and Hook."

Harley 2389 has the following instruction for catching pike: "ever let the nether end of your lyne be towched with asafetida, & your bayte with oyle bendycte or oyle called petrolium & campir."[43] Hanson may be recording some particular recipes available to him in his provincial environment, but with the mention of asafoetida as a key ingredient, the question is raised concerning how such an exotic imported ingredient was made available to him: although this substance was already in use in the fifteenth century,[44] one wonders to what degree it was dependent on the kind of trade with the Far East established by the Portuguese.[45] The reality of the early modern expansion of international trade is implicit, then, in the transmission of homespun knowledge.

Presenting instructions on how to make "an oyntment to anoynte the the [*sic*] bayt for all maner of fyshe," Hanson offers the following advice:

> Take the water of lunare[46] or the water of mortagon[47]
> wythe water of verven and of Jusquyam[48] gathered after the

43. Cited in W. L. Braekman, *The Treatise on Angling in The Boke of St. Albans (1496): Background, Context and Text of "The Treatyse of Fysshynge wyth an Angle"* (Brussels: Scripta Vrijheidslaan, 1980), 40. Braekman, 10–13 and 25–40, offers a short history of fishing manuals from ancient writers such as Aristotle, Aelian, Oppian, and Ausonius through medieval authors such as Aelfric, Peter Cresentius, and Piers of Fulham. He points to a group of late medieval English manscripts of both monastic and secular origins that preserve vernacular fishing lore: BL MSS Sloane 4, 1118, 3153, 3160; Harley 1785, 3371; and Bodleian MS Rawlinson C 506. He cites two short treatises on fishing: "De Arte Piscandi" (BL MS Sloane 1698, ff. 12–13, and "The Harley Tract," BL MS Harley 2389, f.73r–v). Having concentrated on continental documents in his study, Hoffman, *Fishers' Craft*, 345–53, briefly discusses English fishing treatises in manuscript and print. These include a fishing dialogue that survives in only one printed copy, an interesting text that was evidently exploited by Isaac Walton for his *Compleat Angler*: see Gerald Eades Bentley, ed., *The Arte of Angling, 1577*, with an introduction by Carl Otto v. Keinbusch and explanatory notes by Henry L. Savage (Princeton: Princeton University Library, 1956).

44. Hoffman, *Fishers' Craft*, 346, notes that in British Library MS Sloane 4, William Worcester had a recipe for "a bait-enhancing ointment of fennel, asafoetida, and some optional oils and greases."

45. For a discussion of European interest in asafoetida from the time of Alexander the Great through to the early modern era, see Andrew Dalby, *Dangerous Tastes: The Story of Spices* (London: British Museum Press, 2000), 110–12.

46. *OED* defines "lunary" as "the garden plant Honesty *n.*, *Lunaria biennnis*, of the fern Moonwort."

47. The mortagon or martagon is defined by the *OED* as the "martagon lily. Any of certain lilies with strongly reflexed perianth segments (also called *Turk's-cap lily*); *spec.* a lily of this group with dull purple-red flowers, *Lilium martagon*, native to Europe (but perhaps only naturalized in Britain) and widely grown in gardens."

48. The *OED* identifies this as another name for "henbane."

> sone goyng downe (sole exystente in piscile[49]) and take
> powder of valeryan and alytyll honye and myngle all
> in a boxe and anoynt therwyth. (f. 8)

Some of the ointments work on the hands of the fisherman, who can then catch the fish that are attracted by the smell:

> *To take fyshe*
> Take nettylles & howsleke[50] and make Juyce therof and put
> into a pond, and all the fyshe wyll gather together there, and yf
> yowre handes be anoynted therwythe ye maye take theym. (f. 9)

Earlier fishing manuals regularly offer recipes for such ointments. For example, Richard Hoffman translates a 1493 German fishing manual that has the following:

> [I]f you want to catch many fish by hand take a *lot* of camphor, a *lot* of wheat flour, a *lot* of grease from a heron, [and] a *lot* of bone from the aforementioned bird. Crush the bone to powder, mix the other items all together and make a salve of it. You may also add to it a *lot* of olive oil. And when you want to fish, smear your hands and shins, front and back, with it. Thus you will experience great marvels.[51]

To catch trout, the Hanson manuscript offers the following instructions: "Take honye clarefyed and the Juce of vervyn ann and Myngle theym together and anoynt yowre Reade Wormes therwythe" (f. 10v). Like the home remedies we find in so many manuscript documents, such instructions seem to originate in traditional folk practices and from personal experience. It is interesting that we find an addition, at the bottom of f. 10v (see figure 10) in available blank space, of two other fish bait recipes, one for chum, the other for live bait, written in another hand—a fact that suggests that a family member or someone else using the book felt compelled to record additional useful information of this sort under the

49. The *OED* has "pistil" as chiefly a north and midlands spelling of "pestle."

50. *OED*: houseleek, plants of the genus *Sempervivum* with pink flowers and thick stems formerly planted on the roofs of houses to protect against lightning.

51. Hoffman, *Fishers' Craft*, 81 (emphasis in original).

heading "Accipere pisces" ("to catch fish"): "Take vervin rootes & seethe them in sweete worte a good while & sew them in a wollen clowte ix or x fould that the water cannott enter in & hold it in thy hand in aqua et advenient pisces."

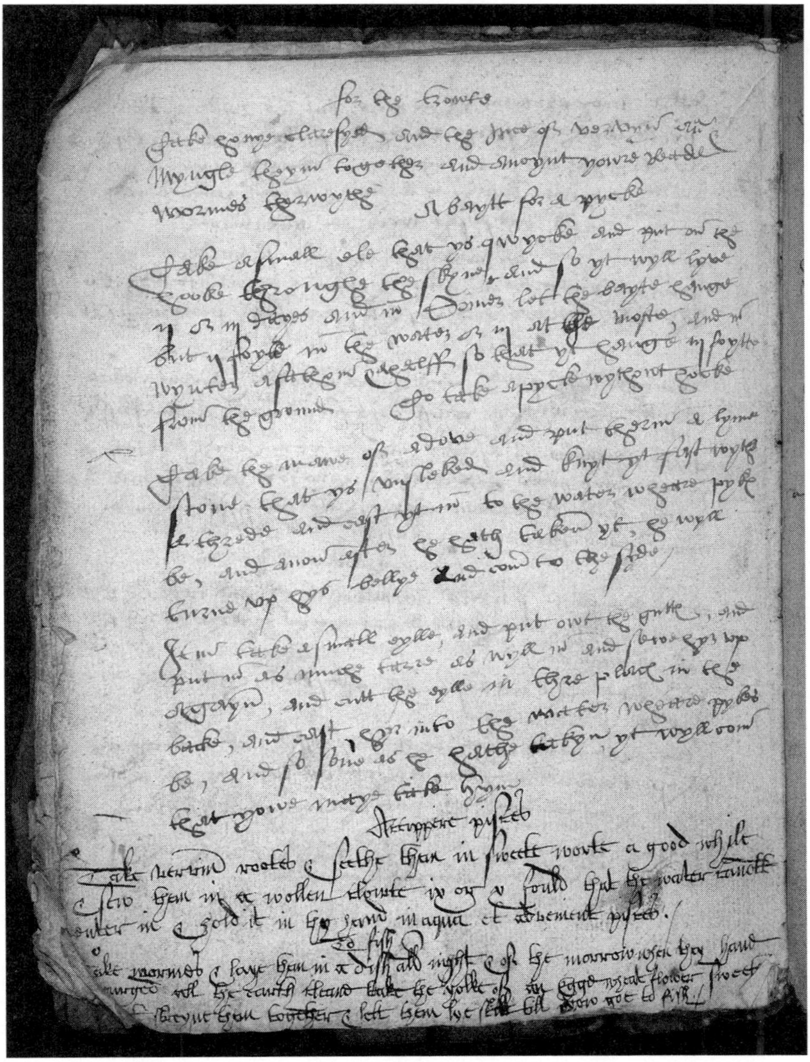

Figure 10. BL Add. MS 82370, f. 10v. Page from fish-bait section showing additions in hand later than that of John Hanson. Reproduced by permission of The British Library Board.

To fish
Take wormes & laye them in a dish all night & of the morrow
when they have
[pu]rged all the earth cleane take the yolke of an Egge wheat flower
sweete
[page torn] t streyne them together & lett them lye still till yow goe to
fish. (f. 10v)

Hanson entered four items dealing with bird catching (f. 11r–v)—all recommending concoctions to attract and drug the prey:[52]

To take wylde geys or cranes
Take leyes of wyne and sethe therin what corne
yowe wyll, and laye yt wheare they hawnt, and
they wyll eate therof, and thowe maye take them
wythe thy handes. (f. 11)

To take all maner of byrdys
Take the Juce of hen bayne and stepe wheate therin
ii Dayes or iii, and cast yt where byrdes ys and as
manye as doth take yt shall not flye awaye (f. 11)

To take foiles° °*fowl*
Take henbane sede, ~~hempe~~ ^popy^ sede and the sede of lettes° °*lettuce*
and the sede of humblokes,° and beytt theym in a morter °*hemlocks*
and then take the powder of wheat flowere and
sede well that powder wythe leys of wyne, and whan
yt ys colde strawe yt in place wheare foyles be
and all that ete therof shalbe so madde that they
maye nether flye ne goo. (f. 11v)

To take byrdes or anye other foole
Take the Rote or sede of humlokes vocat Gonta, the
Royttes° and sedes of henban and the beries of great °*roots*

52. Hoffman, ibid., 83, translates a passage from the 1493 treatise"How to Catch Fish" on fowl catching by such a method: "to catch birds and ducks . . . take the tormentil [root] and boil it in good wine. Then boil grain or barley therein, too, and throw the feed on the site which has been prepared for the birds. That way they will eat the grain together with the aforementioned root, and they will become drunk from it and entirely numb so that they cannot fly any more, and will fall down on the ground. Then you can pick them up by hand without effort."

> morrels and sethe theym in water stronglye than
> sethe barlye or wheate [blank space here] and that yt dry
> and cast yt theras byrdes doe hawnt, and what byrd
> that eatethe of that corne maye not flye awaye. (f. 11v)

In available blank space on this page, the same hand that added two items on folio 10v inserted the following item that is probably not related to fowl catching:

> *To make flesh seeme Rawe*
> Take the blood of a hart or a conye & bake it in oven & doe yt to powder & when thou list put the powder thereon & it shall seeme rawe (f. 11v)

Unless he was offering advice to a deceitful butcher for disguising old or rotten meat, it is hard to imagine why this item is included in Hanson's household book. In any case, this recipe concludes the utilitarian advice found on the first eleven folios of the manuscript. The next entry in the manuscript is the prose account of the Eland-Beaumont feud.

The "Byerley Bouke"

Later in the manuscript, on ff. 30–31v, Hanson has transcribed the "byerley bouke," an informational document related to his legal work with property transactions, in this case explicitly concerned with his own property in the manor of Clifton. The *OED* defines the term "byrlaw" as follows: "The local custom or 'law' of a township, manor, or rural district, whereby disputes as to boundaries, trespass of cattle, etc., were settled without going into the law courts; a law or custom established in such a district by common consent of all who held land therein, and having binding force within its limits. Hence byrlaw-court and *byrlaw-man n.*, bierlaw-grayves *n. at byrlawman n.*" These laws regulated such matters as the dates of ploughing, the turning out of cattle, the number of cattle turned out by each tenant of common land, the fines for trespass and damage done to fences, etc., the keeping up of fences, sea banks, the pound, the "balks" in fields, and the like. Hanson's entry deals with local issues:

f. 30] This byerley bouke Indentyd of the lorshyppe of Clyfton in [the]
County of yorke made the xxv Daye of october in the fyrst & sec[ond]
of Kyng phillipe & quene marye &c by the assent of sir John
Constab[le]
knyght and lady Jane hys wyf and also by the consent and agreme[nt]
of all the freholderes & tennantes and Inhabytantes of the sayd
lordsh[ip]
Fyrst yt ys ordeyned and agreed that yf any of the sayd
tennantes or Inhabytantes from hensefforth at any tyme
herafter for ever do breke the Lordes pynfold by hym selff
or by any other by hys commaundement or procurement shall
fors[f]ayt and lease for every suche Defalte to the lord iij^s^ in
Itm yf any of the sayd tennantes or Inhabytantes have
not suffycyent fuell yeirelye herafter gotten afore the
Feaste of Sanct Mychaell tharchangell That then they
& every of theym so wantyng or offendyng shall forfayt
and lose to the lord for every tyme ij s Itm yf any of the
Lordes tennantes at wyll for yeires or other wyse from
the makyng herof for ever do lett anye parcell or parcelles
of theyr fermholdes to any freholderes or Freholder~~es~~e there
or to any other person owt of the sayd lordshyppe he
shall forfayt for everye tyme so doyng vj s viij d and
also that they and everysuche tennant of the sayd
lordshype as hathe hertofore lett ever any parte or
parcell contrarye to this order and that that they or every
of theym do not Restore the same ageyn to the sayd
Fermhold or Tenement Wythin two yeires next
after the Dat herof to forfayt to the Lord his hole
lease and intrest that he hathe of the sayd Tenement
Itm yf any of the sayd tennantes or Inhabytantes have
not theyr hedges & defences sufficyentlye made abowt
the common pasture of Clyfton before the Feast of
thanuncaicon of owre Lady next & Do not uphold and
mayntene all their sayd Defences Doles gappes *&* yates[53]

53. These words refer, apparently, to the requirement to keep up barriers and divisions between parcels of land and to repair gaps or holes in hedges and fences.

yeirelye & contynuallye for ever, that then they and every of theym shall forfayt and lease to the lord for every

Defalt vj d

f. 30v] A Dole, iij[d] a gappe and xij[d] a yate Itm yf anye of the sayd tennantes and Inhabytantes herafter at any tyme or tymes for ever putt or suffer to go and be anye skalled° horsses or Mares, to the lordes common or pastur ther, shall forfayt for every horsse or mare and for everye tyme v s Itm yf any of the sayd tennantes put or suffer anye swyne to goo upon the sayd common pasture at any tyme herafter that then the person so offendyng shall forfayt for everye tyme to the Lord ij d/ Itm yf they or any of theym have anye of theyr Swyne unrynged by the space of thre dayes at any tyme of the yeire from hensforth for ever, that then he so offendyng shall forfayt to the Lord for everye tyme ij d/ Itm yf they or anye of theym have theyr or anye of theyr swyne unyoked by the space of iij Dayes at any tyme herafter betwyxt the Feast of thanuncacion of our lady and Sanct Mychaell shall forfayt & lose for every suche tyme ij[d] Itm yf they or any of theym putt or suffer flokes of geese to go in theyr commen pasture or into the hall closes at any tyme of the yeire herafter for ever, that everye suche person puttyng or sufferyng theyr sayd flockes of geese so to do to forfayt for every suche Defalt to the Lord xij[d] also that they & everye of theym shall make theyr hedges & defences abowt theyr hardcorne[54] feildes suffy[c]yentlye from alhalowedaye unto the tyme of the sayd hardcorne be gott ever ledd or of suc[he] closes yeirely for ever fromhensforth and yf [they] do not that then suche persons as shall not do the

°*scald, scabby*

f. 31] same shall forfayt for everye dole viij d and for every gapp also yf anye of the sayd tennantes or Inhabytantes have

54. Generally, wheat or rye (first *OED* citation from 1608).

not theyr doles hedges & defences sufficyentlye made
about theyr haver feildes° yeirelye herafter before the °*oat fields*
sayd Feast of thanuncacion of our lady & so to mayntei[ne]
& uphold the same unto the sayd corne be ledd awaye
shall for fayt to the Lord for everye suche defalt, ~~for~~ vi s
for everye dole viij^{d} and for everye gappe iiij^{d} Itm if they
or anye of theym leade theyr hardcorne awaye forth of
the sayd feildes and leave the common gappes open after theym
unmade shall forfayt for every tyme to the lord xij^{d} Itm yf
they or any of theym sell owt any coles or burnyng stone
or other fuell owt of the lordshippe to any stranger or
strangeres shall forfayt for every wayne° lode iij s iiij^{d} °*wagon*
and for every horselod iiij^{d} Itm yf they or any of theym
breke any hedges or carye theym awaye or fell any
grenewodd and carye the same awaye shall forfayt to
the lord for every burdyng° of hedgewodd ij d and for °*load*
every burden of grenewodd iiij^{d} Itm yf any of the sayd tennantes
or Inhabytantes fell down any quyckewodd[55] or thornes
or other wodd in his neighbores hedge to make his owne
wythall wythowt lycence shall forfayt for every tyme
so doyng viij^{d} Itm that non of the sayd tennantes or
Inhabytance shall enclose any parcell or parcells of ground
bylongynge to theyr fermoldes but that they shall ley
the same wythe quyckwodd upon peyn for every
Defalt to the contrarye iij s iiij^{d} Itm yf they or
any of theym have any unrewlye cattell & common hedg
brekeres yf they wyll not the same awaye or laghe° °*catch, capture (Scot.)*
theym Imedyatlye after they shall have sufficyent
warnyng therof to forfayt for every suche defalt xij^{d}
also yf any of theym do lett any beast gates to any
freholderes stranger or strangeres to forfayt & lose to
the lord

f. 31v] Lordes for every suche doynge of everye of theym xij^{d}
also that yf they or any of theym sleate any cattell or
Sheepe wythe Dogges wythin the sayd lordshyppe, that
then they & every of theym to forfayt for everye defalt

55. *OED*: "live plants, especially hawthorn used for hedging."

vi d

thus subscribed John Custable knyght[56]

Itm yf any of the lordes tennantes at wyll within
the sayd lordshippe Do lett of or sett any parte
or parcell of theyr fermoldes to any person or persons
Wythowt lycence of the lord & his ^or^ theire Deputtes
shall forfayt for every tyme so Doyng vi s viij^{d}
Itm that non of the lordes tennantes shall herafter
lopp or topp any trees wythin any parte of this
lordshippe but onely suche as have bene before
topped & lopped & the same to be so topped & lopped
betwixt mychelmes & maye daye upon peyn of every
toppe v s & every loppe ij s
Itm that non of the lordes tennantes breke any hole
grownd for geytyng of coles wythowt leve of
the lordes or of some of theyre officeres upon peyn
of everye defalt v s
Itm that no man sell any Ryse in the oken banke
except he or they leave good & principall wavers
in everye xviij fote one upon peyn of every defalt vi s

Real Estate Notes and the List of Counties of England and Wales

The final items in the manuscript, on folio 50r–v, are both informational, one having to do with the lands assigned to two tenants in the vicinity of Netherwood House and the other listing English and Welsh counties, followed by the number of parishes in each. The first is in Hanson's hand and concerns management of his own property; the second, in Latin, is in Hand B and seems to have been entered into the manuscript later.

f. 50] *The Fyrst Dyvysyon of the netherwod hows*
and of the landes & closes perteinyng to the same

for that moytye which	/For that moytye whiche
was in in the tenure of	/was in the tenure of
Gilberte Crowder	/Gilberte Batleye

56. In margin: "Thus endorsed."

the howse ij gardens the
place betwene the howse
and the gardens and the half
of the lane answeryng wyth
the fold contenyng 3 yerdes
beneth the howse noke[58]
in the northe easte and
west end of batly brodroyd
xviij Ropes
moysye flatte ij acres
I rod xxxj Ropes
Perkyn Royde° iij acres
Stuble close iij rodes x ropes
Crowder crofte j acre iij rod*es*
brodroyde & brodroyd
ynge v acres
yssotroyd leyes° iij rodes
and a half
yssotroyd wod j acre
ij rodes & xxx Ropes
Summa xvj acres
and a half acre

/ longe headles iiij acres
/ nether chofer pighill j acre iij r[ods]
/ xxvi ropes[57]

/ the further tonge ij rodes
/ the nerer tonge ij rodes & demi
/ and sex ropes

/ the spowt close iij acres
/ the fordore & the
/ Todehoyle j acre & j rod
/ the lathe crofte j acre iij Rodes
/ the no[r]th syde of the
/ broderoyd j acre ij rodes &
/ Vij Ropes
Summa/

°*road*
°*untilled land*

f. 50v] *Comitatus Angliae*

1 Cornwall, in quo comitatu sunt par^o^~~a~~chiae 161–161
2 Denshire in quo sunt parochiales ecclesiae 394
3 Dorsetshire, in quo sunt parochiae 248
4 Somersetshire, in quo sunt parochiae 385
5 Wiltshire, in quo sunt parochiae 304
6 Hantshire, in quo sunt parochiae 253 et oppida mercatora 18–18
7 Barkshire, in cuius comitatus complexu sunt parochiae 140–140
8 Suthrie, hic comitatus parochiales ecclesias habet 140
9 Sussex, parochias continet haec prouincia 312
10 Kent, habet haec prouincia paraecias 398
11 Glocestershire, paraeciae 280 in hoc comitatu comprehenduntur
12 Oxfordshire, ecclesias parochiales 280 complectitur hic ager

57. The *OED* defines "rope" as a "measure of length (unspecified), especially for walling or hedging."

58. *OED*: "outside corner of a house."

13 Buckinghamshire, recensentur in hac regione paraeciae 185

14 Bedfordshire, habet haec prouinciol~~a~~^a^ paraecias 116–116

15 Hertfordshire, parochias habet ~~hac~~ ^hic^ comitatus 120

16 Midlesex, paraeciae 73 plus minus in hoc agro extra urbem numerant

17 Essex computantur in hac regione parochiales ecclesiae 415–415

18 Suffolk, habentur in hoc agro parochiae 575

19 Norfolke sunt in hac prounicia parochiales ecclesiae plus minus 660

20 Cambridge shire, parochiae ~~163~~ ^163 in^ hoc comitatu continentur

21 Huntingdonshire numerantur in hac regicuncula paraeciae 78

22 Northamponshire [*sic*], pertinent ad hunc agrum parochhiae 326

23 Leicestershire, intra hunc agrum sunt parochiales ecclesiae 200

24 Rutlandshire, ecclesias parochialibus ornatur haec prouinciola 47

25 Lincolnshire, in hoc comitatu parochiae sunt plus minus 630

26 Nottinghamshire, visuntur [?] in hoc agro ecclesiae parochiales 168

27 Darbishire, paraecias includit hoc comitatus 106

28 Warwickshire, continentur in hoc comitatu parochiales ecclesiae 158

29 worcestershire, hic ager paraecias 152 numerat

30 Staffordshire, habentur in hoc comitatu paraeciae 130

31 Shrappshire, sunt in hac regione parochiae plus minus 170

32 Chesshire, paraecias plus minus 68 habet hic comitatus

33 Herefordshire, continentur in hoc comitatu parochiae 176

34 –42[59] 34 Radnorshire 35 Brecknocshire 36 [illegible] 37 Glamorganshire 38 Caermardenshire 39 Pembrokeshire 40 Cardiganshire 41 Montgomerishire 42 [the rest illegible]

In these two items one finds a conjunction of the local and the national, the very feature of the Hanson manuscript we most want to emphasize. The main compiler and subsequent scribes here and elsewhere in the manuscript were able to focus on local real estate, an old feud that moved from history into legend, and everyday practices, as well as to widen the gaze to take in the English nation as a whole and what was transpiring in the larger world. The utilitarian items in this household book—the recipes for ink and pigments, for fish bait and fowl catching, and for treatment of

59. This is a list of nine Welsh counties, but the bottom of the page is damaged and torn.

parchment as well as the other materials Hanson used in his activities as a legal scribe and agent, his gathering of legal precedents and recording of real estate particulars—all these features reflect both the vocational and the avocational interests and life of this provincial yeoman landowner. They also suggest his desire to pass on to his son and to his descendants valuable information, some of which they eventually supplemented with their own additions to the compilation. Hanson's book was designed to be kept in his household. The accident of its removal to the house of a more socially prominent and wealthier family took it away from the more humble circumstances of its production but happily increased its chances of survival. Unlike most similar documents from the middling classes, it did not perish, so we should treasure it not only for what it contains but also for what it reveals about the complex social and cultural dynamics of the period. It helps us to write a "history from below" that calls into question some of the court- and London-centered narratives of the period. It also allows us to witness some of the processes by which a rural yeoman helped to forge his own personal and social identity by gathering and transcribing items that he thought particularly important in his everyday life.

Conclusion

Despite the growing volume of print publications in the period, early modern English culture was still basically a scribal one: official records, personal correspondence, family histories, practical information, diaries, newsletters, excerpts from one's reading, and historical, religious and literary texts all were at home in the scribal medium. Historians have, of course, calendared or edited correspondence and have drawn selective evidence from archived manuscript documents. Literary scholars have constructed genealogies of texts for their critical editions, using manuscripts that often preserve better and earlier exemplars of works than those that were printed in their own time or shortly after. But the mass of manuscript remains from the early modern period has been only partially explored: there are many historical, literary, and broadly cultural discoveries to be made, valuable texts to unearth in both major and minor repositories. The manuscript we have studied in this book came to the British Library as a miscellaneous item only when, several years ago, the library acquired the Spencer-Stanhope family papers, mainly because of the letters they contain by Lord Nelson's second in command at the Battle of Trafalgar. How many other documents of this sort lie in badly cataloged or uncataloged family muniment rooms, local public record offices, or major manuscript repositories?

In early modern England, students and their teachers at the universities, aspiring lawyers and culturally sophisticated young men at the Inns of Court, men and women at the royal court and in the houses of the gentry and nobility all used the manuscript medium, some of them transcribing and circulating small booklets or what Harold Love has called "separates,"[1] others recording material in commonplace books that preserve excerpts from their reading and pieces they copied individually or in groups from other scribal and print documents to which they obtained access. Although the terminology used to describe whole manuscripts or gatherings of separates is somewhat inconsistent, a basic distinction can be made among the following: (1) the traditional commonplace book, which, in its classical form, arranges its items under preassigned topics or alphabetic headings and preserves texts from an individual's thinking and wide reading in a variety of fields;[2] (2) the manuscript miscellany, which mixes literary and nonliterary texts as well as prose and verse items; (3) the literary collection of one author's or multiple authors' works; and (4) the household book, which resembles the manuscript miscellany in some ways but which also combines materials from high and popular cultures, mixing practical information with aesthetic and intellectual contents. The social and/or educated elite produced all four types of collections, including household books. Those below the social level of the gentry might also have had commonplace books and manuscript poetical anthologies. After all, village lads increasingly attended grammar schools, learned to keep commonplace books, and probably did so in later life even if they had to draw upon books they could only borrow because they couldn't afford to buy them. But literate members of the lower classes more typically compiled

1. Love, *Scribal Publication in Seventeenth-Century England* (Oxford: Clarendon Press, 1993), 9–13.

2. For studies of commonplace books and their importance see Mary Thomas Crane, *Framing Authority: Sayings, Self, and Society in Sixteenth-Century England* (Princeton, NJ: Princeton University Press, 1993), and Peter Beal, "Notions in Garrison: The Seventeenth-Century Commonplace Book," in *New Ways of Looking at Old Texts: Papers of the Renaissance English Text Society, 1985–1991*, ed. W. Speed Hill (Binghamton, NY: Medieval & Renaissance Texts & Studies in conjunction with Renaissance English Text Society, 1993), 131–47.

materials for household books. The problem is that only a few manuscript collections of any kind from this level of society have survived, mainly, as we have suggested, because the families with which they were associated did not have the facilities for their preservation or, perhaps, even the desire to pass on such artifacts to succeeding generations.

John Hanson's household book is, then, a rare and instructive example of an important kind of document from the early modern period—a text compiled by a literate yeoman who had broad interests ranging from the provincial history and culture of his native southwest Yorkshire to the activities and writings associated with London, the royal court, and the larger world. What began as a collection of homespun recipes for inks, fish baits, bird-catching techniques, and other kinds of practical knowledge (ff. 1–11) expanded into a historically, literarily, and geopolitically broader set of texts. The prose and poetic versions of the fourteenth-century revenge story signal the main compiler's interest in local history—including the events that unfolded in connection with the sixteenth-century provincial feud between Sir Richard Tempest and Sir Henry Savile. The historical ballad Hanson copied, the earliest surviving version of which we know, is a remarkable text, one of only seven historical folk ballads from as early as the sixteenth century but one that has been virtually invisible in literary or ballad histories and anthologies. By discussing its multiple contexts and by identifying editions of this poem and of the parallel prose version of the story, we call attention to the importance of this unstudied text. So too, in presenting the texts and discussing the contexts of the two lost Armada Thanksgiving ballads, we hope to restore them to their rightful place in broadside ballad history and call attention to the information they contain that supplements the historical record of the occasion they celebrate. The other items in Hanson's manuscript, copied from either manuscript or print sources, confirm the heterogeneous character of the compilation and the breadth of the compiler's secular and religious interests.

If Hanson's miscellany had originated in London or one of the universities, only a few of its entries would be especially noteworthy, primarily the otherwise lost broadside ballads and the Eland-Beaumont feud narratives. Hanson's compilation is remarkable in large measure because, to date, our understanding of Renaissance scribal culture is almost entirely restricted to documents created by and for members of the gentry and aristocracy and originating at court, the Inns of Court, or one of the universities. Yet this is necessarily a very thin and unrepresentative sample of the realm's voluminous scribal culture. Balancing these few tens of thousands of privileged participants in scribal culture were many hundreds of thousands of their social inferiors who nevertheless created, circulated, and preserved manuscript texts of undeniable cultural value. Fortunately, Hanson's household book made the transition into the Stanhope archive and thus owed its preservation to that family's ever-increasing prosperity. The book offers a unique and rare glimpse into this largely unstudied phenomenon of lower-class texts that, measured by its volume, necessarily comprised the age's dominant public scribal culture.

The evidential importance of Hanson's anthology is thus both social and geographical. It commands particular interest because it reveals in fascinating detail the democratization of discourse created by the mass transmission of texts through the scribal networks. The outlying "benchmark" anthologies with which we have compared Hanson's collection (compiled in the rural Midlands and Norfolk as well as Yorkshire) provide less insight into the kinds of texts available at his social level and the interests that led their compilers in their selection of texts to copy from the available corpus. Hanson was of the yeoman class. His roots remained in the soil despite his occupation as scrivener and freelance legal agent.[3] Henry Gurney was also a yeoman, but his anthology (MS Tanner 175), is dominated by his own records and accounts and, mostly, copies of his own poems. It tells us in detail of his access to printed books but little about the transcribed materials available to yeomen of his rank in rural Norfolk. MS Ashmole 48 may well be an anthology compiled by members of the servant class, a social level below Hanson's, especially if the minstrel Richard Sheale was one of its scribes. Even so, this collection's sampling of regional scribal culture is limited to a brief legal document in Latin, two horoscopes, and a variety of poems. Its poetic highlights are considerable, including an epitaph for the Countess of Derby, the West-Darcy ballad, and Sheale's minstrel repertoire, but there is nothing like Hanson's varied array of recipes or his prose account of the Eland-Beaumont feud, an unparalleled mix of historical

3. E.g., Hanson is termed "yeoman" in grants of 1562 and 1577. WYAS Calderdale, KM: 274, KM: 380. Bequests in his will include several wagons with wheel rims and spokes, three plows, a coulter, and his "Spelded oxe at Swillington." Borthwick Institute, Probate Register 27, ff. 671–671v.

narrative and prose fiction. The two remaining miscellanies were compiled (as were nearly all such anthologies subjected to scholarly analysis to date) by members of the gentry. Both John Kay, scribe of the Folger MS anthologies, and Thomas Brampton, who compiled MS Gough-Norfolk 43, were gentlemen at a social remove one step above Hanson.[4] Yet these gentlemen collectors apparently had access to texts in manuscript circulation no more prestigious than those available to Hanson and the scribes of MS Ashmole 48. In fact, Hanson alone among these anthologists preserved a poem written by the Queen herself. Brampton copied at least two poems written by noblemen, but so did the compilers of Ashmole 48.

Hanson's anthology preserves a much broader spectrum of genres that reflect local culture better than any other household book we have consulted. In part this is because Hanson generated only one of its entries, the list of tenants on folio 50, as compared with the business and family records and original poetry found in the anthologies compiled by Sheale and his associates or by Brampton, Gurney, and Kay. Hanson included a number of practical texts taken from manuscripts available to him locally, especially the "byerley bouke" and the recipes for fish bait.

Finally, as a representative of the household book in its social setting, MS Add. 82370 is a model of transgenerational manuscript culture. Hanson intended to create a useful collection of texts, and there is ample evidence that he succeeded. Later generations of his extended family read and augmented his work in at least six different hands. An unidentified seventeenth-century owner deemed the ballad of the Eland-Beaumont feud sufficiently important to recopy the damaged leaf 15 and replace it in the codex. A different scribe attempted (rather unsuccessfully) to number the ballad's stanzas. Hand D probably belongs to John Stanhope III (1629–93),[5] who signed folios 1, 47v, and 49v, added the date "1579" at the bottom of folio 17 as well as a marginal note on folio 14. Hand B filled folio 50v with the list of English shires and the number of parishes in each

4. J. T. Cliffe, *The Yorkshire Gentry from the Reformation to the Civil War* (London: Athlone Press, 1969), 97, cites the Kayes of Woodsome as representative of the late Tudor Yorkshire gentry. Brampton's father is designated "gentleman" in a receipt dated 1583 (PRO SP 46/17, f. 139) and in his will (Papers of the Consistory Court 62 [10] Sainberbe), 23 July 1591. His heir male, scribe of this anthology, inherited his status as gentleman.

5. This John Stanhope is the only family member of that name whose hand we have not found but whose dates are compatible with this style of writing.

and also used blank space at the bottom of folios 10v and 11v to insert additional recipes for fish bait and for making "flesh seeme rawe." Others with access to the manuscript added the pregnant woman's verse lament on folio 26v (Hand C), pen trials, and further insertions on folios 27v, 40, and 46. Hanson's household book was consulted and expanded well into the seventeenth century and perhaps beyond.

Hanson's miscellany nevertheless displays a conservative insularity with regard to literary taste despite its compilation in the age of Sidney, Spenser, and Shakespeare. One of the cultural changes taking place in the early modern period is a shift in the sphere of what we would regard as the literary, from a moral, rhetorical, and utilitarian conception of literature to a more aesthetic appreciation of literary texts. Literary texts continued to be valued for their didactic and moral value and for their practical usefulness in a variety of social situations—for example, to respond to births, marriages, and deaths, to compliment social superiors, or to make political observations or express political protest—but the artfulness of expression, the skill evident in the handling of traditional genres, the worth and durability of the artifact as artifact (in other words, the "literary" worth of what was written) came to be valued more and more, especially among educated and culturally sophisticated readers. Of course, the linguistic virtuosity that patriots claimed for their native writers was part of their claim to cultural respect—as the arguments for the legitimacy of the vernacular as a sophisticated medium of expression were made in various European countries, including England.[6]

Nevertheless, on a broader popular level, literary texts, including poems, could still be seen primarily as sources of moral wisdom, practical knowledge, and, particularly in the case of ballads, "news." They were valued as equipment for living and as repositories of information, selected for their contents more than for their felicity of expression—the latter seen more often as an aide-mémoire than as self-conscious artfulness. In the Hanson manuscript, there are many "literary" texts, but in virtually every

6. Richard Tottel, for instance, protested that a number of his countrymen had written as well in verse as "divers Latines, Italians, and other," proving "That our tong is able in that kynde to do as praiseworthely as the rest." "The Printer to the Reader," in *Songes and Sonettes, written by the right honorable Lorde Henry Howard late Earle of Surrey, and others* (London, 1557; *STC* 13860), sig. A1v.

case, we believe, these pieces were collected and treasured not primarily for aesthetic reasons but because they were useful. The motives for collecting them might have been old-fashioned and, to us, literarily naive, revealing a primarily utilitarian conception of literature rather than connoisseurship. Thus, the verse calendar (f. 32) and the verse Decalogue (f. 42) probably had mnemonic usefulness; Vaux's "I lothe that I did love" (f. 49v) could have served as a timely moral admonition for the aged scribe; the two Savile epitaphs (ff. 42v–45v) could have reinforced bonds of family and patronage, and Thomas Churchyard's epitaph on the Earl of Pembroke (ff. 47v–49) might have been valued because of that magnate's Yorkshire connections; the two Armada thanksgiving ballads (ff. 19–26v) might have been appreciated for their news value and for their assertion of political orthodoxy; Queen Elizabeth's "The doubt of future foes" might have been read as a political warning seen as particularly relevant to the compiler's home county, which had been a seedbed for political rebellion and religious resistance during both Henry VIII's and Elizabeth's reigns; and the Eland-Beaumont ballad could be read both as an object lesson about the dangers of feuding relevant to the particular circumstances of a contemporary conflict and as a rehearsal of local history that resonated for a sixteenth-century southwest Yorkshire audience. None of these texts was, we believe, perceived by their compiler as fundamentally literary in the modern sense of that term. They were, in a real sense, as utilitarian as the fish-bait recipes, legal information, and proverbs and maxims Hanson also transcribed. All the professional, religious, practical, and recreational contents of Hanson's book were equipment for living. Richard C. Hoffman's description of the cultural hybridity of household books applies to Hanson's manuscript: "As private writings meant to be read . . . household books epitomize full vernacular literacy but reveal in their additive, empirical, and seemingly random qualities their share in popular culture. . . . They revel in intertextuality, the process of making new texts by combining and adapting elements, allusions, and formulas from old ones in a scribal replica of oral composition. Readers glossed and adjusted their manuscripts to their needs."[7]

7. Richard C. Hoffman, *Fishers' Craft and Lettered Art: Tracts on Fishing from the End of the Middle Ages* (Toronto: University of Toronto Press, 1997), 14.

As further evidence of his focus on the value of the texts he transcribed, it is clear that Hanson selected works for his household book with little if any deference to texts transmitted only in manuscript. Nearly 30 percent of his transcriptions were taken from printed sources. All of these works originated in London except for the mnemonic verses on saint's days on folio 32r–v, which derived from a service book printed in France. These sources added a considerable diversity of content to Hanson's anthology: history, politics, philosophy, and wisdom literature dominate the mix taken from printed works, from the formal style of Philip II of Spain, flanked by the two Armada ballads (ff. 19–26v), to the verse epitaph for William, Earl of Pembroke; the Latin epigram memorializing Emperor Frederic (ff. 47v–49); six pages of moral adages from the *Preceptes of Cato* (ff. 27–29v); and Lord Vaux's poetic farewell to worldly vanity (f. 49v). For the most part, of course, Hanson tapped into the manuscript networks that transmitted an even more diverse range of texts throughout the kingdom. His selections, in fact, drew upon two levels of this network. Sources confined to rural Yorkshire and its purlieus contributed the Eland-Beaumont feud narratives in prose and verse (ff. 12–18v, 33–42), the "byerley bouke" (ff. 30–31v), the Savile epitaphs (ff. 42v–45v), and of course the property notes on folio 50. Hanson's unique verses on the Ten Commandments (f. 42), and the visit of the Magi (ff. 46v–47v) may also reflect local rather than national circles of transmission. The dialect of his fish-bait recipes points to their local origins, while his recipes for ink (or their analogues, at least), circulated in the national scribal networks (ff. 1–11v). The two poems attributed to Queen Elizabeth (ff. 45v–46) show that even manuscript texts that originated at court or in court-connected circles became available in time to yeomen scribes residing in the provinces.

In addition to all that it tells us about scribal culture in the hinterlands and at the subgentry social level, Hanson's household book paints a detailed, three-dimensional portrait of its scribe. British Library Additional MS 82370 was for its main compiler an act of self-construction and identity affirmation.[8] John Hanson's choice of items for inclusion reveals who he was as well as who he wanted to be in his immediate sphere of activity. His

8. For an interesting discussion of identity formation through collecting, see Marjorie Swann, *Curiosities and Texts: The Culture of Collecting in Early Modern England* (Philadelphia: University of Pennsylvania Press, 2001), esp. 16–54.

inclusion of the two Armada Thanksgiving ballads was, in effect, a profession of his political loyalty and patriotism. Similarly, the poems attributed to Queen Elizabeth signal Hanson's devotion to the Queen in the context of his home county's problematic history of rebellion and religious resistance. They also evoked the international context of the war with Spain, the latter glanced at in Hanson's reproduction of an edited version of the King of Spain's style. The Nativity poem, verse Decalogue, and the *contemptus mundi* lyric by Lord Vaux express Hanson's personal piety and Protestant orthodoxy. More specifically, Hanson's choices as collector suggest that his household book is an old man's compilation. He no doubt had access to all the love poetry in Tottel's *Miscellany* yet chose to copy from it only Lord Vaux's "I lothe that I did love," a rejection of youthful vanities." "Now leave and let me rest" is a similar rejection of "the toyes, that wretchelesse youthe Requyeres."[9] This poem, however, occurs alongside a wide variety of love lyrics in the manuscript anthologies in which it is found. Thus Hanson may well have had access to amorous verse from both printed and scribal sources, none of which he found worth copying in old age. The Eland-Beaumont prose narrative and long ballad proclaim his Yorkshire identity and his connection with the Saviles, the latter reaffirmed by the two epitaphs written for members of that family. Those epitaphs proclaim Hanson's position as a yeoman and an upwardly mobile client of an important local gentry family. The maxims and proverbs identify Hanson as an educated man appreciative of conventional wisdom. The legal materials signal his professional identity as a legal agent, and the real estate information relates to his involvement in property law and property ownership, the foundations upon which his family would base their ascent in social status in the century following his death. The recipes for various kinds of ink point to his interest in heraldry and his (probable) involvement, like his son's, in illustrating coats of arms. His collection of fish baits and techniques for trapping birds suggests the avocational interests of a yeoman immersed in a local rural culture and its traditional lore. In sum, this household book declares what kind of man—Christian, citizen, professional, and socially networked person—John Hanson was. This dirty, somewhat battered, sloppily written household book is a window onto

9. "Now leave and let me rest," l. 20.

early modern middle-class culture, one through which we can perceive the vital relationship of the political center to the periphery, the confluence of heterogeneous cultural materials from both elite and popular sources, and the personal identity and aspirations of an elderly southwest Yorkshire yeoman compiler whose professional identity and social practices as a legal agent, as well as his personal (recreational) interests, are represented in what he chose to transcribe. The contents of the manuscript collectively define the compiler.

Peter Laslett's term "the world we have lost"[10] applies certainly to the scribal remains of the early modern period. Aside from official records, the vast majority of manuscripts produced during this time have been destroyed—by fire, by being put to culinary or hygienic uses, by rot or rodents, and by similar misfortunes. It is hard to estimate, but certainly, if we are thinking about literary manuscripts, the majority of such documents seem to have disappeared: these include the huge manuscript collection of John Hoskins's poetry that went missing[11] and the numerous manuscript copies of works that were discarded by printers after their need for them ceased. But other manuscripts no doubt are hidden in plain sight—at least if our eyes are pointed in the right direction. They are buried in boxes of uncataloged items in various archives, mislabeled (like the holograph copy of a Donne sermon that Jeanne Shami unearthed several years ago—British Library MS Royal 17.B.XX),[12] or buried in aristocratic and gentry family collections. These "lost" documents we need to find and study. They have the potential to enhance our understanding of early modern English culture in its high and low, literary and nonliterary features. Feminist historians and literary scholars have, to a large extent, led the way in recovering such materials, eager to find new documents that shed light on women's writing and the age's social functioning and practices. Now the recovery efforts need to be expanded so that we can discover and analyze other culturally valuable manuscript texts and collections. John Hanson's

10. Laslett, *The World We Have Lost* (New York: Scribner, 1973).

11. The source of this information is John Aubrey, who wrote of Hoskins, "He had a booke of Poemes, neatly written by one of his Clerkes, bigger then Dr. Donne's Poemes, which his sonn Benet lent to he knowes not who, about 1653, and could never heare of it since." *Aubrey's Brief Lives*, 3rd ed., ed. Oliver Lawson Dick (London: Secker & Warburg, 1958), 170.

12. See Jeanne Shami, ed., *John Donne's 1622 Gunpowder Plot Sermon* (Pittsburgh: Duquesne University Press, 1996).

household book, unknown beyond A. M. W. Stirling's brief excerpts in her early twentieth-century family history of the Stanhopes,[13] is now available at the British Library for scholarly examination. Our task in this book has been to indicate that such study is worth doing. The document we have examined has a striking but in many ways symptomatic heterogeneity that reveals some of the cultural complexities of the time. The fact that such a manuscript has survived is a happy accident for which we are grateful.

13. A. M. W. Stirling, *Life's Little Day, Some Tales and Other Reminiscences* (New York: John Lane, 1924), 277–81.

Bibliography

Primary Sources

The Apologie or Defence, of the Most Noble Prince William, by the grace of God, Prince of Orange. London, 1584. *STC* 15209.

Arber, Edward, ed. *A Transcript of the Registers of the Company of Stationers of London, 1554–1640*. 5 vols. London: Private printing, 1875–94.

Aubrey, John. *"Brief Lives," Chiefly of Contemporaries, Set Down by John Aubrey, between the Years 1669 & 1696*. Edited by Andrew Clark. 2 vols. Oxford: Clarendon Press, 1898.

Bentley, Gerald Eades, ed. *The Arte of Angling, 1577*, with an introduction by Carl Otto v. Keinbusch, and explanatory notes by Henry L. Savage. Princeton: Princeton University Library, 1956.

Bentley, William. *Hallifax, And Its Gibbet-Law . . . To which are added, The Unparallel'd Tragedie committed by Sir Iohn Eland, of Eland, and his Grand Antagonists*. Hallifax, UK: J. How, 1708.

The booke of hauking huntyng and fysshyng with all the properties and medecynes that are necessary to be kept. London, 1566 (?). *STC* 3310.

The Booke of Hawkyng, Hunting, and Blasing of Arms. St. Albans, 1496. *STC* 3308.

A Booke of Secrets: Shewing divers waies to make and prepare all sorts of Inke, and Colours . . . Necessaire to be knowne of all Scriveners, Painters, and others that delight in such Arts. Translated out of the Dutch into English by W. P. London, 1596. *STC* 3355.

A briefe some of the Treason intended against the King and State. London, 1605. *STC* 20960.

Brown, Carleton, ed. *English Lyrics of the XIIIth Century*. Oxford: Clarendon Press, 1932.

Byrd, William. *Psalmes, Sonets, & songs*. London, 1588. *STC* 4253.

Child, Francis James, ed. *English and Scottish Popular Ballads (1882–98)*. 3 vols. 1884–98. Reprint, New York: Dover, 1965.

Churchyard, Thomas. *The epitaphe of the honorable Earle of Penbroke, Baron of Cardiffe, and knight of the most noble order of the garter Who dyed Lord stueward of the Queenes majesties houshold, and of her privie counsell*. London, 1570. *STC* 5227.

Dasent, John Roche, ed. *Acts of the Privy Council of England*. Vol. 30, *A.D. 1599–1600*. London: HMSO, 1905.

Denbo, Michael. *The Holgate Miscellany: An Edition of Pierpont Morgan Library Manuscript, MA 1057*. Renaissance English Text Society, 7th ser., vol. 35. Tempe: Arizona Center for Medieval and Renaissance Studies, 2012.

Elizabeth I. *Elizabeth I Collected Works*. Edited by Leah S. Marcus, Janel Mueller, and Mary Beth Rose. Chicago: University of Chicago Press, 2000.

——. *Poems of Queen Elizabeth I*. Edited by Leicester Bradner. Providence, RI: Brown University Press 1964.

Englands Remembrancer, containing A true and full Narrative of those two never to be forgotten deliverances: The one from the Spanish Invasion in Eighty eight: The other from the Hellish Powder Plot: November 5. 1605. London, 1657. Wing C4510.

Evans, R. H., ed. *Old Ballads, Historical and Narrative, with Some of Modern Date; Collected from Rare Copies and MSS. by Thomas Evans. A New Edition; Revised and Considerably Enlarged . . . by his Son*. 4 vols. London: W. Bulmer and Co., 1810.

Foxe, John. "John Foxe's The Acts and Monuments Online." http://www.johnfoxe.org.

Gouws, John, ed. *Nicholas Oldisworth's Manuscript (Bodleian MS. Don.c.24)*. Renaissance English Text Society, 7th ser., vol. 34. Tempe: Arizona Center for Medieval and Renaissance Studies, 2009.

Gravell, Thomas L. Thomas L. Gravell Watermark Collection. http://www.gravell.org.

The greate Herball. London, 1561. *STC* 13179.

Greene, Richard Leighton, ed. *The Early English Carols*, 2nd ed. Oxford: Clarendon Press, 1977.

Griffiths, Jeremy, ed. *The Tollemache Book of Secrets*. Completed by A. S. G. Edwards. London: Roxburghe Club, 2001.

Halle, Edward. *The Union of the two noble and illustre famelies* (1550), facsimile of *STC* 12723. Menston, UK: Scolar Press, 1970.

Harington, Henry, ed. *Nugae Antiquae*. London, 1769.

Harington, Sir John. *Sir John Harington's A New Discourse of a Stale Subject, Called the Metamorphosis of Ajax*. Edited by Elizabeth Story Donno. New York: Columbia University Press 1962.

Harrington, Richard. *A famous dittie of the Joyful receaving of the Queens moste excellent majestie, by the worthy Citizens of London the xij day of Nouember, 1584, at her graces comming to Saint James*. London, 1584. *STC* 12798.

Hilliard, Nicholas. *Nicholas Hilliard's Art of Limning*. Edited by Arthur F. Kinney. Boston: Northeastern University Press, 1983.

Hughes, Paul L., and James F. Larkin, eds. *Tudor Royal Proclamations*. 3 vols. New Haven: Yale University Press, 1969.

Hughey, Ruth, ed. *The Arundel Harington Manuscript of Tudor Poetry*. 2 vols. Columbus: Ohio State University Press, 1960.

Hume, Martin A. S., ed. *Calendar of Letters and State Papers Relating to English affairs . . . Archives of Simancas*. Vol. 4. London: HMSO, 1899.

Ingledew, C. J. Davison, ed. *The Ballads and Songs of Yorkshire*. London: Bell and Daldy, 1860.

Kinsley, James, ed. *The Oxford Book of Ballads*. Oxford: Clarendon Press, 1969.

Klene, Jean, ed. *The Southwell-Sibthorpe Commonplace Book: Folger MS. V.b.198*. Renaissance English Text Society, 7th ser., vol. 20. Tempe, AZ: Medieval & Renaissance Texts & Studies, 1997.

Knight, Stephen, and Thomas Ohlgren, eds. *Robin Hood and Other Outlaw Tales*. Kalamazoo, MI: Medieval Institute Publications for TEAMS (Consortium for Teaching the Middle Ages) in Association with the University of Rochester, 2000.

Lemon, Robert, ed. *Calendar of State Papers Domestic*, 1581–1590. 1865. Reprint, Nendeln, Liechtenstein: Kraus Reprints, 1967.

Liturgies, Church of England. London, 1588. *STC* 16520.

Louis, Cameron, ed. *The Commonplace Book of Robert Reynes of Acle: An Edition of Tanner MS 407*. New York: Garland, 1980.

Machyn, Henry. *The Diary of Henry Machyn*. Edited by John Gough Nichols. London: Camden Society, 1848.

Mascall,Leonard. *A Booke of fishing with Hooke & Line*. London, 1590. *STC* 17572.

May, Steven W., ed. *Henry Stanford's Anthology: An Edition of Cambridge University Library Manuscript Dd.7.75*. New York: Garland, 1988.

———. *Queen Elizabeth I: Selected Works*. New York: Washington Square Press, 2004.

Melville, Sir James. *Memoirs of His Own Life, by Sir James Melville of Halhill M.D.XLIX.–M.D.XCIII*. Edinburgh: Roxburgh Club, 1827.

A Memorable song made upon the unhappy hunting in Chevy Chase. London, c.1625. *STC* 5129.5.

Morley, Henry, Lord. *Lord Morley's Tryumphes of Fraunces Petrarcke*. Edited by D. D. Carnicelli. Cambridge, MA: Harvard University Press, 1971.

Natura Exenterata; or Nature Unbowelled. London, 1655. Wing N241.

A New Book of Knowledge; Treating of Things, Whereof some are Profitable, some Precious, and some Pleasant and Delightful. London, 1697. Wing N585.

Nichols, John. *Progresses and Public Processions of Queen Elizabeth*. 3 vols. 1823. Reprint, New York, AMS Press, n.d.

Olsen, Thomas G., ed. *The Commonplace Book of Sir John Strangeways (1645–1666)*. Renaissance English Text Society, 7th ser. vol. 29. Tempe: Arizona Center for Medieval and Renaissance Studies, 2004.

Peacham, Henry. *The Art of Drawing with the Pen, and limming in Water Colours*. London, 1606. *STC* 19500.

Owen, G. Dyfnallt, ed. *Historical Manuscripts Commission, Marquess of Bath, Talbot, Dudley and Devereux Papers 1533–1659*. Vol. 5. London: HMSO, 1980.

Puttenham, George. *The Arte of English Poesie*. London, 1589. *STC* 20519.

Rhodes, John. *The Countrie Mans Comfort*. London, 1637. *STC* 20961.

Rollins, Hyder E., ed. *Tottel's Miscellany (1557–1587)*. Rev. ed. 2 vols. Cambridge, MA: Harvard University Press, 1965.

Shakespeare, William. *The Arden Edition of the Works of William Shakespeare: Romeo and Juliet*. Edited by Brian Gibbons. London: Methuen, 1980.

——. *The Riverside Shakespeare*. Edited by G. Blakemore Evans. Boston: Houghton Mifflin, 1974.

Shami, Jeanne, ed. *John Donne's 1622 Gunpowder Plot Sermon*. Pittsburgh: Duquesne University Press, 1996.

Shuffleton, George, ed. *Codex Ashmole 61: A Compilation of Popular Middle English Verse*. Kalamazoo: Medieval Institute Publications, 2008.

"The Sonnge of Sir Andraye Barton, Knight." In *A Volume of English Miscellanies Illustrating the History and Language of the Northern Counties of England*, edited by James Raine, 64–65. Surtees Society, vol. 85. Durham, UK: Surtees Society, 1890.

Spenser, Edmund. *The Works of Edmund Spenser, A Variorum Edition*. Edited by Edwin Greenlaw et al. Vol. 1. Baltimore: Johns Hopkins University Press, 1932.

Stow, John. *The Annales of England*. London, 1592. *STC* 23334.

——. *The Chronicles of England*. London, 1580. *STC* 23333.

Sullivan, Ernest W., II, ed. *The First and Second Dalhousie Manuscripts: Poems and Prose by John Donne and Others, a Facsimile Edition*. Columbia: University of Missouri Press, 1988.

Third Report of the Royal Commission on Historical Manuscripts. London: HMSO, 1872.

Tottel, Richard, ed. *Songes and Sonettes, written by the right honorable Lorde Henry Howard late Earle of Surrey, and others*. London, 1557. *STC* 13860.

A very proper treatise, wherein is briefly sett forthe the arte of Limming. London, 1573. *STC* 24252.

Warkentin, Germaine, ed. *The Queens Majesty's Passage and Related Documents*. Toronto: Centre for Reformation and Renaissance Studies, 2004.

Watson, John. *History and Antiquities of the Parish of Halifax, in Yorkshire*. 1775. Reprint, Manchester: E. J. Morten, 1973.

Weikel, Ann, ed. *The Court Rolls of the Manor of Wakefield from October 1550 to September 1552*. Leeds: Yorkshire Archaeological Society, 1989.

——. *The Court Rolls of the Manor of Wakefield from October 1583 to September 1585*. Leeds: Yorkshire Archaeological Society, 1984.

The whole booke of Psalmes . . . by Thomas Sternhold, John Hopkins and others. London, 1567. *STC* 2438.

Wright, Thomas, ed. *Songs and Ballads with Other Short Poems, Chiefly of the Reign of Philip and Mary*. 1860. Reprint, New York: Forgotten Books, 1970.

Secondary Sources

Armytage, George John. "Ancient Pedigree of Hanson of Rastrick." *Yorkshire Archaeological Journal* 1 (1870): 80–81.

Bajetta, Carlo A. "'Most peereles Poëtresse': The Manuscript Circulation of Elizabeth's Poems." In *Representations of Elizabeth I in Early Modern Culture*, edited by Alessandra Petrina and Laura Tosi, 105–21. New York: Palgrave/Macmillan, 2011.

Baker, J. H. *An Introduction to English Legal History*. 4th ed. Oxford: Oxford University Press, 2007.

Barrett, Jr., Robert W. *Against All England: Regional Identity and Cheshire Writing, 1195–1656*. Notre Dame, IN: University of Notre Dame Press, 2009.

Beal, Peter. *A Dictionary of English Manuscript Terminology 1450–2000*. Oxford: Oxford University Press, 2008.

——. "Notions in Garrison: The Seventeenth-Century Commonplace Book." In *New Ways of Looking at Old Texts: Papers of the Renaissance English Text Society, 1985–1991*, edited by W. Speed Hill, 131–47. Binghamton, NY: Medieval & Renaissance Texts & Studies in conjunction with Renaissance English Text Society, 1993.

——. "Poems by Sir Philip Sidney: The Ottley Manuscript," *The Library* 33 (1978): 284–95.

Beal, Peter, and Grace Ioppolo. "Elizabeth's Execution Warrants." In *Elizabeth I and the Culture of Writing*, edited by Peter Beal and Grace Ioppolo, 173–200. London: British Library, 2007.

Boffey, Julia. "Bodleian Library, MS Arch. Selden. B.24 and Definitions of the 'Household Book.'" In *The English Medieval Book: Studies in Memory of Jeremy Griffiths*, edited by A. S. G. Edwards, Vincent Gillespie, and Ralph Hanna, 125–34. London: British Library, 2000.

Braekman, W. L. *The Treatise on Angling in The Boke of St. Albans (1496): Background, Context and Text of "The Treatyse of Fysshynge wyth an Angle."* Brussels: Scripta Vrijheidslaan, 1980.

Brewer, John. "Microhistory and the Histories of Everyday Life." *Cultural and Social History* 7, no. 1 (2010): 87–109.

Broadway, Jan. "Hopkinson, John." *ODNB*. http://www.oxforddnb.com/view/article/13757?docPos=1.

Brooks, C. W. *Pettyfoggers and Vipers of the Commonwealth: The "Lower Branch" of the Legal Profession in Early Modern England*. Cambridge: Cambridge University Press, 1986.

Brown, Alan. "Bull, John." *ODNB*. http://www.oxforddnb.com/view/article/3905?docPos=1.

Brown, Carleton, and Rossell Hope Robbins, eds. *The Index of Middle English Verse*. New York: Columbia University Press, 1943.

Brown, Mary Ellen. "The Popular Ballad and Oral Tradition," *Oral Tradition* 18 (2003): 176–77.

Buchan, David. *The Ballad and the Folk*. 1972. Reprint, East Linton, Scot.: Tuckwell Press, 1997.

Bühler, Curt F. "At Thy Golg First eut of the hous vlysse the saynge thus." *Studies in the Renaissance* 6 (1959): 223–35.

Burke, Peter. *Popular Culture in Early Modern Europe*. New York: New York University Press, 1978.

Campbell, Heather. "'And in their midst a sun': Petrarch's *Triumphs* and the Elizabethan Icon." In *Goddesses and Queens: The Iconography of Elizabeth I*, edited by Annaliese Connolly and Lisa Hopkins, 83–100. Manchester, UK: Manchester University Press, 2007.

Caraman, Philip. *Henry Garnet 1555–1606 and the Gunpowder Plot.* New York: Farrar, Straus, 1964.

Chambers, E. K. *The Elizabethan Stage.* 4 vols. 1923. Reprint, Oxford: Clarendon Press, 1961.

Chartier, Roger. "Leisure and Sociability: Reading Aloud in Modern Europe." Translated by Carol Mossman. In *Urban Life in the Renaissance*, edited by Susan Zimmerman and Ronald F. E. Weisman, 103–20. Newark: University of Delaware Press, 1989.

Clay, John William, ed. *The Registers of Elland, Co. Yorkshire.* 2 vols. Leeds, UK: J. Whitehead and Son, n.d.

——. "The Savile Family." *Yorkshire Archaeological Journal* 25 (1920): 1–47.

Cliffe, J. T. *The Yorkshire Gentry from the Reformation to the Civil War.* London: Athlone Press, 1969.

Coffin, Tristram P. "The Folk Ballad and the Literary Ballad: An Essay in Classification." *Midwest Folklore* 9 (1959): 5–18.

Coogan, Robert. "Petrarch's 'Trionfi' and the English Renaissance." *Studies in Philology* 67, no. 3 (1970): 306–27.

Crabtree, John. *A Concise History of the Parish and Vicarage of Halifax.* Halifax, UK: Hartley and Walker, 1836.

Crane, Mary Thomas. *Framing Authority: Sayings, Self, and Society in Sixteenth-Century England.* Princeton, NJ: Princeton University Press, 1993.

Cressy, David. *Bonfires and Bells: National Memory and the Protestant Calendar in Elizabethan and Stuart England.* Berkeley: University of California Press, 1989.

Dalby, Andrew. *Dangerous Tastes: The Story of Spices.* London: British Museum Press, 2000.

Dictionary of the Scots Language. http://www.dsl.ac.uk.

Duffy, Eamon. *The Stripping of the Altars: Traditional Religion in England 1400–1580.* New Haven: Yale University Press, 1992.

——. *The Voices of Morebath: Reformation & Rebellion in an English Village.* New Haven: Yale University Press, 2001.

Firth, C. H. "The Ballad History of the Reigns of Henry VII. and Henry VIII." *Transactions of the Royal Historical Society*, 3rd ser., 2 (1908): 21–60.

Foster, Joseph, ed. *Alumni Oxonienses.* Vol. 3. Oxford: Parker, 1891–92.

Fowler, David C. *A Literary History of the Popular Ballad.* Durham, NC: Duke University Press, 1968.

Fox, Adam. *Oral and Literate Culture in England 1500–1700.* Oxford: Oxford University Press, 2000.

Goring, Jeremy. "Social Change and Military Decline in Mid-Tudor England." *History* 60 (1975): 185–97.

Griffin, Carrie. "Instruction and Information from Manuscript to Print: Some English Literature, 1400–1650." *Literature Compass* 10, no. 9 (2013): 667–76.

Hackett, Helen. "Courtly Writing by Women." In *Women and Literature in Britain, 1500–1700*, edited by Helen Wilcox, 169–89. Cambridge: Cambridge University Press, 1996.

Hands, Rachel. "Juliana Berners and *The Boke of St. Albans*." *RES*, n.s., 72 (1967): 373–85.

Hannawalt, Barbara A. "Ballads and Bandits: Fourteenth-Century Outlaws and the Robin Hood Poems." In *Robin Hood: An Anthology of Scholarship and Criticism*, edited by Stephen Knight, 263–84. Cambridge: D. S. Brewer, 1999.

Hansard, George Agar. *The Book of Archery, Being the Complete History and Practice of the Art, Ancient and Modern*. London: Henry G. Bohn, 1851.

Hasler, P. W. *The House of Commons 1558–1603*. 3 vols. London: History of Parliament Trust, 1981.

Helgerson, Richard. *The Elizabethan Prodigals*. Berkeley: University of California Press, 1976.

——. *Forms of Nationhood: The Elizabethan Writing of England*. Chicago: University of Chicago Press, 1992.

Hoffman, Richard C. *Fishers' Craft and Lettered Art: Tracts on Fishing from the End of the Middle Ages*. Toronto: University of Toronto Press, 1997.

Holt, J. C. *Robin Hood*. London: Thames and Hudson, 1982.

Hunter, Joseph. "Antiquarian Notices of Clay House, in Greteland, in the Parish of Halifax, and County of York." Edited by Thomas James. *Yorkshire Archaeological and Topographical Journal* 2 (1871): 129–70.

——. *Familiae Minorum Gentium*. Edited by John W. Clay. Vol. 2. Harleian Society Visitation Series 38. London, Harleian Society, 1895.

——. *South Yorkshire*. 2 vols. 1828–31. Reprint, Sheffield, UK: E. F. Publishing, 1974.

Iamartino, Giovanni, and Angela Andreani. "In the Queen's Name: The Writings of Elizabeth I between Public and Private Communication." In *The Language of Public and Private Communication in a Historical Perspective*, edited by Nicholas Brownlees, Gabriella Del Lungo, and John Denton, 116–34. Newcastle Upon Tyne: Cambridge Scholars' Press, 2010.

Ibbetson, David. "Savile, Sir John (1546–1607)." *ODNB*. http://www.oxforddnb.com/view/article/24741?docPos=2.

Index of Wills in the York Registry, A.D. 1594 to 1602. Yorkshire Archaeological Society, Record Series 24. Leeds, UK: Yorkshire Archaeological Society, 1898.

James, Mervyn. *Society, Politics and Culture: Studies in Early Modern England*. Cambridge: Cambridge University Press, 1986.

Kaye, J. M. "The Eland Murders, 1350–51: A Study of the Legend of the Eland Feud." *Yorkshire Archaeological Journal* 51 (1979): 61–79.

Kesserlring, K. J. *The Northern Rebellion of 1569: Faith, Politics, and Protest in Elizabethan England*. Houndmills, UK: Palgrave Macmillan, 2007.

Kirby, Joan. "Savile family (*per* . 1480—1644), gentry." *ODNB*. http://www.oxforddnb.com/view/71873.

Klein, Ursula, and E. C. Spary, eds. *Materials and Expertise in Early Modern Europe: Between Market and Laboratory*. Chicago: University of Chicago Press, 2010.

Laslett, Peter. *The World We Have Lost*. New York: Scribner, 1973.

Leach, A. F. "St. Paul's School before Colet." *Archaeologia*, 2nd ser., vol. 62 (1910): 191–238.

Leahy, William. *Elizabethan Triumphal Processions*. Aldershot, UK: Ashgate, 2005.

Lees-Jeffries, Hester. "Location as Metaphor in Queen Elizabeth's Coronation Entry (1559): *Veritas Temporis Filia*." In *The Progresses, Pageants, and Entertainments of*

Queen Elizabeth I, edited by Jayne Elizabeth Archer, Elizabeth Goldring, and Sarah Knight, 65–85. Oxford: Oxford University Press, 2007.

Love, Harold. *Scribal Publication in Seventeenth-Century England*. Oxford: Clarendon Press, 1993.

Marcus, Leah. *Puzzling Shakespeare: Local Reading and Its Discontents*. Berkeley: University of California Press, 1988.

Mattingly, Garrett. *The Armada*. 1959. Reprint, Cambridge, MA: Harvard University Press, 1962.

May, Steven W. *The Elizabethan Courtier Poets*. Columbia: University of Missouri Press, 1991.

———. "George Puttenham's Lewd and Illicit Career." *Texas Studies in Literature and Language* 50 (2008): 143–76.

———. "Henry Gurney, a Norfolk Farmer, Reads Spenser and Others." *Spenser Studies* 20 (2005): 183–223.

———. "Matching Hands: The Search for the Scribe of the 'Stanhope' Manuscript." *Huntington Library Quarterly* 76, no. 3 (Autumn 2013): 345–75.

———. "Queen Elizabeth's 'Future Foes': Editing Manuscripts with the First-Line Index of Elizabethan Verse (a Future Friend)." In *New Ways of Looking at Old Texts*, no. 3, edited by W. Speed Hill, 1–9. Renaissance English Text Society Special Publication. Tempe: Arizona Center for Medieval and Renaissance Studies and Renaissance Studies, 2004.

———. "Queen Elizabeth's Performance at Paul's Cross in 1588." In *Paul's Cross and the Culture of Persuasion in England, 1520–1640*, edited by Torrance Kirby and P.G. Stanwood, 300–313. Leiden, Neth.: Brill, 2014.

May, Steven W., and William A. Ringler, Jr. *Elizabethan Poetry: A Bibliography and First-Line Index of English Verse, 1559*–1603. 3 vols. London: Continuum, 2004.

McAleer, John J. "Ballads on the Spanish Armada." *Texas Studies in Literature and Language* 4, no. 4 (1963): 602–3.

McGinley, J.K. "Burrant, Robert." *ODNB*. http://www.oxforddnb.com/view/article/4097.

Mears, Natalie. "Public Worship and Political Participation in Elizabethan England." *Journal of British Studies* 51 (2012): 4–25.

Miller, Anthony. *Roman Triumphs and Early Modern English Culture*. Houndmills, UK: Palgrave, 2001.

Monson, Craig. "Byrd, William." *ODNB*. http://www.oxforddnb.com/view/article/4267?docPos=2.

Mueller, Janel. "Elizabeth I: Poet of Danger." In *Approaches to Teaching Shorter Elizabethan Poetry*, edited by Patrick Cheney and Anne Lake Prescott, 202–15. New York: Modern Language Association of America, 2000.

Nebeker, Eric. "Broadside Ballads, Miscellanies, and the Lyric in Print," *ELH* 76, no. 4 (Winter 2009): 989–1013.

Nelson, Alan H. *Monstrous Adversary, The Life of Edward de Vere, 17th Earl of Oxford*. Liverpool: Liverpool University Press, 2003.

Nelson, William. "From 'Listen Lordings' to 'Dear Reader.'" *University of Toronto Quarterly* 46 (1976–77): 110–24.

Owen, Hugh. *Stanhope, Atkinson, Haddon & Shaw, Four North Country Families*. Chichester, UK: H. Owen, 1985.

Page, William. *Victoria County History, York*. Vol. 1. London: Constable, 1907.

Parkes, M. B. "The Literacy of the Laity." In *Literature and Western Civilization: The Mediaeval World*, edited by David Daiches and Anthony Thorlby, 555–77. London: Aldus Books, 1973.

Perry, Ruth. "War and the Media in Border Minstrelsy: The Ballad of Chevy Chase." In *Ballads and Broadsides in Britain, 1500–1800*, edited by Patricia Fumerton, Anita Guerrini, and Kris McAbee, 251–70. Farnham, UK: Ashgate, 2010.

Pritchard, Arnold. *Catholic Loyalism in Elizabethan England*. Chapel Hill: University of North Carolina Press, 1979.

Quitslund, Beth. *The Reformation in Rhyme: Sternhold, Hopkins and the English Metrical Psalter, 1547–1603*. Aldershot, UK: Ashgate, 2008.

Rieuwerts, Sigrid. "The Folk-Ballad: The Illegitimate Child of the Popular Ballad." *Journal of Folklore Research* 33 (1996): 221–26.

Ringler, Jr., William A. *Bibliography and Index of English Verse in Manuscript 1501–1558*. Edited by Michael Rudick and Susan J. Ringler. London: Mansell, 1992.

——. *Bibliography and Index of English Verse Printed 1476–1558*. London: Mansell Publishing Limited, 1988.

Robbins, Rossell Hope, and John L. Cutler, eds. *Supplement to the Index of Middle English Verse*. Lexington: University of Kentucky Press, 1965.

Rollins, Hyder E. *An Analytical Index to the Ballad-Entries (1557–1709) in the Registers of the Company of Stationers of London*. 1924. Reprint, Hatboro, PA: Tradition Press, 1967.

——. "Concerning Bodleian MS. Ashmole 48." *Modern Language Notes* 34 (1919): 343–49.

Seng, Peter J., ed. *Tudor Songs and Ballads from MS Cotton Vespasian A-25*. Cambridge, MA: Harvard University Press, 1978.

Sharpe, Kevin. *Selling the Tudor Monarchy: Authority and Image in Sixteenth-Century England*. New Haven: Yale University Press, 2009.

Shuffleton, George. "Is There a Minstrel in the House? Domestic Entertainment in Late Medieval England." *Philological Quarterly* 87 (2008): 51–76.

Sil, Narasignha P. "William Herbert, First Earl of Pembroke." *ODNB*. www.oxford.dnb.com/view/13055.

Simmon, J. S. G., and Bé van Ginnekan-Van de Kasteele, eds., *Likhachev's Watermarks in English-Language Version*. Vol. 2, *Plates and Indexes*. Amsterdam: Paper Publication Society, 1994.

Simpson, James. *Reform and Cultural Revolution*. The Oxford English Literary History, vol. 2, 1350–1547. Oxford: Oxford University Press, 2002.

Smith, R. B. *Land and Politics in the England of Henry VIII, the West Riding of Yorkshire: 1530–46*. Oxford: Clarendon Press, 1970.

Spufford, Margaret. *Small Books and Pleasant Histories: Popular Fiction and Its Readership in Seventeenth-Century England*. Cambridge: Cambridge University Press, 1985.

Stirling, A. M. W. *Annals of a Yorkshire House: From the Papers of a Macaroni & His Kindred*. 2 vols. London: John Lane, 1911.

———. *Life's Little Day, Some Tales and Other Reminiscences*. New York: John Lane, 1924.

Summitt, Jennifer. "'The Arte of a Ladies Penne': Elizabeth I and the Poetics of Queenship." *English Literary Renaissance* 26 (1996): 395–422, reprinted in *Reading Monarch's Writing: The Poetry of Henry VIII, Mary Stuart, Elizabeth I, and James VI/I*, edited by Peter C. Herman, 79–108. Tempe: Arizona Center for Medieval and Renaissance Studies, 2002.

Swann, Marjorie. *Curiosities and Texts: The Culture of Collecting in Early Modern England*. Philadelphia: University of Pennsylvania Press, 2001.

Taylor, Andrew. "Bodleian MS Ashmole 48 and the Ballad Press." *English Manuscript Studies 1100–1700* 14 (2008): 219–43.

———. "The Myth of the Minstrel Manuscript." *Speculum* 66, no. 1 (January 1991): 43–73.

———. *The Songs and Travels of a Tudor Minstrel: Richard Sheale of Tamworth*. York, UK: University of York, 2012.

Tilley, Morris Palmer. *A Dictionary of the Proverbs in England in the Sixteenth and Seventeenth Centuries*. Ann Arbor: University of Michigan Press, 1950.

Turner, J. Horsfall. *Biographia Halifaxiensis: or, Halifax Families and Worthies*. 2 vols. Bingley, UK: T. Harrison, 1883.

———, ed. *The Elland Tragedies*. Bingley, UK: T. Harrison, 1890.

———. *History of Brighouse, Rastrick, and Hipperholme*. Bingley, UK: T. Harrison, 1893.

Ward, B. M. *The Seventeenth Earl of Oxford*. London: John Murray, 1928.

Watson, John. *The History and Antiquities of the Parish of Halifax, in Yorkshire*.1775. Reprint, Manchester, UK: Morten Publishers, 1973.

Watt, Tessa. *Cheap Print and Popular Piety 1550–1640*. Cambridge: Cambridge University Press, 1991.

Weinreb, Ben, and Christopher Hibbert, eds. *The London Encyclopedia*. London: Macmillan, 1993.

Wernham, R. B. *After the Armada: Elizabethan England and the Struggle for Western Europe 1588–1585*. Oxford: Clarendon Press, 1984.

Whitaker, Thomas Dunham. *Loidis and Elmete; or, an Attempt to Illustrate the Districts Described in Those Words by Bede*. Halifax, UK: T. Davison, 1816.

Wightman, W. E. *The Lacy Family in England and Normandy 1066–1194*. Oxford: Clarendon Press, 1966.

Withington, Phil. *The Politics of Commonwealth: Citizens and Freemen in Early Modern England*. Cambridge: Cambridge University Press, 2005.

Woolf, D. R. "The 'Common Voice': History, Folklore, and Oral Tradition in Early Modern England." *Past and Present*, no. 120 (August 1988): 26–52.

Woolf, Daniel. *The Social Circulation of the Past: English Historical Culture 1500–1730*. Oxford: Oxford University Press, 2003.

Woolf, Rosemary. *The English Religious Lyric in the Middle Ages*. Oxford: Clarendon Press, 1968.

Wright, Joseph, ed. *The English Dialect Dictionary*. 6 vols. Oxford: Oxford University Press, 1898.

Würzbach, Natascha, and Simone M. Salz. *Motif Index of the Child Corpus: The English and Scottish Popular Ballad*. Translated by Gayna Walls. Berlin: Walter de Gruyter, 1995.

Index